9/04

History
—of—
World War I

Volume 1

War and Response
1914–1916

Marshall Cavendish
New York • London • Toronto • Sydney

Marshall Cavendish Corporation
99 White Plains Road
Tarrytown, New York 10591

Website: www.marshallcavendish.com

Library of Congress Cataloging-in-Publication Data
History of World War I
    p. cm.
    Includes bibliographical references and index.
    Contents: 1. War and response, 1914-1916 – 2. Victory and defeat, 1917-1918 – 3. Home fronts. Technologies of war.
    ISBN 0-7614-7231-2 (set) – ISBN 0-7614-7232-0 (v. 1) – ISBN 0-7614-7233-9 (v. 2) – ISBN 0-7614-7234-7 (v. 3)
    1. World War, 1914-1918.   I. Marshall Cavendish Corporation.

D521 .H48 2001
940.3–dc21

                   2001017413

Printed in Malaysia

Brown Partworks
Managing editor: Tim Cooke
Project editors: Ian Westwell, Dennis Cove
Designers: Duncan Brown, Paul Griffin
Picture manager: Susannah Jayes
Cartographers: Duncan Brown, Bob Garwood, Mark Walker
Indexer: Kay Ollerenshaw

Marshall Cavendish Corporation
Editor: Peter Mavrikis
Editorial director: Paul Bernabeo

Authors
Mike Sharp, Ian Westwell, John Westwood

Consultants
Oscar Lansen, University of North Carolina, Charlotte
Professor John H. Morrow Jr., University of Georgia
Professor William R. Keylor, Boston University

Picture credits
AKG London: 8-9 , 10 , 19, 20, 22, 26, 28-29, 33, 35, 37, 45, 48, 50-51. 56, 57, 58-59, 66, 67, 76, 78, 79, 86, 87, 88-89, 101, 271, 282-283, 289, 292-293, 302-303, 305, 308, 309.
Archive Photos: 39, 234, 274, 282, 290b; Hirtz 236; US Army 285.
Corbis: 40, 42, 268, 290-291tc, 296; Bettmann: 263, 270-271, 272-273, 298, 299 ; Underwood & Underwood 276-277; UPI : 69, 279, 280-281, 284, 286-287, 303, 306-307; Baldwin H Ward & Kathryn C Ward 269.
Mary Evans Picture Library: 15, 17, 18-19, 21, 24-25, 32, 34-35, 36, 43, 44, 52, 54, 55, 60, 82, 83, 91, 93, 104-105, 117, 118, 119, 237, 247, 261, 278, 304, 311.
Robert Hunt Library: 12, 13, 27, 31, 38, 46, 47, 53, 61, 62, 63, 64, 68-69, 70, 72, 73, 74-75, 77, 80, 81, 84, 85, 88, 92-93, 94, 95, 96, 97, 98, 102, 103, 105, 107, 108, 109, 110, 111, 112, 114-115, 116, 121, 122-123, 124, 125, 126, 127, 128-129, 130, 131, 132, 133, 134, 135, 136, 137, 138, 139, 140, 141, 142, 143, 144, 145, 147, 148, 149, 150, 151, 152, 153, 154, 155, 156, 157, 158, 159, 160, 161, 162, 165, 166, 167, 168, 169, 170, 171, 172, 173, 174, 175, 176, 177, 178, 179, 180, 181, 182-183, 185, 187, 188, 189, 190, 191, 192, 193, 194, 195, 196-197, 198, 199, 201, 202-203, 204, 205, 206-207, 208, 209, 210, 211, 213, 214, 215, 216, 217, 218, 219, 220, 222, 223, 224, 225, 226, 227, 228, 229, 231, 232, 235, 238, 239, 242-243, 248, 249, 250-251, 252, 253, 254, 256, 257, 258-259, 262, 264, 265, 275, 288-289, 294, 295, 300-301.
Hulton Archive: 65, 90, 118, 119, 120, 266-267, 297.
MARS: US Marine Corps 281.
Peter Newark Pictures: 241, 244, 245, 260, 277, 286, 291br, 310.
U.S. Library of Congress: 240, 246.

SET CONTENTS

Volume I: War and Response, 1914–1916

continued

Volume 2: Victory and Defeat, 1917–1918

continued

Volume 3: Home Fronts / Technologies of War

continued

Map Key

This reference work uses color maps to illustrate many of the major battles and strategic operations of the war. For ease of use, each of the important warring powers is represented by the same color in all maps and diagrams.

These colors are shown below, along with the various symbols used on the maps. While precise heights of the terrain may vary from map to map, darker colors are always higher, and paler colors are closer to sea level.

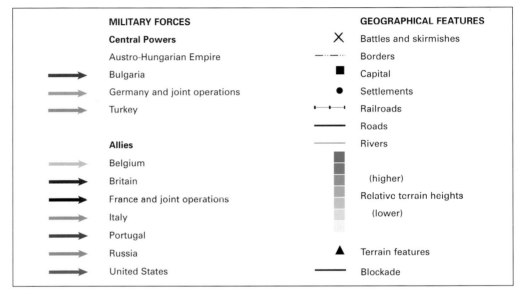

MILITARY FORCES

Central Powers

Austro-Hungarian Empire
Bulgaria
Germany and joint operations
Turkey

Allies

Belgium
Britain
France and joint operations
Italy
Portugal
Russia
United States

GEOGRAPHICAL FEATURES

X Battles and skirmishes
Borders
■ Capital
● Settlements
Railroads
Roads
Rivers

(higher)
Relative terrain heights
(lower)

▲ Terrain features
Blockade

▶ *This is a sample map from* History of World War I. *It shows the whole area covered by the European theaters in the conflict. Many other maps are far more detailed, and focus on military engagements on the western and eastern fronts, and on other fronts in Italy, the Middle East, and at sea.*

Maps and Diagrams

Introduction

Although very few people survive today who fought in or directly experienced World War I, the conflict continues to fascinate historians and students around the world. This is hardly surprising: The four years of terrible conflict between 1914 and 1918 affected not only those who fought but also those at home and those who came after. The fighting and its inconclusive aftermath, which would spark an even more terrible second world war a mere two decades later, dominated the history of the 20th century. Without an understanding of the first global conflict, its causes, and its aftermath, the course of the 20th century cannot be fully comprehended.

World War I marked the end of one age and the beginning of what can be termed the modern world. Before the United States entered the conflict in 1917, the war was fought mainly by the great powers of Europe, most of which could boast prestige and world influence stretching back many decades if not centuries. These powers were run by small elites—members of the aristocracy, top-ranking bureaucrats, and senior military figures—who habitually settled international matters among themselves. Because the European powers held colonies throughout the world, the decisions and agreements made by and between their controlling elites had global impact. Democracy,

▼ *A British soldier examines German dead in a captured machine-gun nest on the western front. Over nine million people died in combat during the war.*

where it existed, was at worst seen by those in power as a dangerous and threatening aberration; at best it was grudgingly accepted.

World War I changed the balance of power in the world, both for nations and their peoples. Four great empires—Austria-Hungary, Germany, Russia, and, shortly after the end of the war, Turkey—were swept away, along with their autocratic rulers. New nations, many of them fledging and fragile democracies, emerged in their place. The old powers that survived, especially Britain and France, faced renewed and increasing demands from their own citizens for increased democratic rights and an end to the secret international political systems that had previously existed.

World War I brought about a decisive shift in the world political order. First, the preeminence of Europe was dealt a decisive blow. Four years of intense conflict left its leading states politically, economically, and emotionally weakened. Second, new powers emerged on the global scene that would dominate the years between the two world wars and beyond. Chief among these emerging powerhouses were Japan, communist Russia, and above all, the United States, whose resources and industry had proved decisive in World War I. The United States' new position as the world's major superpower, however, brought with it responsibilities that some Americans had no wish to accept. The high cost of what many saw as a European war convinced U.S. citizens and politicians alike to attempt in the 1920s to isolate themselves from international affairs.

World War I also brought about a transformation in the way that world affairs were conducted in the future. Revulsion at the sheer violence and waste of the conflict inspired the creation of the League of Nations. The brainchild of U.S. president Woodrow

Wilson, the League was conceived idealistically as a forum at which international disputes could be settled in the open by discussion and arbitration among its member states. The U.S. Congress failed to ratify U.S. membership in the League; as a consequence the League was never fully effective and was often ignored. It played an important role, however, as the precursor of the modern United Nations.

By any measure World War I was fought on a scale so massive and unrelenting that it fully deserves the names given to it by contemporaries who called it "the Great War" and "the war to end all wars." Probably more than 70 million men from every corner of the globe took up arms; around nine million were killed in battle. Many more were left horribly wounded or psychologically damaged. Estimates of the total number of wounded begin at around 20 million. Millions of families around the world were left to grieve the loss of loved ones. This shockingly high level of casualties resulted from the development of new military technologies, including more effective guns, artillery, and bombs, as well as the struggle of an older generation of generals to come to terms with the tactics needed to best exploit or counteract these new weapons of war. Submarine

▲ *A French battleship fires on the Turkish coast in 1915. At sea and in the air, as on land, new technologies made weapons more effective and killing more efficient.*

▲ *American infantry during an operation in the Argonne region of France, October 1918. For many Americans, as for other combatants, war profoundly altered how they looked at the world.*

warfare and the introduction of fighter planes and Zeppelin bombers were other significant developments that pointed the way toward the type of fighting to come in World War II. Of major consequence for future wars was the introduction toward the end of the conflict of the first tanks.

Physical destruction took place on an unimaginable scale, leaving whole regions of northwestern and eastern Europe devastated. New artillery weapons obliterated entire towns. The war, the first truly total conflict, was fought between entire nations and their peoples, not only their armies. No one, from the soldier in the front line to his family at home, could escape the impact of war. Fighting drove millions of people from their homes and refugees drifted across Europe searching for security. When the war itself and the peace settlements that ended it redrew the continent's political boundaries, these refugees either moved to

join their compatriots in new states or found themselves part of ethnic minorities in their own homelands. In both cases the suffering of the dispossessed continued. Refugees received a cold welcome from previous inhabitants who saw them as more competition for scarce work and food, and minority groups everywhere were easy targets for prejudice.

During the conflict, government intervention on an unprecedented scale ensured that whole economies were directed toward just one goal—winning the war. In all combatant countries, all other considerations, from political rights to artistic expression, were subordinated to one aim. Modern industry and mass production ensured that once the killing began it would be sustained with astonishing precision and on a massive scale. The result was a dramatic leap forward in many types of technological development and, in countries including the

United States, a profound reexamination of the role of government in citizens' private and business lives.

The aftermath of the war brought other profound changes to U.S. daily life. In politics a generation attempted to turn its back on international affairs, only to discover that the nation's new world standing would not allow it such isolation. Millions of troops returned from France to rejoin the workforce, and many felt resentful about the way their noncombatant contemporaries had prospered from the economic boom during the conflict. The return of the troops also displaced many of the female workers who had been drafted into factories and offices to support the U.S. war effort. Women who had enjoyed the experience of independent working life were reluctantly forced back into the role of housewife, although their contribution to the Allied victory was a major factor behind the granting of woman suffrage in 1920.

Many African Americans also felt that their contribution to the war effort was poorly rewarded. Black troops returned from the front line to face a society in which segregation, prejudice, and sometimes lynching and burning, remained common. In the South and Midwest, the Ku Klux Klan had been revived during the course of the war, fueling fear and hatred of African Americans, Catholics, and Jews. Many of the hundreds of thousands of African Americans who had migrated to work for war industries in the cities of the Northeast were put out of work by returning white troops; race riots drove others from their urban homes.

The war brought dislocation for a whole generation of Americans. Millions had experienced European culture at first hand. Millions more were affected by the industrial boom during the war and the rapid urbanization that followed. U.S. cities became exciting centers of energy and creativity where artists, writers, and musicians sought to produce work that reflected the times. Abstract art and mass-produced design, experimental poetry and novels, jazz and blues, and other new forms of creativity reflected the belief of many Americans that the conflict had marked the end of one world and the beginning of another, the modern world.

History of World War I consists of three volumes. The first volume, "War and Response, 1914–1916," discusses the causes of the conflict, the reactions around the world to its outbreak, the course of the fighting in the first years of conflict, and the United States' move toward declaring war in April 1917. The second volume, "Victory and Defeat, 1917–1918," charts the U.S. contribution to the war and the fighting between 1917 and 1918, as well as the war's aftermath and impact around the globe during the 1920s and beyond. The third volume, "Home Fronts and Technologies of War," divides into two strands. The first looks at the impact of the war on the lives of ordinary civilians, while the second studies the military innovations, tactics, and weapons that made World War I a conflict of a ferocity that remains virtually unparalleled.

▼ *Women who had experienced factory work, like these British women preparing soldiers' rations, often felt betrayed and frustrated when they were forced back into their traditional roles as housewives at the end of the conflict.*

The World before the War

World War I began a month after the assassination of the heir to the throne of the Austro-Hungarian Empire, Archduke Franz Ferdinand, at Sarajevo in Bosnia on June 28, 1914. Decades later the local authorities tried to boost their tourist trade by laying a small rectangle of concrete on the sidewalk from where the shots that killed the archduke were fired. As the concrete was setting, the outline of a foot was imprinted in it to match the spot on the sidewalk where the assassin stood.

In the late nineteenth century the world was dominated by the relationships between a handful of European powers that were colonial, economic, and military rivals.

Over the following years some visitors went away under the impression that the shots that brought about the first global conflict were fired by a one-legged man standing in wet concrete. This was a minor misunderstanding compared with the greater misunderstandings, inadvertent or engineered, that actually sparked World War I. There is no undisputed answer as to why World War I came about, and historians remain divided on where to apportion blame. For various reasons, a complex series of events, most dating back to the final quarter of the nineteenth century and the first years of the twentieth, had impelled Europe's great powers, some more so than others, toward belligerency. The assassination

▶ *Archduke Franz Ferdinand of Austria-Hungary and his wife Sophie make their way to the town hall in Sarajevo, June 28, 1914. On their return journey, both were assassinated by a Serbian nationalist, an event that was to provoke the outbreak of the war.*

at Sarajevo was no more than a catalyst or, as some claimed at the time, a justification for total war.

Before looking at the world in the late nineteenth century it is worth making a few general points. Most obviously, it was a very different world from that of today. Full democracy was rare. No European country allowed women to vote on the eve of World War I, for example. Most European countries had full male suffrage (Britain and Hungary being the exceptions) before 1914, but voters had limited power over national and international policy. This right was strongly reserved for the unelected upper classes, usually drawn from the aristocracy and military, hereditary rulers, who had a great say in senior appointments, and elected representatives, most drawn from and favoring the upper classes and their interests. In reality, most of the ruling elites actively feared the spread of democracy, believing that it would create instability, possibly revolution, and thus endanger their positions. Consequently, national policies were dictated by a tiny minority whose self-interest they equated with their country's national interest.

Equally, international affairs or crises were not dealt with by bodies such as today's United Nations. No such permanent bodies existed. The great powers, acting alone or in concert, usually dealt with problems and issues concerning them as they arose. This system worked when there was broad agreement, in cases where their self-interests were roughly similar, but proved woefully inadequate when such national interests were widely divergent. Finally, many of the world's countries were colonies and were often used as pawns in the wranglings between the great powers. The idea of a community of world

▼ *After the Franco-Prussian War, Paris was seized by revolutionaries known as Communards. Here, they topple a statue in one of the city's squares.*

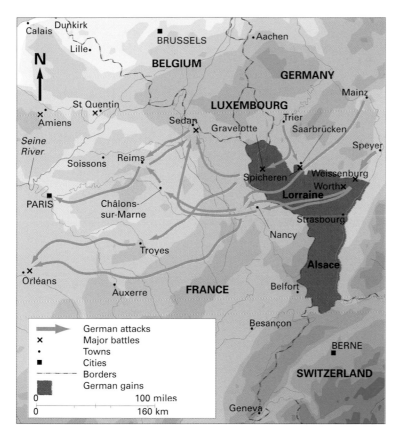

The new German Empire

It is difficult now, after two world wars, to appreciate the military and political drama of the Franco-Prussian War (1870–1871). Never before had armies been so fast-moving, so enhanced in their destructiveness by new technology, and their actions so closely followed by newspaper readers. Several major battles were fought within just a few weeks. The Battle of Sedan on September 1, 1870, when the Prussians effectively destroyed the French Army, saw 100,000 French troops killed, wounded, or captured. The surrender of the French fortress of Metz with its 170,000 defenders on October 27 was the biggest military surrender to date.

Paris, regarded as the world's center of luxury and refinement, was besieged for four months, from September 1870 to January 1871, and much of it destroyed. It was then torn apart by a civil war between rival French political factions. From March to May 1871, in what was called the Commune, thousands of French citizens died at the hands of their fellows, and even more of the city was razed.

This was a European war on a grand scale, one unseen since the Napoleonic Wars that ended in 1815. It involved the total defeat of a major power and changed the geopolitical map of the entire continent. International backing at the outset of the Franco-Prussian War was with the Prussians, but the enormous scale of the French defeat changed this. When the victorious Prussians demanded not only massive financial reparations from the French (who had been effectively tricked into declaring war on Prussia in the first place) but also possession of the whole of Alsace and part of Lorraine—provinces in eastern France—Britain's Queen Victoria was disturbed enough to telegraph her misgivings to the Prussian king, Wilhelm I. Victorious Prussia was increasingly seen internationally as a bully.

nations, as embodied in today's United Nations, was unknown, unwanted, and unthinkable to those in power.

In the latter part of the nineteenth century Europe dominated the world in every aspect. It contained the greatest powers, economically, militarily, and politically, although both the United States and Japan were fast becoming significant world players. Nevertheless, the European powers—Austria-Hungary, Britain, France, Germany, Italy, and Russia—were preeminent. They had gone about their own business with a degree of accord for much of the nineteenth century. They had acquired prestige, to a greater or lesser degree, through European or overseas empires, had developed industrial might, and had large armed forces. Although rivals, for several decades they had avoided direct conflict that might have seriously threatened their status. However, in 1870 matters changed.

▲ *The course of the war between France and Prussia during 1870 and 1871, in which France was humiliated and Prussia emerged as the head of a unified and powerful German Empire.*

11

German Unification

The Prussian victory in the Franco-Prussian War (1870–1871), in which other German states also participated by sending troops to fight alongside the Prussians, laid the foundations for the creation of a unified German state. There was already the North German Confederation, which had been formed following Prussia's victory over the Austro-Hungarian Empire in the Seven Weeks' War (1866). The confederation integrated the Protestant north, but many Germans in the south, mainly Catholics, had resisted its expansion until the Prussian success in 1871.

To secure the support of Prussian traditionalists the king of Prussia, Wilhelm I, was persuaded to become kaiser (emperor) of the new Germany. At Versailles, the former residence of French kings, the German Empire was proclaimed on January 18, 1871, and the reluctant Wilhelm received the German crown amid acclamation from officers representing the various German units around Paris. Nothing could have better emphasized that the new German Empire had been, and would remain, a creation of the Prussian Army.

Many of the still-independent German states were reluctant to join, but had been carried along, as Chancellor (prime minister) Otto von Bismarck had expected, by the tide of Prussian success. Nevertheless, Bavaria, the large southern Catholic state, secured various exemptions, and all of the south German states were exempted from the northern beer tax, which ended one of the popular objections to unification.

▶ *Wilhelm I (1797–1888) was crowned the king of Prussia on January 2, 1861.*

▲ *French cavalrymen and Prussian infantry clash during the first days of the Franco-Prussian War.*

Both Wurttemburg and Bavaria were allowed to continue organizing their own railroad and postal services. In effect, to maintain the pace on which Bismarck counted in order to get the empire accepted, the existing North German Confederation was expanded to include the new states. In the new Federal Council Bavaria had six votes out of the 58, with Prussia having the most—17, enough to block any constitutional change.

The Bavarian Army was allowed to be independent in peacetime, and even kept its own general staff. However, the German emperor could inspect it whenever he wished, and it was to be merged into the German Army in wartime. The Bavarians, like the other German states, also had to organize their army on Prussian lines, with the same length of service.

Bismarck was well aware that there were many people, particularly in southern Germany, who had not wanted his Prussian-dominated Germany. In the following years he tried to weaken the two forces that he thought were most opposed to unification: the socialists and the Roman Catholic Church.

Bavaria and the other southern states that joined the empire in 1871 were Catholic, but Catholics were a minority overall in Germany. Bismarck regarded them as potentially disloyal, and their establishment of a Center Party to defend their interests further alarmed him. He took several measures to take education away from the Roman Catholic Church and to require state approval of appointments to the priesthood. The Roman Catholic Church resisted, and by 1876 most bishops were in prison or in flight. But the Catholic-dominated Center Party actually grew stronger as people rallied against Bismarck's oppressive measures. In the end the campaign petered out.

The same happened with Bismarck's campaign against the socialists. He persecuted leading German Social Democrats like August Bebel, who was sent to prison on several occasions on various charges, including "spreading doctrines dangerous to the state," and "libel of Bismarck." Bismarck also acted more generally, enacting the Anti-Socialist Law in 1878. However, the repressions failed. The 1878 law was ended in 1890, a year in which the Social Democrats won 20 percent of the vote. By 1912 they formed the largest group in the German parliament, a source of major concern to the traditionalists.

KEY FIGURES

CHANCELLOR OTTO VON BISMARCK

Otto von Bismarck (1815–1898) was the creator of modern Germany. Undoubtedly the towering statesman of his age, he also strove to protect Germany from future aggression by forming a series of Europe-wide alliances.

Bismarck studied law before becoming a member of the Prussian parliament and then serving as ambassador to Russia and then France. He was made chancellor (prime minister) of Prussia in 1862 and embarked on a course that would lead to the unification of all of Central Europe's German states under Prussian dominance.

His successive military victories over Denmark (1864), Austria-Hungary (1866), and France (1870–1871) culminated in the foundation of the German Empire, with Bismarck as its first chancellor. He then constructed a complex series of alliances as protection against possible French revenge, particularly the Triple Alliance with Austria-Hungary and Italy in 1882.

Bismarck's internal policies mixed ruthlessness, as in his unsuccessful repression of the Catholic Church and the socialists, with reforms, such as social security and workers' insurance plans. However, Bismarck was sacked by Emperor Wilhelm II on March 18, 1890.

vinced that its military elite had made the country great and would ensure its future greatness. Second, there was a widely held view that future wars would be short and would be contested by fast-moving forces.

Previously the European states had consciously sought to avoid major wars against each other, quite successfully at first, but with subsequent failures like the Crimean War (1853–1856) that had seen Britain, France, and Turkey combine against Russia. Normally the big powers settled disputes among themselves through diplomatic horse-trading without resorting to war—crises but without conflict. This was the so-called Concert of Europe, and it often worked, usually by a majority of the great powers coming together when needed to block the aggressive intentions of one or other of their members. Sometimes they would call an international conference to settle a big issue.

The architect of German unification in 1871 and its subsequent greatness was the prime minister of Prussia, Otto von Bismarck, who was the first chancellor of united Germany. Initially Bismarck relied on military might to increase Prussia's prestige. In 1864 Prussian troops successfully invaded Denmark to take over the province of Schleswig-Holstein, thereby putting down a marker for future expansion. In 1866 Prussia embarked on a brief conflict with the Austro-Hungarian Empire, which most countries recognized as the dominant power in Central Europe. Prussia's swift victory in the Seven Weeks' War, which culminated in the routing of the Austro-Hungarian Army at the Battle of Königgratz on July 3, fatally weakened Austria-Hungary's power in the region and allowed Bismarck to proclaim a confederation of north German states, with Prussia at its head. The process of unifying the remaining states in southern Central Europe into Germany was completed by the Franco-Prussian War. However,

Nevertheless, the Franco-Prussian War changed the entire political face of Europe. France, seen by many contemporaries as the continent's leading power, had been humiliated and left resentful toward Prussia. More importantly, victory allowed Prussia to complete the unification of Germany, previously a loose coalition of states that had been in train since the mid-nineteenth century, and become a European power to be reckoned with. In addition, the war also had some long-lasting military consequences. Germany was recognized as a military superpower, and itself became con-

Bismarck's use of force to promote German unification clearly went against the spirit of the Concert of Europe.

Within newly founded Germany, Prussia was clearly the dominant state. Containing most of the total land area and population, it was also an economic powerhouse. Politically, the prime minister of Prussia was the chancellor (prime minister) of Germany, the king of Prussia was the kaiser (emperor) of Germany, and the capital of Prussia (Berlin) was also the capital of united Germany. Although the states in the new empire had rudimentary forms of popular assemblies, they were far from a full democracy. Most power resided with those of the upper classes close to the kaiser and the military.

In Prussia, members of the conservative landowning class, known as junkers, had dominant influence in elections. The Prussian prime minister therefore owed his position to the landowners, and it was he, as Germany's chancellor, who governed all Germany in the name of the emperor, to whom he was answerable. There was a German parliament (Reichstag), elected by male voters, but although it could debate issues it did

▲ *The conservative landowning class in Prussia prospered following German unification in 1871, as this painting of ladies taking tea and playing cards at the spa town of Marienbad in 1899 clearly shows.*

not govern in the modern sense. Its main power was its right in theory to approve or reject the German budget, but in practice, when there was a budget the chancellor was always able to persuade enough of the political parties to vote in the government's favor.

European militarism

The Prussian tradition of a dominant military class drawn from the great landowners was transferred to the new Germany. What used to be said about Prussia—"Whereas most states have an army, in Prussia the army has a state"— also became true of Germany. Military minds guided the state to an unprecedented degree. A possible advantage of the military mind in some circumstances is that it tends to take prompt and firm action rather than pause for thought. The corresponding disadvantage is that it can act with little thought.

In the second half of the nineteenth century the military mind served Prussia well, as the rapid victories over Austria-Hungary, Denmark, and France indicated. New developments in science and technology were exploited for military rather than for civil ends. It was seen that military power would need an educated population, so schools were built to inculcate children with the necessary beliefs. It was also seen that some industries, initially steel and chemicals, were becoming of military importance, so they were fostered. The Prussian military mind soon grasped what railroads could do for strategy, so railroads were built with this in mind.

However, the dominance of the military mind can also lead a state in the wrong direction. The military mind develops a contempt for civilian government, even for non-military advisers. It reacts strongly against real or imagined threats, when a diplomatic approach might be less dangerous and actually achieve more. Its behavior frightens its neighbors, who also begin to think in terms of war, and so the stage is set for conflict. The military mind believes that it alone understands war, but all too often it discovers that war takes its own violent and uncontrollable course.

Militarism was not confined to Prussia, or to Germany, before World War I, although in other European countries it was not so intense. Britain and the United States were lucky. Protected by their surrounding seas, they did not face hostile forces on their borders, so did not need to maintain large land armies. Their civilian leaders were not overawed by the military class.

Matters were not so simple in France. With Germany on their doorstep, the French felt a great need for an effective military, but a succession of events undermined their faith in both the institution and its leaders. Total defeat in the Franco-Prussian War had severely dented the French Army's prestige and its role at the center of the country's life. A general, Georges Boulanger, almost seized power in 1889, further undermining the wider country's faith in its armed forces. The Dreyfus Affair in 1894, in which a French Army officer of Jewish background was twice wrongly convicted of treason on false charges of spying for Germany, created splits within the French Army itself, as well as among the wider French public.

Austria-Hungary was influenced by militarism, chiefly because its power and influence had been seriously weakened in the second half of the nineteenth century, not least due to Prussia and then Germany usurping its authority in Central Europe. Its senior generals believed that war, or the threat of war, was the best means for the empire to regain some of its lost power, or at least not to lose any more.

In Russia, too, military leaders took a major share of public offices. The czar, Nicholas II, like many of his royal contemporaries, had spent his youth in the Russian Army and was never happier than when on parade.

The Balkans

After 1871 Bismarck had effectively completed his plan to unify Germany and place the state at the center of European affairs. Thereafter his plan was to secure the new state's future through diplomacy rather than through conflict. In a sense, therefore, Germany was a potentially stabilizing element in European affairs under Bismarck's chancellorship, possessing a strong military, being at the heart of Europe, and wanting peace above all. However, it had frontiers with Austria-Hungary, France, and Russia, the latter two seen as threats. France, still smarting from the Franco-Prussian War, could never be accommodated but by itself could not match Germany. In alliance with another power, though, it might well feel it had a chance of righting its deeply felt wrong. Much of Bismarck's international diplomacy after 1871, until his dismissal in 1890, was designed to keep France isolated. Again, this form of single-minded diplomacy went against both the spirit and previous reality of the Concert of Europe.

However, Bismarck initially attempted to secure the future peace of Europe. Evidence of this first came with the Congress of Berlin. Held in June and July 1878 at the behest of the Austro-Hungarian foreign minister, Gyula Andrassy, it was dominated by Bismarck. The congress attempted to bring order to the confused and fractious relations between the dominant powers in the Balkans. It was agreed that the tottering Turkish Empire would be maintained, Britain's concerns over Russian naval expansion were assuaged, and Austria-Hungary was allowed to take over the regions of Bosnia and Herzegovina in the Balkans. However, Russia considered such agreements humiliating, because they conflicted with its own geopolitical aims. Nor did the congress address the aspirations of the peoples of the Balkans, an oversight that was to have major consequences.

THE DREYFUS AFFAIR

The Dreyfus Affair, which arose in 1894, sparked a bitter controversy in France that lasted for some 12 years and brought a polarization in French political life, between left-wing and right-wing groups, that would continue into World War I.

In 1894 Captain Alfred Dreyfus, a French Army officer of Jewish background, was accused of selling military secrets to the Germans. He was convicted of treason and sentenced to life imprisonment in a distant French colony. Initially, the French public supported the conviction, which was used by sections of the press to whip up anti-Semitism by claiming that French Jews were disloyal.

However, doubts grew that Dreyfus was guilty. It was discovered after the conviction that a colleague of his, Major C. F. Esterhazy, had been engaged in espionage, but that the French military had covered up the evidence. Esterhazy was eventually tried but acquitted, an event that prompted novelist Emile Zola to pen a damning indictment of the trial and the French military's deliberate suppression of evidence, entitled *J'Accuse* (*I Accuse*), in February 1898. Zola was found guilty of libel, fined, and sentenced to a year in prison.

However, support for a retrial for Dreyfus was growing, and he was brought back to France and faced a second court martial in 1899. Again he was found guilty, but the French president freed him on compassionate grounds. However, Dreyfus continued to press for complete exoneration, which he finally won in 1906. Nevertheless, the bitter splits the case highlighted and exacerbated would dog French political life for years to come.

Captain Dreyfus stands trial for the second time.

▲ *Constantinople (now Istanbul) was the capital of the crumbling Turkish Empire, a source of instability in the Balkans and Middle East throughout the second half of the nineteenth century.*

A year later Bismarck engineered even closer ties with the Austro-Hungarian Empire. The two powers were reconciled and created a powerful military alliance in Central Europe. In 1881 Bismarck was partially successful in organizing a major treaty between Austria-Hungary, Germany, and Russia. It became known as the Alliance of the Three Emperors (Wilhelm I of Germany, Franz Joseph of Austria-Hungary, and Alexander II of Russia), and was intended to bolster the tottering Turkish Empire at the expense of Britain. However, Russian support for the alliance was never more than halfhearted, due to its antagonisms with Austria-Hungary over the Turkish-controlled Balkans. Also, Alexander II, who favored the

alliance, was assassinated in March 1881 and replaced by his son, Alexander III, a nationalist opposed to any accommodation with Austria-Hungary.

However, the treaty that was to have the most impact on future events in Europe was not the partly successful Alliance of the Three Emperors, but the Triple Alliance. Signed on May 20, 1882, this secret agreement involved Austria-Hungary, Germany, and Italy, and was primarily directed against France. Among its provisions were that Austria-Hungary and Germany would support Italy if it was attacked by France; that Italy would support Germany if it was attacked by France; and that Italy would remain neutral in any future conflict between Austria-Hungary and Russia.

corrupt, and resentful of the growing foreign involvement in its affairs. Its provincial governors often treated the empire's subject peoples with great cruelty. There were revolts and, more important, independence movements. If the latter could obtain outside support, they had some hope of success.

Russia—until the emergence of a fully independent Serbia in 1878, the only Slavic state—felt responsible for the fate of Slavs under foreign rule. At the same time it had what it saw as a religious mission to restore Constantinople to the Orthodox Church. This holy mission coincided with a more materialistic

Turkey and Russia

At the other end of Europe, around the eastern end of the Mediterranean, lay another, older, source of instability between the great powers: the Turkish Empire. Constantinople, the Turkish capital, had once been the seat of the Eastern Orthodox Church, a Christian rival to Roman Catholicism. After the Turks captured Constantinople in 1453, Russia became the center of that church, which evolved into the Russian Orthodox Church. In the European parts of what became the Turkish Empire, the parallel Greek Orthodox Church was the bedrock of Christian communities under Turkish rule.

By the second half of the nineteenth century the large Turkish Empire was a shadow of its former self—it was weak,

▶ *Born in 1830, Franz Joseph was emperor of Austria-Hungary from 1848 until his death in 1916. He believed that World War I would be a disaster for his realm.*

object, namely control of the narrow sea channel of the Bosporus (through Constantinople) and the Dardanelles, which was the only way that Russian ships from the Black Sea could enter the Mediterranean. Thus Russia was deeply concerned with the fate of the Turkish Empire. Other powers realized, with varying degrees of concern, that if Slavic states were created from the ruins of the Turkish Empire, then those states might give Russia the vital foothold it desired in the Mediterranean, thereby altering the balance of power between the great powers in the region.

The health of Turkey, the so-called sick man of Europe, had been a main concern of the European powers throughout the nineteenth century. For a long time the British government followed a policy of encouraging Turkey to cure itself, to become strong enough to maintain its possessions in some kind of tolerable order. However, the decline continued and the idea of creating new nations in the Balkans found increasing

▼ *In the second half of the nineteenth century, Russia wished to win control of Constantinople, the Turkish capital, as it guarded the narrow but deep Bosporus seaway that linked the Mediterranean and Black Seas.*

favor. Indeed, there was already the example of Greece, which declared its independence in 1822 with the support of the European great powers.

Turkey recognized Serbian independence in 1878, although the area of the new Serbian state was smaller than the Serbian Empire that the Turks had overthrown in 1389 at the Battle of Kosovo. Henceforth, Serbian political life would be dominated by the struggle, often lethal, between two rival ruling families, and by the re-creation of the old Serbian Empire under a new name, Greater Serbia. Some Serbs lived in Montenegro, a small mountainous principality that had managed to keep the Turks more or less at bay over the centuries and was regarded as semi-independent.

Among the other nationalities of the Balkans were the Croats, a Slavic people who had embraced both the Catholic Church and the Roman alphabet, but who spoke the same language as the Serbs. There were the Bulgars, another Slavic people who spoke a language of a

◀ This cartoon by
Alfred Schmidt,
depicting Turkey's
power in Europe
being shaken by its
Balkan neighbors,
appeared in the
Danish magazine
Klods-Hans in 1912.
Turkish control of
the region was
severely under-
mined during
the Balkan Wars
(1912–1913), when
it was forced to
surrender large
tracts of its
European territory.

background very similar to Russian; the Macedonians; the Romanians, who believed that they were the true descendants of the ancient Romans; the Slavic Bosnians and Slavic Herzegovinians; and sundry tribal groups that had embraced the religion of Islam and were known collectively as Albanians.

The fallacy that determined the policy of the great powers was that it would be possible to transplant the idea of the nation state to this region, separating the different peoples into their own states. It was not realized that although these people resented the Turks, they feared and hated their neighbors even more. The

▲ *Several different nationalities lived in the Austro-Hungarian Empire, but German-speakers were dominant in Vienna, the capital city. They held most key political posts, a situation that was resented to a lesser or greater degree by many others.*

greater wisdom would have been for the powers to stand clear of the Balkans and let history take its slow, sometimes cruel, course. Bismarck once stated that the troubles of the Balkans were not worth the bones of a single Prussian soldier.

However, several of the powers felt that they could not ignore the Turkish problem. In Russia, the czar had to take into account the powerful pro-Slavist movement, which regarded the Slavic Balkan peoples as relatives who were in need of protection. Austria-Hungary, which had millions of Serbs and Croats within its frontiers, could not ignore the Balkan region. Britain, sensitive about its route to India, was interested in the eastern Mediterranean and did not relish Russia gaining a foothold.

The unsettled Balkans complicated Bismarck's diplomatic plans. In his need to protect Germany from France,

Bismarck developed a series of treaties that tended to replace the old Concert of Europe method of keeping the peace. Russia was his primary concern, for not only was there a big Russian Army but any Franco-Russian alliance would mean that Germany might have to fight on both its eastern and western frontiers simultaneously. Bismarck's efforts to keep Russia in some kind of alliance were repeatedly endangered by the conflict of interests between Austria-Hungary, Germany's constant ally, and Russia, Germany's necessary friend. Austria-Hungary and Russia feared what the other might do in the Balkans.

The Austro-Hungarian Empire
The great power closest to the Balkans danger zone was itself a troubled anomaly and, appropriately enough, was known by several names. It had once

been the Holy Roman Empire, then the Hapsburg Empire, and after the defeat by Prussia in 1866 it became the Dual Monarchy of Austria-Hungary. Like Russia, it was not a nation state but a fractious multinational empire.

Not one of its dozen or so nationalities was a majority. Germans were the most numerous and influential, being dominant in the empire's and Austria's capital, Vienna, and in a few of the provinces. Germans were also the backbone of the civil service. Other major nationalities in Austria were the Poles, who occupied that part of Poland that was controlled by Austria-Hungary (the other parts were occupied by Prussia and Russia). Poles were Slavs, and so were the Czechs in Austrian Bohemia. Other Slavs were the Slovaks and the Ruthenians, the latter being close to the Ukrainians of the Russian Empire. In the empire's south there were more than 500,000 Italians, most of whom backed the cause of irredentism, political reunification with Italy.

To the east of Vienna lay the other half of the Dual Monarchy, Hungary. This was the homeland of the Magyars, who racially and linguistically were quite distinct from other Europeans in Central Europe. Within Hungary there were also important minorities, including Serbs and Croats. The Magyar ruling class of landowners had insisted on a degree of independence, and the Dual Monarchy was the result. The emperor of Austria was also the king of Hungary, but there was an independently minded Hungarian parliament, elected in effect by the landowners. There was a Hungarian prime minister, and only war, foreign affairs, and finance were dealt with jointly as Austro-Hungarian matters, with their ministers answerable to the king/emperor, to two prime ministers, and, in theory, to two parliaments.

German was the language of the administration and of the armed services, but in Hungary the non-Magyars were subject to "Magyarization," with Hungarian the language of the schools. Some of the constituent peoples were beginning to hanker for independence. Political parties multiplied, with some arising purely to represent a single nationality, while broad parties like liberals and conservatives were divided by nationality into sub-parties. All in all, this was not an easy empire to govern.

Austria-Hungary appeared strong militarily, but its political weaknesses were obvious. The loyalty of its multitude of nationalities could not be taken for granted. Moreover, some nationalities could look to their own national states already functioning to a greater or lesser degree outside the empire's frontiers. Italians could look enviously at their co-nationals in the recently independent and united Italy, while Serbs could look to independent Serbia.

POLITICAL WORLD

IRREDENTISM

Irredentism originated from the Italian words *Italia irredenta* ('unredeemed Italy') and referred to nationalists who sought to liberate both Italian lands and Italian people from foreign rule.

To Italians, irredentism was the wresting of control of the Trentino (southern Tyrol), Gorizia, Istria, Trieste, Ticino, Nice, Corsica, and Malta from the Austro-Hungarians, the Swiss, French, and British. However, the movement concentrated on those areas controlled by Austria-Hungary.

The irredentists also opposed Italy's signing of the Triple Alliance with Austria-Hungary and Germany, because they believed it would harm their cause, and they were one of the key groups that led Italy to abandoning its alliance obligations at the beginning of World War I and eventually siding with the Allies. After victory over the Central Powers in 1918 the aspirations of most irredentists were satisfied by the acquisition of the Istrian Peninsula and the southern Tyrol from Austria-Hungary. However, a number of extremist Italian nationalists sought further gains in the postwar period.

For these reasons, Vienna was unlikely to favor the creation of new states out of the Turkish Empire and had a vested interest in the continuation of that empire. Nor could it regard Russia with anything but suspicion when many influential Russians talked of a Greater Slavdom. Austria-Hungary was the only great power to feel itself threatened by small nations. Small wonder that its rulers felt anxious and increasingly relied on alliance with Germany for protection of their interests.

Imperialism

Well before the end of the nineteenth century, colonization had given way to imperialism, in which the exploitation of colonial resources was supplemented by a complete system of government imposed by the home country. Empires became status symbols, and the point was reached when states felt that they could only truly be "great" if they possessed overseas domains. Germany, only recently created, lacked such imperial status and felt it acutely.

The British Empire was by far the biggest and stretched all around the globe, so it could truly be described as the empire on which the sun never sets. However, countries that were late in appearing as world powers missed out on the early bout of colonizing and therefore lacked empires. Japan was one of these countries and by the late nineteenth century was seeking to annex parts of the Asian mainland. The United States was another. Initially preoccupied with expanding westward and southward overland, and with anticolonialism as one of its founding principles, it was late in seeking overseas territories. Russia, having reached the Pacific in 1860, was interested both in the Far East and in Central Asia. In the latter, Russia seemed, to the British, to be threatening British India. Meanwhile Germany and Italy, only recently emerged as nations, produced politicians and publicists who proclaimed

they would only be taken seriously as leading world powers if they acquired their own empires.

In previous centuries major wars had been fought for the acquisition or retention of overseas possessions. At first, colonies had been regarded as useful for obtaining raw materials and thereby enriching the nation that possessed them. Later, when vast areas of territory were added to empires, the cost of defending and administering those empires was greater than any economic gain derived from them. British India might have provided a secure market for a few British industries, but

exports it could send in return, like textiles, tended to be items that the British were already producing. The advantages gained by a few home industries were outweighed by the sheer cost of administering and defending India. Nevertheless, India had its value as a long-held possession in which British citizens could take great pride.

Similarly, the U.S. acquisition of the Philippines at the end of the nineteenth century, due to victory in the Spanish-American War of 1898, was expected to open up a new field for U.S. products and investment, both locally and in nearby China, but brought few such gains. Ordinary people believed that overseas possessions were of economic advantage, but the acquisitions of empire made in the late nineteenth century rarely produced economic gain for the possessing nations, although they often greatly benefited a few individuals. However, the empire as a national status symbol was a very real phenomenon. The chief problem for the emerging imperialist powers in the last quarter of the nineteenth century was that there was an increasing shortage of countries to colonize. There was growing competition among the great powers for those uncolonized countries that remained.

▼ *India was the jewel in the crown of the British Empire in the nineteenth century and it was guarded jealously. This colorized photo of Calcutta was taken in the 1890s.*

▲ German forces on the move in German East Africa (now Tanzania) in 1885. Imperial acquisitions in the late nineteenth century helped raise Germany's status as a world power. However, its colonial empire was much smaller that those of most other major powers. The situation was a cause of deep frustration among the country's ruling elite in the years before World War I and particularly irritated Emperor Wilhelm II.

What imperial rivalries did do was to make international relations more volatile and less certain, thereby further undermining the Concert of Europe. Governments began to consider imperial issues when forming alliances. For example, when in 1881 the French occupied Tunis, which the Italians were coveting, the Italian response was to make a treaty, the Triple Alliance, with Austria-Hungary and Germany. When the British and French clashed over Egypt in 1898, the British drew closer to Germany, whose diplomatic help was seen to be useful.

Austria-Hungary, already having in its realm more nationalities than it wanted, refrained from the imperialist urge, but Italy and Germany were determined to raise their imperial profiles. However, Italy was humiliated while attempting to secure colonies in East Africa. Its invasion of Ethiopia (1895–1896) was repulsed, with the Ethiopians emphatically defeating the invaders at the Battle of Adowa. Germany acquired territory in Africa with British and French acquiescence. German South West Africa (Namibia) was one gain, and German East Africa (Tanzania) was another. Following fierce competition with the United States, Germany also managed

to pick up part of the Samoan Islands in the Pacific and also established a base, Tsingtao, on the coast of China.

The scramble for Africa, most of which was divided among several European nations by 1900, was followed by the scramble for China, as the old Chinese Empire disintegrated. The Japanese sought to acquire Manchuria and Korea, just as the Russians had the same idea, while the French, British, and Germans established their own treaty ports, where they exercised control and obtained access for their exports and imports. China was seen as a big potential market for the industrialized nations that were beginning to fear that their productive capacity was far greater than was needed for their own domestic use. Both Britain and the United States feared that if the Chinese Empire collapsed there would be a general war as each imperial power sought to take over the ruins to the exclusion of the others.

Partly to moderate competition in this region, in 1898 the United States proposed the open door policy, which envisaged equal trading access for all through treaty ports. The policy was never agreed, but the Boxer Rebellion (1900–1901) did briefly indicate that the imperial powers could act in self-interested concert if their rights were threatened. This uprising by Chinese nationalists—the Boxers—who enjoyed support from the Chinese authorities, was directed against both foreigners and Chinese Christians. Random murders and massacres were followed by the Boxers attacking the diplomatic compounds of the imperialist powers in the Chinese capital, Peking (Beijing).

A multinational force was eventually sent to restore order and reassert foreign rights. It proved successful, and China returned to effective foreign dominance. However, as soon as the Boxers were defeated the great powers attempted to pursue their own interests in China. Ironically, the troops that comprised the multinational force were drawn entirely from those countries that would take part in World War I.

Empires generally needed to be defended, chiefly against other imperial powers. The British were particularly sensitive about any threat to their lines of communication to India and beyond to Australasia. For the British and other powers, imperial defense was a reason to maintain large naval forces.

When Admiral Alfred von Tirpitz, head of the German Navy, sought to build up his country's naval power from the late 1890s, the necessity of colonial defense was one of the arguments he used. Navies needed coaling stations around the world where their warships could refuel, and, for example, the U.S. acquisition of islands in the Caribbean and Pacific at the end of the Spanish-American War in 1898 was largely intended to provide for these needs.

Situations arose in which a territory was acquired to provide a base for land or naval forces, and then another one had to be acquired to defend the first. The Russian Empire in Central Asia had expanded because as soon as a new frontier was established as defense against hostile tribesmen, it

needed another piece of territory to provide a buffer. In this way Russian territory neared that of British India, causing considerable tension between the two powers as well as goading Britain into costly advances into Afghanistan. These imperial clashes of interest repeatedly brought the powers involved close to war, but the powers, fearing a general conflagration, always drew back in time. However, events in the late nineteenth and early twentieth centuries combined to make a decision to pull back from war all the more difficult.

▼ *German cavalry, part of a multinational force, march into Peking (Beijing) in 1901 after the collapse of the Boxer Rebellion. This demonstration of unity borne out of self-interest among the world's leading powers proved short-lived.*

The United States before the War

In the decades following the American Civil War (1861–1865), the United States underwent a profound transformation, economically, socially, and politically.

In 1865, U.S. life was dominated by Reconstruction, the rebuilding and reintegration of the war-devastated Confederacy. This was a major program that was painful. Abraham Lincoln, the U.S. president, had believed that if the Confederacy was to be fully reintegrated into the United States it had to be aided. However, politics and Southern resentment at some of its aspects made Reconstruction traumatic.

Lincoln's successor, Republican Andrew Jackson, believed that he had the powers to direct the program, but this right was challenged by the U.S. Congress. Congress won the argument and Radical Republicans, as they were called, took charge. Under their direction, the First Reconstruction Act was passed in 1867, despite the president's veto. The act divided the South into five military districts, each subject to martial law. The Southern states were ordered to elect new conventions based on universal male suffrage, to create new governments guaranteeing African-American voting rights, and they also had to ratify the 14th Amendment of 1868, which confirmed the status of African Americans as U.S. citizens with rights equal to those of whites.

Such sweeping reforms, undertaken under what was effectively military rule, were anathema to many people in the South, and Reconstruction progressed slowly and acrimoniously. Additional acts followed, only adding to the bitterness between North and South. The period of Reconstruction continued into the 1870s and subsided only with the inauguration of Rutherford B. Hayes in 1877, an event that, in effect, marked the end of the Radical Republicans' stranglehold on the South.

Settling the continent

Attempts to bind the country together and open up the West to settlement began while the civil war was still in progress and they continued during the

▼ *The burned ruins of Richmond, Virginia, the former capital of the Confederacy, in 1865 at the end of the American Civil War.*

period of Reconstruction. On July 1, 1862, the Pacific Railroad Act permitted the Union Pacific Railroad to construct a transcontinental route from Iowa to Utah, where it would meet with a route being constructed eastward from California by the Central Pacific Railroad. The two lines finally met at Promontory Point, Utah, on May 10, 1869, heralding the white settlement of the far West. Finance to open up these lands came from two sources—the federal government, which gave the railroad companies land to exploit along their routes, and the nation's major banks, not least that of J.P. Morgan.

Other routes followed over subsequent years. For example, in 1860 the United States had some 30,000 miles (48,000 km) of track, but by 1900 had some 250,000 miles (400,000 km). Between 1900 and 1910, an additional 100,000 miles (160,000 km) were built, binding the country together more than ever before, and allowing people and various produce and goods to flow in ever-greater volumes.

The railroads not only united the country from coast to coast as never before, but they also heralded a new era in the colonization of the continent. Settlers flooded into the new lands along the various routes. The majority of them became farmers, while others tried their luck at exploiting the region's rich natural resources, such as minerals and timber. Small settlements were established in order to serve the incoming settlers' various needs.

The country was also undergoing an unprecedented increase in population— from 31 million in 1860 to 76 million in 1900, and then to 92 million by 1910. Most of the growth between 1860 and 1900 was due to births exceeding deaths within the United States, but after 1900 the previous, steady stream of immigrants—mostly from Ireland, Germany, and Scandinavia, between 1820 and 1880—turned into a torrent.

Many of this new wave of immigrants came from Austria-Hungary, Italy, and Russia, and an estimated 26 million of them arrived between the end of the American Civil War in 1865 and 1915, some nine million alone between 1880 and 1900. Many settled in the larger cities of the East and West Coasts, but many others, tempted by offers of a new start and free lands to farm, moved into the lands opened up by the new railroads in the region west of the Mississippi River. The percentage of U.S. citizens who were living west of the Mississippi rose from 22 percent in 1880 to 27 percent by 1900.

The Native-American experience

This new colonization increased the frictions between Native Americans and the predominantly white settlers. Many Native Americans had already been pushed out of their traditional eastern homelands by the steady westward expansion of European settlers, and once in the West, the Native Americans

had nowhere else to go. Inevitably they fought back to stem the tide of settlement and between the end of the American Civil War and their final defeat at Wounded Knee in 1890, numerous wars were fought. The Native Americans won occasional, if spectacular, victories, such as the Battle of the Little Big Horn in 1876, but they had little hope of winning the longer war. Wounded Knee, really more of a massacre than a battle, was the final episode in Native American attempts to maintain a separate existence. All of these wars and campaigns had a profound impact on the Native Americans—confined to reservations, disenfranchised and with rising death rates, the Native American population declined from 125,000 in 1890 to 120,000 by 1900.

▶ *In May 1869 the great transcontinental railroad route was completed when the Central Pacific and Union Pacific railroads met near the Great Salt Lake.*

▼ *The building of railroads in the late nineteenth and early twentieth century bound the United States and its people together as never before.*

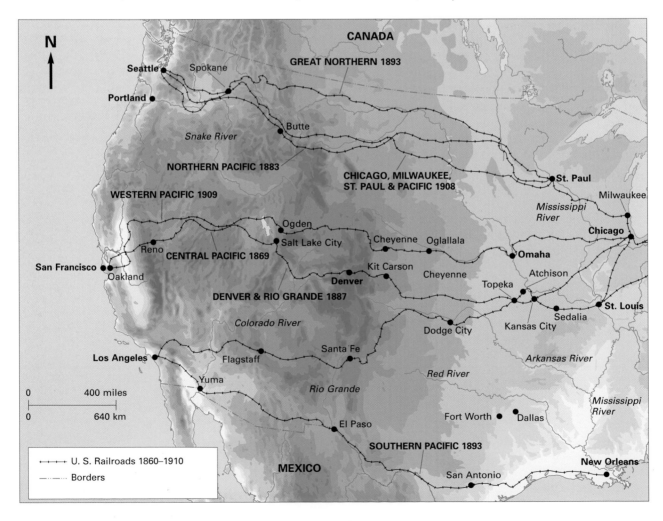

The African American Experience

The decades preceding World War I were years of disappointment for those who, after the American Civil War, had been hoping for a sweeping improvement in the rights and status of African Americans.

Literacy tests and other discriminatory devices intended to disenfranchise African Americans without blatantly violating the U.S. Constitution became even more widespread in the South as the twentieth century dawned. In the South, African Americans were no longer recognized as part of the electorate, except in a few cities where the incumbent party relied on their vote. Also in the South, systematic segregation, known as Jim Crow, was being extended in the early twentieth century. The first such devices had appeared as early as the 1890s, when railroads in the South were required to separate African Americans from whites.

By the turn of the century it was no longer just the South that upheld the Jim Crow system. An 1896 U.S. Supreme Court decision concerning streetcar segregation ruled that, so long as the facilities were "separate but equal," discrimination did not exist. This encouraged new discrimination in the North and the South.

▶ *A former slave, educator Booker T. Washington set up the Tuskegee Institute in Alabama to provide African Americans with further education.*

▲ *A French magazine of May 7, 1911, depicts the brutal murder of an African American at the hands of a white theater audience.*

Racist lynchings also became more common. The statistics are not wholly reliable, but 1915 seems to have been a record year for this, with 79 African Americans killed. Lynchings were imposed by white mobs on black men "suspected" of raping white women or killing white people. Such horrific events were regarded as public entertainment and had a carnival atmosphere.

Almost as repugnant as lynching was the race riot. Early twentieth-century race riots in the United States had much in common with the anti-Jewish pogroms then occurring in Russia. The worst was at Atlanta in 1906, when swathes of the city were burned and 11 African Americans were killed. In August 1908 there was the first major riot in Springfield, Illinois.

African Americans soon found ways of fighting back. Under the inspired leadership of Booker T. Washington, many people sought an education and in just 10 years (1900–1910) the number of African Americans able to read and write rose from about 35 to 70 percent. Washington, having done much to raise self-respect, was criticized for his apparent acceptance of white domination. He was challenged by William Du Bois, who favored concentrating attention on the top 10 percent of blacks, while demanding complete freedom and equality for all. The splitting of the movement probably did no long-term harm, However. Du Bois and his friends, with the support of some Northern whites, created an organization in 1909, the National Association for the Advancement of Colored People (NAACP), which would come to play a decisive role in African American affairs.

Reflecting this pattern of white settlement was the admission into the union of new states, chiefly in the West. Excluding former Confederate states that were readmitted after the civil war, Nebraska (1867) was the first territory to achieve statehood after the conflict and others followed steadily over the decades. The political union of the country gathered pace with the Omnibus Bill of February 1889, which allowed for the admission of North Dakota, South Dakota, Montana, and Washington. Oklahoma, formerly known as Indian Territory, was admitted in 1907, and Arizona and New Mexico in 1912. The modern political map of the continental United States was effectively completed shortly before the outbreak of World War I.

Although the settlement of the West was one phenomenon of the period, another was the urbanization of the population. While people were moving to the rural West in considerable numbers, the greater trend was the expansion of urban settlements. In 1880 the Bureau of the Census reported that 28 percent of the population lived in urban areas, but by 1900 the figure increased to 40 percent.

Industrialization

Hand in hand with urbanization went industrialization. The period between the end of Reconstruction and the dawn of the twentieth century, from roughly 1878 to 1898, saw an unparalleled expansion of the economy. During these two decades, U.S. industrial production, the number of industrial workers, and the number of factories all doubled. For example iron and steel output rose more than sevenfold between 1880 and 1900. However, such economic figures were not confined to purely traditional businesses. The annual value of manufactured goods produced in the United States during the same period more than doubled.

The emergence of the United States as an industrial giant was due to many factors. The opening of the West by the railroads greatly boosted the demand for iron and steel, while the West's resources, chiefly the mining and lumber industries, provided capital that could further spur industrial development in the East. Equally, the United States soon harnessed the most up-to-date technologies and manufacturing processes in larger factories. Output rose dramatically and costs fell. New methods of production were introduced—Henry Ford, one of the leading industrialists of his age, pioneered the cost-saving concepts of standardization and the production line.

The final quarter of the nineteenth century also saw many new inventions that were to have lasting importance. Among these were the automobile, the electric light, the telephone, and refrigeration. Each of these offered an opportunity to develop wholly new industries, and big business responded. Petroleum,

▲ An engraving taken from a work titled **Darkness and Daylight** *showing a typical New York tenement yard in 1891, places that housed many of the latest immigrants to the United States from Europe.*

34

too, was becoming a major enterprise, initially in industry but increasingly for public and domestic use. This economic dynamism was orchestrated by a new breed of entrepreneurs, men who ran vast businesses that were effectively monopolies. John D. Rockefeller was dominant in oil, Andrew Carnegie in steel, and Cornelius Vanderbilt and a few others controlled the railroads.

However, rapid industrialization and the dominance of big businesses and entrepreneurs did bring social and political problems in their wake. For much of the period, industrial tensions—mainly centered around wages, hours, and working conditions—rose. The living conditions of ordinary citizens in the fast-growing towns and cities were also frequently extremely squalid. Buildings were often poorly maintained and lacking in basic amenities, not least sanitation. The combination of poor working conditions and substandard dwellings led many to form associations to press for change.

KEY FIGURES

HENRY FORD

Henry Ford (1863–1947) was the embodiment of the U.S. success story. Born in Greenfield, Michigan, to a family of average means, Ford grew up to become head of an industrial empire.

Ford arrived in Detroit in 1891 and worked as an engineer, while experimenting on gasoline engines in his spare time. His first automobile was produced in 1896 and he formed the Detroit Automobile Company three years later. In 1903 he created the Ford Motor Company and pioneered new production methods, including mass production based on the standardization of parts and the use of the production line.

In 1908 he unveiled the Model T, which embodied all of his beliefs. It was the first automobile that the masses could realistically afford, and it remained in production until 1927. Thanks to a moving production line, Ford was producing some 2,000 cars a day by 1916.

Although conservative in nature, in some ways Ford was an enlightened employer. He fought hard against unionism (Ford did not recognize any union until 1941), but did attempt to improve the lot of his workers—in 1915, for example, he doubled their wages.

Industrial unrest

The first significant labor union was the Knights of Labor, which was founded in 1869 and also supported wider political and social reform. The impetus for its expansion came during the general economic depression that swept the country between 1873 and 1878. Matters came to a head in July 1877, shortly after railroad bosses in the East had agreed among themselves to cut workers' wages by 10 percent. On July 14, workers on the Baltimore and Ohio Railroad went on strike, quickly followed by colleagues on other railroads. Workers in other industries, chiefly mining, then walked out in sympathy and by the end of the month much of the country was paralyzed.

The response of business and government to the unrest was to use force. Police, many hastily sworn-in, state militias, and federal troops were all deployed. The confrontations became increasingly violent and culminated in the events at Pittsburgh, Ohio, on the 21st. A demonstration by local railroad workers and ordinary citizens was met by lethal force. In the ensuing riot some 2,000 freight cars were destroyed and the rail companies suffered property damage estimated at $10 million. By the end of the month, despite the use of troops, the railroad owners had agreed to drop the plan for the 10 percent reduction in wages.

The Knights of Labor rekindled interest in unions among the wider U.S. population and the movement was able to boast a membership of 700,000 by the mid-1880s. However, the Knights of Labor was undermined in 1886, a year in which the United States was deeply troubled by worker unrest. Some 1,600 strikes were recorded, involving 600,000 workers. Matters reached crisis point in Chicago on May 4, when strikers from the McCormick Harvesting Machine Company of Chicago held a meeting in Haymarket Square. The meeting was

▼ *In July 1894, a strike by railroad workers in Chicago brought chaos to communications. In this scene from the periodical* Graphic *of July 28, troops are escorting the Western Mail Service to protect it from mob attack.*

taken over by anarchists and local police were called in to restore order. A bomb was thrown, killing seven policemen. Eight of the anarchists present were arrested and four were hanged. The public identified the Haymarket events with the union movement in general and the Knights of Labor in particular, and both suffered as a result. Union membership declined markedly.

However, a new type of unionism was developing. The American Federation of Labor (AFL), founded in 1881, was very different from the Knights of Labor. Its membership was drawn only from skilled workers and its leadership rejected any wider political reform to concentrate on matters of greater concern to its memberships—union recognition, shorter hours, and better wages. Although by 1900 union membership had only returned to its 1880 levels, the AFL, which was led by Samuel Gompers, would thrive in the first decades of the twentieth century.

Nevertheless, the last 20 years of the nineteenth century saw considerable labor unrest, particularly in the four years following a crash on the New York Stock Exchange in 1893. One of the most contentious began when the Pullman Palace Car Company employees based in Chicago called a strike on May 11, 1894, to protest job losses, reduced wages, higher rents, and high prices in company-owned houses and stores. Refusing to negotiate, the company hired some 3,600 marshals to break the strike, while left-wing leader Eugene Debs called for a strike by all of the country's railroad workers.

As the crisis deepened, U.S. Attorney General Richard Olney, who had close ties with the railroad companies, persuaded President Grover Cleveland to take legal action against Debs as his strike call would interfere "with interstate commerce and postal service," although the Pullman Company did not in fact carry mail. To enforce the injunction, Debs later received a six-month jail sentence for his activities.

On July 3 U.S. troops were sent to break the strike, and greater violence erupted. Several strikers and hangers-on were killed before the troops were withdrawn on the 20th. The strikers agreed to call off their action on August 3, by which time some $80 million in property and wages had been lost. Although the strikers won public sympathy, they gained no concessions.

▲ *Living conditions for American workers were often pitiful, particularly during strikes. On many occasions striking workers, such as this man, were reduced to living in squalid shanty towns.*

A fairer society

The imbalances and injustices in U.S. society, in which a very rich few lived well and wielded enormous power while the masses lived in appalling conditions, was seen by some politicians as unacceptable. Known as Progressives, they were to be found in both the Republican and Democratic parties, and their main concern was redirecting society so that it approached more closely the one they had known in their younger days, in which the ideals of the Founding Fathers were, by and large, observed. Progressives felt that the existing society contained too much unnecessary misery, injustice, corruption, violence, and waste, largely due to the dominance of big business.

▲ *President William Howard Taft of the Republican Party was on the Progressive wing of his party and held office from 1909 to 1913.*

While the Progressives aimed at bringing big business to heel, they simultaneously wanted to maintain the economic benefits that big business brought to the economy. Expressed differently, they wanted to travel backward to a past age while moving forward with technology and economic development. Wanting to progress simultaneously in opposite directions, their achievements tended to be less impressive than they might have been, and in subsequent decades the United States continued to depart from the ideals of its founders. Nevertheless, with three Progressive presidents—the Republicans Theodore Roosevelt (1901–1909) and William Taft (1909–1913), then the Democrat Woodrow Wilson (1913–1921)—following each other in the decade preceding World War I, much was done to moderate the uglier features of U.S. society.

However, the struggle against the big monopolies, or trusts, was not really won. This was partly because these agglomerations seemed to be doing a good job in terms of production. With the Supreme Court favoring the big trusts, successive antitrust legislation usually succeeded only in putting an end to blatantly unfair competition. Nevertheless, the mania for trusts continued. In February 1901, for example, the United States Steel Corporation was incorporated under the direction of financier J. P. Morgan, becoming the first billion-dollar business. Morgan himself is believed to have profited to the tune of $80 million. It has been estimated that by the dawn of the twentieth century, men such as Morgan, who together formed just one percent of the U.S. population, owned some 87 percent of the wealth. Meanwhile, despite repeated attempts to reduce import tariffs, the U.S. industries they controlled remained well protected, to the detriment of the U.S. consumer.

It was at local and state level that the Progressive Movement had its greatest beneficial effects. Corruption in local government, with businesses buying influence and privilege, was never eliminated, but it was at least checked in an increasing number of states and cities. This, in turn, made it harder for businesses to rely on local police forces in labor conflicts. Workers at the time were grievously underpaid and when they asked for a "living wage" they meant precisely that, because their pay was often not enough to sustain their families. The tide was gradually turning, though, and a landmark came when President Theodore Roosevelt intervened in a miners' dispute.

The issue revolved around a strike in May 1902 by 140,000 members of the United Mine Workers led by John Mitchell. The owners refused to negotiate, believing the federal authorities would eventually send in troops to break the strike, but the dispute dragged on until the fall. Roosevelt finally intervened in October, but the owners refused to compromise. The president then sent in troops—not in support of the miners, but in the public interest. On October 16, a Commission of Arbitration was formed to investigate the miners' grievances. When it reported in March 1903, the miners gained higher wages, shorter hours, and a measure of union recognition.

Justifying expansionism

By the last decade of the nineteenth century, some leading Americans began to look for another stage for U.S. expansionism. The nation was economically strong, it had a higher, if still

▼ *President Woodrow Wilson, a leading Progressive from the Democratic Party, making an impassioned speech in 1917 from a banner-draped booth.*

▶ *Alfred Mahan was an ardent advocate of U.S. naval expansion, believing that a strong fleet of warships was necessary to protect the country's economic interests and enhance its position as a major world power.*

imperfect, degree of social stability than ever before, yet it remained an essentially regional power in global terms. Prominent among those who were advocating a greater international presence were men such as Theodore Roosevelt, senior politicians John Hay and Henry Cabot Lodge, and the naval theorist Alfred Thayer Mahan. What was needed was a justification for American involvement and, equally important, a means.

Part of the justification for the expansionist policy lay with the Monroe Doctrine. Named after James Monroe, president between 1817 and 1825, the doctrine was publicly acknowledged in 1852, it being claimed that the United States had the right to consider as a hostile act any attempt by a European power to colonize any independent nation in the western hemisphere. The United States would act, therefore, to prevent further interference in a region it considered within its sphere of influence. By the mid-nineteenth century, however, the western hemisphere's greatest European colonial power, Spain, had surrendered its South American colonies to independence movements, and its grip elsewhere, chiefly in Central America and the Caribbean, was failing as the century drew to a close.

Clearly, a power vacuum was developing and it was one that the United States had the resources to fill. However, as a former colony itself, one that prided itself on freedoms and rights, it did not wish to be seen as an aggressive colonial power. A way around this was sought. First, a policy of so-called Dollar Diplomacy was developed, which used U.S. diplomacy to support home-grown business interests overseas. In effect, U.S. businesses were allowed to colonize some countries to such an extent economically that they effectively ran them through little more than puppet regimes. Most such regimes were despised by the people they purported

to rule and many faced internal political unrest that they were hard pressed to control and which then threatened U.S. economic interests.

Second, there were attempts to forge closer ties between the United States and the states of Latin America. Discussions held between October 1889 and April 1890, organized by Secretary of State James Blaine and involving 17 countries, led to the creation of the International Bureau of American Republics. Established to further cultural, economic, and political links in the region, it was renamed the Pan-American Union in 1910.

A more aggressive U.S. political strategy was signaled by President Theodore Roosevelt in December 1904. In what became known as the Roosevelt Corollary, the president argued that the United States had the right to act as an "international police power" in those countries included in the Monroe Doctrine. The basis for military intervention would be in cases where domestic unrest was evident and U.S. business interests were threatened.

American naval power
In 1890 Captain Alfred Mahan, historian at the U.S. Naval War College, published his *The Influence of Sea Power Upon History 1660–1783*, a book which quickly became the favorite of the advocates of naval power in many countries. It was not at first a best-seller, but it was read by a number of very influential people, including the future U.S. president Theodore Roosevelt and the German emperor, Wilhelm II.

The book argued that the outcome of great wars was determined not so much by the clash of land forces as by the activity of navies. Command of the sea secured communication and supply, advantages without which armies could hardly function. He who mastered the seas mastered the world, was the message. One of Mahan's theses was that a navy did not necessarily have to fight in

POLITICAL WORLD

THE GREAT WHITE FLEET

The Great White Fleet was a U.S. naval flotilla that circumnavigated the world between 1907 and 1909, thereby heralding the United States as a leading maritime nation and therefore one of the world's great powers.

The idea for the worldwide flag-showing cruises was that of President Theodore Roosevelt, who hoped that the operation would lead to more funds being earmarked for further naval expansion. Some 12,000 U.S. naval personnel and a fleet of 16 battleships, all of which were painted white for the occasion, set sail from Hampton Roads in December 1907 led by the *Connecticut*. Sailing from east to west around the globe, the fleet broke its journey at Australia, New Zealand, the Philippines, China, and Japan. Returning by way of the Suez Canal and the Atlantic, the fleet arrived home in February 1909.

Roosevelt's hopes for greater naval finances were only partly successful, but the cruise did convince the American public that he was the greatest supporter of the U.S. Navy. After his death, there was a popular movement to have October 27, Roosevelt's birthday, commemorated as Navy Day.

Theodore Roosevelt's Great White Fleet in December 1907.

order to be effective; he wrote of the "fleet in being," whose mere existence would force an enemy to change his plans. He also wrote about the theoretical clash of fleets that would finally decide which of the belligerent powers would win that decisive command of the world's seas.

What Mahan had done was to provide a convincing argument for naval power. It was just what "navalists" in various countries had been waiting for, and Mahan's theories spurred national ship-building programs around the globe. His work was less influential in Britain, because the British had been acting on its assumptions for decades, but it was extremely influential in the United States. In 1890, having no overseas interests, relying on Britain's Royal Navy to check any threat from Europe, and with a constitutional aversion to standing armies and armed force, the United States possessed negligible naval forces. This was soon to change. Despite strong opposition in Congress, the construction of three modern battleships was authorized on June 30, symbolizing a radical change in what the United States stood for.

Between 1890 and 1914, U.S. naval power increased enormously, chiefly under the administrations of Theodore Roosevelt and William Howard Taft. Naval expenditure rose more than six-fold during this period, so that on November 1, 1909, Secretary of the Navy Meyer was able to report that the U.S. Navy was the second largest in the world, still behind Britain but now ahead of Germany. This new-found naval strength was clearly demonstrated in December 1907, when Roosevelt sent a large group of battleships, known as the Great White Fleet, on a world cruise that only ended in February 1909.

Overseas expansion

Mahan also advocated a U.S.-controlled canal across the Panama Isthmus, which would enable the prompt union of the U.S. Pacific and Atlantic fleets. He further argued that to protect the proposed canal a base would be needed in Cuba, then a Spanish possession, and also in Hawaii.

It would not be long, however, before these territorial requirements were satisfied. The United States itself had begun as a revolt against empire and its national character remained opposed to empires. Its own expansion was regarded simply as movement toward its natural frontiers—those within the continent, in accordance with the doctrine of Manifest Destiny that had been first espoused by John L. O'Sullivan in the

POLITICAL WORLD

THE PANAMA CANAL

The Panama Canal, which opened on August 15, 1914, was created to link the Atlantic and Pacific Oceans and thereby remove the necessity of traveling around Cape Horn at the tip of South America.

In 1903 the Hay-Bunau-Varilla Treaty between Panama and the United States permitted the latter the right to build and operate the canal, as well as the right to control what eventually would become known as the Canal Zone. Plans for the project were finalized by the U.S. Isthmian Canal Commission in 1906, although the construction work had actually begun two years before.

The building work was undertaken by the U.S. Corps of Engineers under Colonel Charles Goethals, and it was aided greatly by Colonel William Gorgas's destruction of the breeding sites of mosquitoes transmitting malaria and yellow fever. Stretching some 40 miles (64 km), the canal cost $365 million to build.

Apart from any commercial benefits derived by the United States, the canal also permitted the U.S. Navy, which was divided into Atlantic and Pacific Fleets, to combine much more rapidly in either ocean if the situation so demanded.

Constructing one of the Panama Canal's massive locks.

Democratic Review of July 1845. He stated that it was "our manifest destiny to overspread the continent allotted by providence for the free development of our yearly multiplying millions."

Some new territory was bought. For example, the Louisiana Purchase in 1803 that added some 830,000 square miles (2,150,000 sq km) to the country at a cost of $15 million, and the purchase of Alaska from the Russian government at two cents an acre in 1867. Other territory was acquired by conquest. For example, all of the land that comprises what is now Arizona, California, Nevada, and Utah, as well as parts of Colorado, New Mexico, and Wyoming, was secured by the Treaty of Guadalupe Hidalgo that concluded the Mexican War (1846–1848). However, all of these territorial gains, with the sole exception of Alaska, were just overland extensions. U.S. expansion overseas was a different matter, came somewhat later, and took different forms.

The ability of business to influence government was the major factor in early overseas expansion. An early example of U.S. military power in support of trade came with Commodore Matthew Perry's two expeditions to Japan in 1853–1854. The Japanese wanted to avoid contact with other peoples, while the United States wanted to trade with Japan and use its ports. On the first visit the Japanese rebuffed Perry's advances. Subsequently, the guns of Perry's squadron were enough to change Japanese minds and thereby open Japan to outside contact.

Ordinary Americans long resisted the idea of overseas expansion, but there were always some who were advocating it. Prominent among this group were

▼ *General Winfield Scott's force takes the important city of Veracruz in March 1847 during the Mexican War.*

those representing commercial interests. In the Pacific Ocean, U.S. speculators would buy land in distant islands and then agitate for U.S. government protection or the acquisition of those islands, which would immediately result in rising land values. This system provided much of the impetus for the major friction between the United States and Germany over the possession of the Samoan Islands, a quarrel that might well have ruptured into open conflict had not a timely storm disturbed the naval preparations of the various parties involved in the incident. Eventually, the U.S. flag did rise above part of Samoa in 1899.

Also finally accomplished in 1899 was the annexation of Hawaii. This had been a longer process, but U.S. sugar interests had simply pursued their goal with persistence to see it achieved eventually. When rule passed to a nationalist queen, who advocated "Hawaii for the Hawaiians," U.S. settlers organized a scuffle that was portrayed as a revolution and the U.S. Navy intervened, deposing the queen. The recently inaugurated president, Grover Cleveland, refused to approve the treaty of annexation that had been forced on the Hawaiians, and it was his successor, McKinley, who finally took possession of the islands.

▲ *A dinner given for the Japanese commissioners aboard the U.S. warship* Powhatan *in 1854, hosted by Commodore Perry.*

The Spanish-American War

The emergence of the United States as a fully fledged imperial power occurred in the late 1890s with the eviction of much-weakened Spain from its Caribbean and Pacific colonies. Many influential U.S. politicians had long been thirsting for war—men like Roosevelt and Cabot Lodge who believed it was time for the country to assert itself through military power. This had little to do with commercial advantage, but was an emotional affair. War was still considered a test of manhood, both for individuals and nations, and it could bring feelings of national greatness and self-worth.

Not far from Florida lay the island of Cuba, a Spanish colony. Cubans had been in revolt sporadically for decades, and this guerrilla warfare was accompanied by barbarities inflicted by both sides. In 1895 the United States raised tariff barriers against Cuban sugar exports to make life easier for U.S. sugar producers. This act added deeper economic depression to the sufferings imposed on the Cubans by the Spanish occupiers. Native Cubans decided in

▲ *Henry Reuterdahl's painting of the U.S. battleship Maine, sunk mysteriously in Havana Harbor, Cuba, on February 15, 1898. The event led to a press campaign for a declaration of war against Spain.*

1895 that a final determined effort should be made to win independence. The result was a particularly savage guerrilla war, one in which the Cubans were herded into so-called "reconcentration camps," where thousands died from neglect and disease.

Some prominent Americans had long advocated the annexation of Cuba as part of Manifest Destiny, and this war seemed an opportunity to intervene. President Cleveland and business interests, who saw no likely profits and an all-too-likely loss from intervention, were against any venture. The mood changed, however, with the accession of President William McKinley in 1897. All that was needed was a reason to intervene that would be palatable to the wider U.S. public. This came on February 15, 1898, when the battleship *Maine*, sent to protect U.S. citizens in Cuba, mysteriously blew up in Havana harbor.

An ultimatum was sent to Spain, and although its government showed signs of accepting its terms, Congress voted for war on April 25. The Spanish-American War has been described as the most popular in U.S. history and the country's most artificially contrived war. Both are true. Popular indignation against the Spanish was whipped up until most people did indeed want war. The popular press, especially the "yellow press," played a key role by publishing on a daily basis accounts of real and purely fictitious Spanish atrocities, and demanding U.S. intervention as a matter of national honor and humanity. Two of the country's great press barons, Joseph Pulitzer and William Randolph Hearst, used their rival New York papers, the *World* and *Journal*, to whip up anti-Spanish feeling.

The small U.S Army was ill-equipped to fight the war, and it was the U.S. Navy that spearheaded the campaign against the weaker Spanish forces in the Pacific and Caribbean. On May 1 a U.S. fleet under the command of Commodore George Dewey sailed into Manila Bay in the Philippines. In the ensuing battle Dewey's forces completely destroyed the rival Spanish force of Admiral Patricio Montojo, paving the way for an amphibious landing by 10,000 U.S.

troops under General Wesley Merritt on June 30. Manila, the capital, surrendered to Merritt on August 13.

In the Caribbean, U.S. troops commanded by Major General William Shafter landed near to Santiago in late June, and then advanced toward the city. The capture of San Juan Ridge by U.S. forces on July 1 effectively sealed the fate of Santiago. U.S. naval forces under Commodore Winfield Schley then crushed the Spanish squadron of Admiral Pascual Cervera at the Battle of Santiago Bay on July 3. Santiago itself surrendered two weeks later. The final act of the short war was the landing of U.S. troops on the Caribbean island of Puerto Rico on July 25. Spanish resistance had been virtually eliminated by the time the war ended in mid-August.

The Treaty of Paris, signed on December 10, brought a conclusion to the war. Spain surrendered its sovereignty, ceded Puerto Rico and the island of Guam to the United States, which also bought the Philippines off the Spanish for $20 million. McKinley,

▼ *The Battle of San Juan Hill, Cuba, in July 1898 was a hard-fought encounter in which Theodore Roosevelt's volunteer "Rough Riders" received much popular press coverage.*

▲ *Cuban guerrillas fighting the Spanish colonial power during the Spanish-American War in 1898.*

own independence. Indeed, a leader of the rebels, Emilio Aguinaldo, had declared the Philippines independent on January 20, 1899.

The U.S. occupying forces, however, did not depart and the Filipinos rose against them on February 4. What followed was a protracted and bloody guerrilla war, one that dragged on until 1905, when the Filipinos were finally defeated. The campaign had forced the United States to deploy some 100,000 men to the Philippines, of whom 8,000 were killed or wounded in action. Some 16,000 Filipinos were killed in the fighting and 100,000 more died of famine.

The Caribbean island of Cuba was treated differently. A U.S. military government under General Leonard Wood was installed with the intention of smoothing the path for Cuban independence. However, there was a further increase in U.S. dominance of the island's economy, chiefly based on sugar production, tobacco, and mining, and the island's presidents were little more than unpopular figureheads and U.S. puppets. Indeed, the United States found it necessary to intervene there militarily on two occasions before World War I. President Theodore Roosevelt sent in troops in 1906, and they remained in Cuba until 1909. Roosevelt's successor, President William Howard Taft, followed a similar course, dispatching U.S. Marines in 1912. A third intervention was also ordered by President Woodrow Wilson in 1917.

At the beginning of the twentieth century, the United States became increasingly involved in China. U.S. policy toward China had been characterized by the desire to maintain equal opportunities of trade for all. However, the European powers and Japan were carving up China between themselves. In September 1899 Secretary of State John Hay attempted to win the agreement of the great powers involved in China to a system of free trade, or what was termed an "open door." He also requested that

soon to win a second term in office on the back of victory, later explained his decision to effectively assume control over the people of the Philippines— "There was nothing left for us to do but to take them all, and to educate the Filipinos, and to uplift and civilize and Christianize them, and by God's grace do the very best we could by them as our fellow men for whom Christ also died." However, the U.S. Army was shown to be in need of a major overhaul. Due to plans laid by Secretary of War Elihu Root, a general staff was created in 1903 and the U.S. Army War College was founded four years later.

A Pacific and Latin American power

The Filipinos, like the Cubans, had been fighting the Spanish before the arrival of the U.S. forces, and expected the defeat of Spain would lead to their

---

KEY FIGURES

WOODROW WILSON

Woodrow Wilson (1856–1924), who entered politics as the governor of New Jersey in 1912 following a career as an educator and academic, led the United States into World War I in April 1917.

Wilson, a Democrat, was a member of the Progressive Movement and following his inauguration in 1913, he introduced legislation to curb the excesses of big business. Although pacifist in outlook, he backed overseas interventions by U.S. forces, chiefly against Mexico in 1914 and 1916. However, with the outbreak of World War I, he strove to maintain U.S. neutrality while attempting to broker a peace between the belligerents.

Germany's decision to reintroduce unrestricted submarine warfare, and the revelations of the Zimmermann telegram in 1917, finally pushed Wilson toward a declaration of war. Nevertheless, he continued to search for a just peace, publishing his 14 Points program in January 1918. At the end of the war he attended the Versailles peace talks, where most, if not all, of his program was adopted. However, Wilson was unable to win U.S. ratification of the treaty or secure the country's entry into the League of Nations, both of which events were a major disappointment to him. He was seriously incapacitated by a stroke in 1919, but served out his second term in office.

China's political independence should be respected. Hay was mostly successful. On March 20, 1900, he announced that Britain, France, Germany, Italy, Japan, and Russia had agreed to his proposal.

U.S. interest in China and the Pacific intensified. In 1900, U.S. troops took part in an international military mission to rescue foreign nationals besieged by Chinese nationalists, the Boxers, in Peking (Beijing). U.S. mediation also helped bring an end to the Russo-Japanese War (1904–1905). In the latter case, Roosevelt chaired the peace discussions that were concluded by the Treaty of Portsmouth on September 6, 1905. Roosevelt's efforts were rewarded with the Nobel Prize for peace the same year.

As these previous pages have revealed, by the eve of World War I, U.S. politics were overwhelmingly dominated by domestic issues and the nation's involvement in its spheres of influence, chiefly Latin America and the Pacific. Between 1900 and 1914, U.S. troops continued to intervene in several Latin American countries in order to bolster U.S. imperial ambitions.

Therefore, by 1914 the United States had been, for the most part, disengaged from Europe and its affairs for some 100 years and most American citizens saw no reason for this situation to change. Yet within the space of three years the nation would be drawn into the world's first truly global conflict.

The Move to War

Germany's Emperor Wilhelm II finally dismissed Chancellor Otto von Bismarck in 1890, but Bismarck's successors did not possess his level of diplomatic skill. However, even if they had been as adept in such matters, it is doubtful that his system of Europe-wide peace-keeping alliances would have held firm. The highly volatile personality of Wilhelm II, a ruler with grandiose plans to greatly boost Germany's international standing, coupled with the mediocre

From the late 1890s Europe's powers made alliances, faced crises, embarked on rearmaments programs, and engaged in military brinkmanship.

▼ *By World War I, Europe was divided into two armed camps—the Triple Alliance and the Triple Entente.*

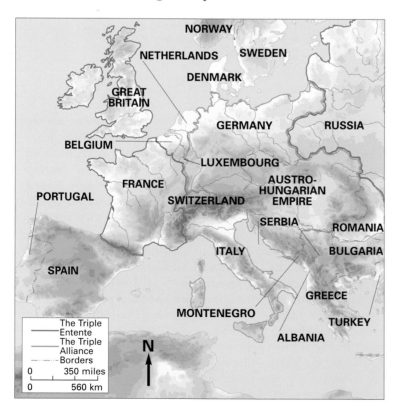

NORWAY
NETHERLANDS
SWEDEN
DENMARK
GREAT BRITAIN
GERMANY
RUSSIA
BELGIUM
LUXEMBOURG
FRANCE
AUSTRO-HUNGARIAN EMPIRE
PORTUGAL
SWITZERLAND
SERBIA
ROMANIA
ITALY
BULGARIA
SPAIN
GREECE
MONTENEGRO
TURKEY
ALBANIA

The Triple Entente
The Triple Alliance
Borders
0   350 miles
0   560 km

N

figures whom he chose as his chancellors after Bismarck, simply ensured that trouble would come sooner rather than later.

The first diplomatic setback for Germany was a Franco-Russian alliance signed in 1894. The two governments had little in common, but a shared fear of German attack pushed them into this treaty, which became known as the Dual Alliance. The alliance was essentially military. It stated that at least a third of the Russian Army would mobilize against Germany if Germany attacked France. In return, France would mobilize, although not necessarily go to war, if Austria-Hungary mobilized against Russia. Closer ties also came when the French began to invest in Russia, which was attempting to industrialize. The

French were eager for the Russians to extend its railroad system, on which the mobilization of its forces relied, but the work progressed slowly.

Consequently, by the mid-1890s Europe was effectively divided between the Franco-Russian bloc and the Triple Alliance of Austria-Hungary, Germany, and Italy. Outwardly these alliances were purely defensive. They would only come into play if a member of the same treaty agreement was attacked. The general feeling was that, because all the signatories had declared that national defense was their only priority, war could not take place.

Equally, it seemed that the rival powers had few areas of major disagreement in Europe that might lead to war. Germany seemingly had no further desire to expand its frontiers in Europe; the French might wish for the return of the province of Alsace and the part of the province of Lorraine that they had lost following their heavy defeat in the Franco-Prussian War (1870–1871), but they were not willing to initiate a war to recover the territory; and Russia might have liked to have control of the Turkish Bosporus and Dardanelles, but seemed content that no other leading power had control of the vital seaway. Some Italians might have desired the return of Italian-speaking lands under the control of the Austro-Hungarian Empire, but the country was too weak to press its claim militarily.

Europe seemed at peace, as it had been since the Franco-Prussian War. However, the great powers had several

▲ *King Edward VII of Great Britain (seated on the left) with Germany's Emperor, Wilhelm II, in Berlin during 1909. At this time, tensions between Europe's great powers made war seem inevitable to some people. Wilhelm was greatly envious of Britain's power and prestige.*

areas of potential conflict outside Europe, chiefly relating to their spheres of influence and colonies, or colonial ambitions. These issues sparked numerous crises or incidents before World War I, but were solved diplomatically, usually after an initial round of saber-rattling. Nevertheless, Germany's continuing inability to make significant colonial gains caused considerable pain to Emperor Wilhelm II, who believed that Germany was being thwarted by the other European powers.

However, the Dual Alliance seemed to threaten Germany with war on two fronts in Europe. The German general staff, headed by Count Alfred von Schlieffen between 1891 and 1906, evolved what it considered to be the only viable military plan to stave off defeat. It was a strategy for waging a short, aggressive war, one initiated by Germany, against France and Russia. What was called the Schlieffen Plan relied on the notorious slowness of Russian mobilization. It also assumed that Britain would remain neutral while France was invaded through Belgium.

Although the secret Schlieffen Plan was just that, a military scheme, to make it credible Germany had to have the armed forces to carry it out and the systems in place, chiefly railroad transportation, to make it work. Two Army bills, in 1911 and 1912, were enacted to strengthen the already mighty German Army. In December 1912, Emperor Wilhelm II called a war council where the likelihood of conflict in the future was accepted. The head of the German general staff at the time, Field Marshal Helmuth von Moltke, went further,

---

KEY FIGURES

EMPEROR WILHELM II

Wilhelm II (1859–1941), who was not only emperor of Germany but also king of Prussia, succeeded his father, Frederick III, in 1888. A monarch with little time for democracy, he oversaw Germany's economic and military expansion prior to World War I.

Wilhelm also believed that Germany, although Europe's leading power, had an almost divine right to even greater status, chiefly by acquiring colonies. However, his attempts to follow this course were frequently frustrated by Germany's international rivals. During his reign he surrounded himself with conservative politicians, right-wing industrialists, and aggressive militarists, all of whom became increasingly alarmed at attempts to make Germany a more democratic state.

Historians have suggested that this fear of democracy and failure to engage in diplomacy predisposed Wilhelm to war in August 1914. However, when the conflict began, he generally did no more than just endorse the plans of his generals, and became a figurehead. At the end of World War I, Wilhelm was forced to abdicate. He spent the remaining years of his life as an exile in the Netherlands.

This Belgian cartoon satirizes Wilhelm II's ambitions by depicting him as a saber-rattler at the head of a toy army.

informing the emperor that it would be better to go to war as soon as possible, as Germany's potential enemies would only get stronger.

Moltke's proposal was rejected, and it was decided to put off any firm decision on whether to go to war or not for 18 months. The head of the German Navy, Admiral Tirpitz, advocated the delay. He argued that 18 months would allow the naval and military preparations necessary to fight a successful war to be completed, not least the widening of the Kiel Canal, which would allow Germany's largest warships to move safely between the Baltic and North Seas. Thus by 1912 Germany was prepared to initiate a European war, and only its timing was a matter of debate. Why had this situation come about?

Germany's preparations to wage war reflected its wariness of Britain's new-found interest in gaining allies. For decades Britain had adopted a policy of aloofness from Europe, one that was termed splendid isolation. It had signed no treaties in peacetime and relied on its large navy, which Germany feared

and was attempting to emulate, to enforce its security. However, Britain began to look around for friends at the turn of the century. It had felt isolated when most of world opinion turned against its conduct of the Second Anglo-Boer War (1899–1901) in South Africa, a war in which the Boers received financial and military aid from Germany. Britain's leaders were also beginning to realize that, because of Germany's ongoing naval expansion, they could not gather enough naval strength in European waters to match Germany while simultaneously maintaining warships all around the globe to defend their widespread empire.

At first, Britain considered an alliance with Germany, but the German government indicated that Britain should join the Triple Alliance if it wanted friendship. Britain would not do this and in 1902 ended its splendid isolation by making an alliance with Japan, whose large navy the British had helped to create. The alliance stated that each would come to the aid of the other if it was attacked by a third power. This alliance

▲ Widening the Kiel Canal was an essential part of Germany's naval expansion plans, because it provided a secure link between the Baltic and North Seas for the country's growing fleet of warships.

▶ *This illustration in France's* Le Petit Journal *of April 9, 1899, depicts Britain's prime minister and foreign secretary, Lord Salisbury (right), and France's Paul Cambon signing an agreement on Africa following the Fashoda Incident in 1898, a crisis that brought the countries close to war. In the first decade of the following century, relations between the two former historical rivals steadily improved.*

made it possible for Japan to fight Russia without Russia's main ally, France, joining in. The Russo-Japanese War (1904–1905) was fought, and Russia was thoroughly defeated.

Russia's defeat at the hands of Japan, which led to a short-lived revolution in 1905, was seen as advantageous by several European powers. Germany was relieved that the Russian Army had been defeated and its many shortcomings exposed, but this view was short-sighted, as Russia soon embarked on a massive rearmaments program, which alarmed Germany. The British saw the Japanese victory as undermining Russian influence on the borders of India. Equally, Russia's severe defeat was

welcomed by Austria-Hungary. Russia had long backed Slavic nationalist movements in the Balkans, an area important to the Austro-Hungarian Empire. The empire itself also contained sizable Slavic groups who craved independence, but these groups were less likely to flourish without Russian support.

Meanwhile Britain, whose advances Germany had discouraged, was about to take the unexpected step of allying with France, its traditional enemy in Europe, by agreeing to the Entente Cordiale ('Friendly Understanding') in 1904. Certain key personalities smoothed the path for this development. In France there was a gifted foreign minister, Théophile Delcassé, while in Britain there was a new prime minister, Arthur Balfour, and a new king, Edward Vll, both of whom were Francophiles.

The Entente Cordiale, the discussions of which lasted 10 months, solved most of the grievances that had long troubled the two countries and had brought them close to war on occasion. They had nearly gone to war in 1893 over control of Siam (now Thailand), and again in 1898 as both tried to spread their influence along the Upper Nile. This latter event, the Fashoda Incident, ended only when Britain rushed forces from the Sudan under General Herbert Kitchener to confront a French expedition led by Jean-Baptiste Marchand.

However, such problems were mostly in the past. Under the Entente Cordiale, the French accepted Britain's control of Egypt, while Britain promised to raise no objections should France take over Morocco. Britain was willing to state that the maintenance of French independence was vital to its interests, but no promise of military support was forthcoming. However, in January 1906, discussions on military matters did begin and these formed the basis for military cooperation in World War I.

Crises, but no war

At about the same time, France secretly agreed with Italy that France could extend its influence over independent Morocco and Italy was allowed to take over the Turkish province of Libya in North Africa, and that each country would remain neutral in the event of the other being attacked. This secret

▼ An unattributed illustration from Le Petit Journal, August 13, 1905, showing the French fleet visiting Portsmouth on the coast of England as part of the Entente Cordiale between Britain and France.

agreement conflicted with Italy's obligations to the Triple Alliance, but the German chancellor felt that the Franco-Italian and Franco-British friendships were a bluff. He arranged to call the bluff in 1905, risking war. This arrangement of a preventive crisis was not Wilhelm II's idea, and he was against it.

The emperor, enjoying a cruise in the Mediterranean, found himself diverted to the Moroccan port of Tangiers, where he paid his respects to the sultan and thereby implied Germany's support for him against the French. This caused an international crisis, and a conference was called to solve it in 1906. This conference, at Algeciras in southern Spain, resulted in France, Britain, and Italy remaining solid. When it was concluded in 1907, France and Spain were given a free hand in Morocco, a decision that humiliated Germany.

Meanwhile, diplomatic moves by France succeeded in encouraging Britain to move closer to Russia. In the spirit of the Anglo-French Entente Cordiale, this consisted in settling long-lived differences which, with goodwill, were quite soluble. Britain and Russia had some areas of friction, primarily in Afghanistan, Persia (now Iran), and the Far East. What emerged in 1907 was the Triple Entente of France, Britain, and Russia. This was not a formal treaty, but simply an understanding.

In this atmosphere of increasing trust within the Triple Entente, some preparations for military cooperation were indeed quietly worked out. By 1914 it was clearly understood by the general staffs and politicians of Britain and France that in the event of war a British force would be promptly sent to northern France, and that while Britain's Royal Navy protected the ports on the English Channel, the French Navy would patrol the Mediterranean, where Austria-Hungary and Italy both had potentially hostile fleets. A naval agreement between Russia and Britain and France was being worked out when war came. These agreements, although not binding, made it easier for each to aid the other in a crisis.

A further crisis between France and Germany over Morocco developed in June 1911. The French were attempting to formalize their influence over the country by establishing a protectorate in the face of local uprisings. The French moves threatened German economic interests in the region and Germany sent a gunboat, the *Panther*, to Agadir, under the pretext of protecting its nationals and their business from the violence sparked by the uprising. The gun-boat arrived on July 1. Tensions ran high and war seemed likely. Yet the crisis was resolved by November.

So, less than two years before the outbreak of World War I, Europe appeared peaceful, at least on the surface. There were tensions between the two great

▼ *A cartoon relating to the Morocco crisis of 1911. Morocco is shown as a reluctant patient, while in the center four doctors representing the European powers involved in the crisis argue over how to divide up the patient.*

◀ *In this cartoon on the Morocco crisis of 1911, the European great powers are depicted as vultures hovering over Morocco (in the form of a camel) and squabbling over it, with Germany staking the first claim.*

alliances, and also some tensions within them, but various crises had been dealt with and outright conflict avoided. Although diplomatic talks had been conducted, often informally, between individual foreign ministers and ambassadors, and there was no formal international body in existence to arbitrate between those countries in dispute, the existing system appeared to work, at least on the most recent evidence. If a major crisis developed, like the one at Agadir, then an international gathering of those involved, directly or indirectly, could be called and the issue resolved peacefully. In part, this almost haphazard diplomatic system also reflected the close, often familial, links between the rulers of the various leading European powers at the time, rulers who played an often significant role in the foreign policies of their respective countries.

▶ *Taken during the Balkan Wars, this photograph shows an abandoned Turkish gun emplacement in Macedonia. The brief wars saw Turkey lose almost all of its major Balkan territories.*

The Balkan question

The outbreak of general war in 1914 was preceded by a decade in which the Balkans region was rent by instability. This had two results: a number of wars and near-wars that did not really decide anything, and the creation of a view that another war was not only likely and imminent, but also welcome as a way to clear the air.

As in the nineteenth century, the weakening of the Turkish Empire gave opportunities for the nations of the Balkans to pursue their different paths to independence. Several of these nations were Slavic and looked to Russia for support. Some of the Slavic nations, particularly Serbia, which was already independent but believed it had a right to expand its territory, were conscious that millions of its people were under Austro-Hungarian rule.

Austria-Hungary feared that Slavic states would encourage their nationals within the Austro-Hungarian Empire to demand their own independence or union with their national states. The likelihood that Slavic aspirations would have Russian support made it difficult for Austria-Hungary to take, or even to threaten, military reprisals. Austria-Hungary's failure to force Serbia to abandon ideas of a Greater Serbia only emboldened Serbia and demoralized the empire's ruling circles. In the latter, only the Archduke Franz Ferdinand, the heir to the empire's ruler, Emperor Franz Joseph, seemed to sympathize with the empire's Serbian subjects. He favored the idea of changing the Dual Monarchy into a Triple Monarchy by creating a separate but integrated state for Slavs inside the empire. However, his views were in the minority, because Austria-Hungary had plans to expand its rule in the Balkans further. These plans centered on Bosnia.

The Bosnian crisis of 1908 resulted from Austria-Hungary's decision to consolidate its position in the two Slavic, but formally Turkish, territories of

Herzegovina and Bosnia by annexing both of them. Neighboring Serbia was furious at this, and there were vague Serbian threats of declaring war on Austria-Hungary, threats that encouraged many senior Austro-Hungarian military figures to make plans for a preventive war that would put an end to the Serbian nuisance once and for all.

Russia backed Serbia, but Germany assisted its ally Austria-Hungary by making warning noises toward Russia, which eventually and reluctantly accepted Austria-Hungary's annexation of Bosnia and Herzegovina. The Russian government was heartily criticized by its pan-Slavists for this and this reaction made its members less likely to accept compromises in the future. Serbia felt humiliated and betrayed. More importantly, Germany had set itself a precedent by supporting Austria-Hungary more or less unconditionally and, indeed, by accepting that Austria-Hungary had a right to make war on Serbia should that seem necessary.

Hardly had the Bosnian crisis been diffused than the Balkan Wars (1912–1913) broke out. These began with a joint offensive by Bulgaria, Serbia, Montenegro, and non-Slavic Greece against Turkey. Instigated in part by Russian diplomats, this alliance forced Turkey to abandon its domains in the Balkans. In 1913 a peace conference in London confirmed Turkish withdrawal from almost all of its possessions in Europe. However, Bulgaria, which had done most of the fighting, suspected that its former allies Serbia and Greece were plotting against it, and attacked them, but was then itself invaded by Turkey and Romania.

The resulting defeat and loss of territory left Bulgaria resentful. Meanwhile, Serbia had practically doubled in size due to the acquisition of most of Slavic Macedonia. Serbian secret nationalist societies continued to be active both inside and outside Austria-Hungary, spreading pro-Serbian propaganda and plotting to carry out assassinations.

EYEWITNESS

M. EDITH DURHAM

Few Europeans fully appreciated the ethnic and political tensions that dominated the Balkans before World War I. Most agreed that the region was unstable because of friction between nationalists who opposed Turkey's control of the region. However, they did not appreciate that the tensions ran deeper and that those under Turkish rule were disunited. Durham, an English woman, caught a flavor of the animosity between the various ethnic groups opposed to Turkey during a visit to Macedonia after a rising by Bulgarians:

"I condoled with the Bulgar bishop of Ochrida on the terrible massacre of his flock by the Turks. He replied calmly that to him it had been a disappointment. He had expected quite half the population to have been killed, and then Europe would have been forced to intervene. I suggested that, had the Bulgars risen in 1897 when the Greek made war on the Turk, the whole land could have been freed. He replied indignantly, 'I would rather the land should remain forever under the Turk than that the Greeks should ever obtain a kilometer.'

"Later I met his rival, the Greek bishop. To him I suggested that if Greece aided the Bulgar rising the Christian might now be freed. The mere idea horrified him. Sooner than allow those swine of Bulgars to obtain any territory he [said the bishop], 'would prefer that the land should be forever Turkish.'"

From M. Edith Durham's Twenty Years of Balkan Tangle, *published in 1920.*

To the Austro-Hungarian general staff the Balkan situation seemed intolerable. Hostile Serbia, they believed, was intent on detaching part of Austro-Hungarian territory, probably with the assistance of not only Russia, Romania, and Montenegro, but also of Italy. The empire's only true ally, Germany, was hemmed in by France, Russia, and maybe Britain. Meanwhile, not only the German general staff, but the German emperor and his chancellor, Theobold

▶ *Serbian nationalist pride during the Balkans Wars is the subject of this illustration from* Le Petit Journal, *December 1, 1912. It portrays 19-year-old Sophia Iovanovitch, who, along with her fiance (behind her), fought bravely against the Turks as a Serbian volunteer for the duration of the wars.*

von Bethmann Hollweg, were urging Austria-Hungary to take a firm line with Serbia and promising their support.

However, the Balkan Wars were seen by many European politicians and diplomats as confirming the desire for peaceful coexistence in Europe. They continued to believe that the general accord between the leading powers that had prevented war from breaking out between them in Europe was still working. After all, none of the European powers had been drawn into the fighting in the Balkans.

This was in part due to agreements engineered between the two powers most concerned with the Balkans, Austria-Hungary and Russia, by Britain's foreign secretary, Edward Grey. Austria-Hungary demanded that Serbia be denied access to the Adriatic Sea, and Russia would not tolerate a Bulgarian take-over of Constantinople, the Turkish capital, or control of the Bosporus and Dardanelles seaway. Both requirements were met, partly due to the course of the wars and partly to thinly veiled threats from the European powers. Equally, the Balkan Wars seemed to settle the long-standing problem of Balkan nationalism. Turkish rule had finally been removed from a region previously rent by unrest, and several independent nations had emerged.

The German Navy Laws

The Balkans problem, from which the spark igniting World War I would come, was the result of a long historical process with which diplomacy, try as it might, could not cope. However, one of the main factors in creating an atmosphere in which a stray spark would initiate a world war was the rapid expansion of the German Navy.

Admiral Alfred von Tirpitz shared Emperor Wilhelm II's addiction to the naval theories of Alfred Thayer Mahan. Mahan, once head of the U.S. Naval War College, had argued that colonial expansion was coming to an end and

---

KEY FIGURES

ALFRED VON TIRPITZ

Admiral Tirpitz (1849–1930) was the architect of the military expansion program that transformed Germany's naval might from a relatively small coastal defense force into one of the world's most powerful fleets of warships.

Tirpitz joined the German Navy in 1865, and by 1896, he was commanding the squadron that secured the Chinese port of Tsingtao for Germany. A year later he became the effective head of the entire German Navy and embarked on a program to transform its forces and equipment that was wholeheartedly supported by Wilhelm II.

The financing of this huge expansion program came chiefly through the Navy Law of 1898, which was sponsored by Tirpitz. Similar legislation followed, particularly after the British launched the revolutionary battleship *Dreadnought* in 1906. By 1914 Germany had the second largest fleet in the world, which alarmed the British.

On the outbreak of war, Tirpitz recommended himself as the country's naval operational commander-in-chief, but his offer was rejected. When it became clear that his beloved High Seas Fleet was not going to be risked against the British, he was one of those calling for unrestricted submarine warfare. However, Tirpitz resigned in 1916 out of frustration.

that trade and the search for foreign markets would dominate future maritime strategy. Thus, he argued, conflicts would revolve around the defense or blockade of trade routes, and that battles between rival fleets would be part of blockades and blockade-breaking. Both Tirpitz and the emperor wanted Germany to become a great naval power. The core of their argument was that Germany should plan a fleet with the most dangerous potential enemy in mind. This automatically meant that the future German fleet would need to be powerful enough to impress the British.

Britain, whose power and influence were based on its huge Royal Navy, had maintained its "two-power standard." This propounded that the Royal Navy should be big enough to cope simultaneously with the second and third biggest of the world's navies. Tirpitz persuaded Wilhelm II that as soon as the German Navy was big enough to threaten the British, not with defeat, but with enough damage to reduce its prospects in a conflict with a third power, then the British would be forced to concede Germany a share of maritime power. Naval theorists, steeped in Mahan, believed that to have any chance of crippling or defeating an enemy fleet the challenger would have to be at least two-thirds the size of the latter, and Tirpitz's aim was to build a fleet two-thirds the size of Britain's

Royal Navy, with its ships designed to fight not in the great oceans but in the smaller North Sea.

By the last decades of the nineteenth century, Germany had overhauled Britain as an industrial power, and Tirpitz believed Britain would lack the will or the means to match his shipbuilding program. Even if it did, Britain would not be able to crew a bigger navy, because whereas German sailors were conscripts, its fleet was manned by volunteers. Tirpitz conceded there would be a period in which the German Navy would be weak and that Britain, if it realized what was happening, might make a preemptive strike. He relied on diplomacy to take his country through that dangerous period, and in the meantime, the first Navy Law was modest in scope, so as not to arouse suspicion.

In the Navy Laws, Tirpitz pursued the idea of laws that would provide not just an annual building program, but a program for the years ahead, which would specify not just the new ships but also their replacement ships when they became obsolete. Once a Navy Law was in place, the shipbuilding budget would not be subject to interference or resistance by the German parliament.

The Navy Law of 1898 provided for 19 new battleships by 1905. The Navy Law of 1900, passed when Britain was preoccupied with the Second Anglo-Boer War, showed the true reality of Tirpitz's plans by increasing the German fleet to

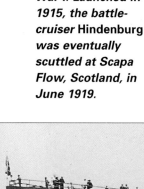

▼ German warship construction carried on into World War I. Launched in 1915, the battlecruiser Hindenburg was eventually scuttled at Scapa Flow, Scotland, in June 1919.

POLITICAL WORLD

DREADNOUGHT IS LAUNCHED

Britain's revolutionary battleship *Dreadnought* marked the arrival of a new era in naval warfare and added fuel to the ongoing naval arms race between Britain and Germany in the years leading up to World War I.

Dreadnought, the brainchild of First Sea Lord Admiral John Fisher, was not only the first "all big-gun" battleship but also the first to use the more economical turbines in place of steam engines. The ship was completed in record time, with keel-laying at the state dockyard in Portsmouth on October 2, 1905, and its official launch on February 10, 1906.

At a stroke *Dreadnought* made all of the world's battleships obsolete, a situation that Germany, among other maritime powers, found intolerable. A dreadnought shipbuilding race ensued, with Britain and Germany competing to build as many of the new warships as possible. These armaments programs greatly increased the political tension between the two countries. *Dreadnought* itself saw little active service during World War I.

38 battleships. Tirpitz intended to lay down three new battleships each year, which in 20 years would produce a fleet of 60 battleships and oblige the British, if they wanted to maintain the theoretical ratio, to build a fleet of 90 battleships, which Tirpitz considered they would not do.

The creation of a German Navy aroused great popular enthusiasm, and to a limited extent Tirpitz was right when he claimed it would slow the advance of democracy, much feared by Germany's traditional ruling elite, by whipping up enthusiasm for a national cause and by boosting employment. The German Navy League organized meetings, publications, and demonstra-tions to gain popular support for the cause. Other countries, including Britain and the United States, also had navy leagues, but only Germany's had a truly mass membership.

By 1905 a naval race was developing between Britain and Germany, but in 1906 the situation was transformed with the appearance of the British battleship *Dreadnought*. This rendered all preced-ing battleships obsolete because it carried more than double their number of heavy guns, was faster, and was better armored. The naval race would hence-forth be measured in terms of the new battleships. Britain's existing pre-dread-noughts, which greatly outnumbered German ones, lost their relevance.

The naval race was now measured in terms of new dreadnoughts, and the annual number of new ships laid down became a matter of excited public interest. What Tirpitz and his circle seemed to have overlooked was that what for them was an endeavor aimed at influence and prestige was for the British a matter of sheer survival. The British people fully realized that their food and materials were largely imported and that only naval supremacy could protect that vital flow. The British public fully supported the construction of as many dreadnoughts as needed to keep British naval strength ahead of Germany's.

In fact, when one British government, horrified by the diversion of so many resources to battleships, sought to reduce the program, British public opinion soon forced it to change its mind. In the end it was Germany that showed signs of weakening, when in 1913 its government rejected Tirpitz's plea for a supplementary law providing for extra ships. About the same time, a British delegation tried to reach a deal with Germany to limit the pace of construction, but it returned empty-handed, having discovered that the price for such an agreement was an end to the Franco-British Entente Cordiale.

▶ Admiral Alfred von Tirpitz, the architect of Germany's naval expansion, misjudged the importance of the Royal Navy to Britain, which could not stand by and allow the German Navy to rival its own. By 1914 the British fleet was larger and more powerful than ever before.

◀ *Enormous crowds gathered in the streets of Berlin to hear Emperor Wilhelm II's various declarations of war. War enthusiasm swept through most European countries in the summer of 1914.*

The result of Tirpitz's plan was therefore a diversion of funds, in both Britain and Germany, to the building of ships. Both nations began World War I with expensive fleets that had little to do except watch each other. Germany's fleet was an extreme example of Mahan's theoretical "fleet in being," but in practice turned out to be little more than an expensive luxury.

Its expense was not just a matter of money. The German program had so alarmed the British as to push them into their Entente Cordiale with France and led to, first, mistrust of Germany, and, second, a feeling that sooner or later Germany would provoke a war.

For and against war

In most European countries, public opinion in the years preceding 1914 had accepted the likelihood, to some extent even the desirability, of war. Many authors even published fictionalized books that described their country being weakened by foreign agents or overrun by a foreign enemy, or told of an enemy's build-up of military forces—all of which fueled the prevailing mood.

POLITICAL WORLD

WAR LITERATURE

Prior to World War I the tensions between Europe's leading nations led to numerous books being published that fueled the fears of ordinary people. Generally, they told of a country under threat from a ruthless enemy. They were particularly common in Britain, France, and Germany.

One of the earliest of such books was George Chesney's *Battle of Dorking*, which the author wrote with the express intention of "securing the defense of the nation by the enforced arming of the people." First published in 1871, it recounted a successful German invasion of Britain.

Similar books tended to coincide with heightened international tension. For example, the Moroccan crisis of 1906 led to the publication of books such as *Der Deutsch-Englische Krieg* (*The Germany-English War*) and, from England, the *Invasion of 1910* by William Le Queux, which sold more than one million copies around the world.

Such publications reflected, and probably fueled, the prevailing mood, but most proved poor guides to World War I, which was far longer, more destructive, and less glorious than the authors ever imagined.

Nationalism, intense love of one's country, was a potent force, and most people were strongly patriotic.

Fearing the worst, governments and their general staffs had come to the same conclusion, and many countries, like Germany, had devised strategies to fight a general war in Europe. Some even considered preventive wars, which were simply a device to ensure that when war did come, it would come at exactly the most favorable moment. An increasing number of influential figures came to believe that war was necessary, because so many long-standing international rivalries seemed insoluble by conventional diplomatic means.

In fairness both to the unashamed warmongers and to those who believed war had become a regrettable necessity, it needs to be emphasized that they believed the future war would be short and relatively bloodless. A short war was also seen as a great political asset to the victor in an age when public opinion was becoming important to national leaders. The Spanish-American War (1898) had been acclaimed as such a conflict, and in the political events leading to the Russo-Japanese War at least one Russian leader had advocated war

in the same terms, although the actual conflict that followed turned out to be neither short nor victorious for Russia.

When people envisioned war they tended to think about Bismarck's short, victorious wars that had changed the map of Europe to Germany's advantage. They forgot about the American Civil War (1861–1865), which had been a punishing four-year conflict that cost many thousands of lives. In any case, war over the centuries had become an institution, providing a profession and ethos for many, economic prosperity for others, and the possibility of glory for the participants. On the other hand, an increasing section of the public was aware that war was changing and that it was a phenomenon to be avoided at all costs. Pacifist movements founded in the nineteenth century gained strength in the early twentieth century as war became more likely and technology would likely make it more destructive.

There were official attempts to limit Europe's growing arsenal. The first, although limited, success came when Czar Nicholas II organized the First Hague Peace Conference in 1899. It was true that it was less morality, and more the crippling cost of rearmament, that

▼ Tens of thousands of men died in the bloody Battle of Gettysburg in 1863 during the American Civil War—but most Europeans in 1914 had forgotten that such carnage was likely in a modern conflict and few people were aware of the unparalleled destructive power of the most up-to-date weapons.

motivated Nicholas II, but it was a step forward, one undertaken in the face of hostility, even mockery, from his fellow rulers. Most countries sent as delegates their most aggressively minded soldiers or politicians, and not much progress was made. However, the establishment of an arbitration court to settle dangerous differences had some impact, and it may have helped to avoid war when warships of the Russian Baltic fleet, on their way to take part in the Russo-Japanese War, accidently opened fire on British fishing vessels. However, influential Germans in particular hated the idea of arbitration proceedings and limits on armaments. One German delegate present at the conference acknowledged that his task was to ensure that "everything turns to sand that we can throw in the eyes of public opinion."

The Second Hague Peace Conference, held between June and October 1907, met with equally little success. Some laws concerning the conduct of war were defined and codified, and an international court of arbitration was established, but little else was achieved. A final attempt to control the armaments race took place during the London Naval Conference (1908–1909). Those present did agree to certain proposals, but these were never ratified in a period of increasing tension.

Although Europe was on the surface peaceful by 1914, there were strong antagonisms between its great powers. Most of these great powers, particularly Germany, had been engaged in major rearmament programs, and most had unresolved international political issues. Diplomats had resolved various crises, but they lacked the formal links to deal quickly with such situations involving several countries.

There was also a general belief that war was likely to break out at some time in the future, although most people expected it to be short. Finally, few people outside Germany were fully aware of Germany's belligerence, which had its origins in a leadership that believed its country was destined for even more greatness. However, no one could anticipate that the assassination of an Austro-Hungarian archduke in a Balkan city on June 28, 1914, would precipitate an international crisis that would lead to the outbreak of World War I within little more than four weeks.

▲ *The Second Hague Peace Conference took place between June 16 and October 18, 1907, Those present failed to ease the increasing tensions among Europe's great powers.*

Who Was to Blame?

Although the assassination of Austria-Hungary's Archduke Franz Ferdinand by a Serbian nationalist in June 1914 sparked World War I, the conflict's underlying causes ran deeper and were much longer-standing.

Historians still do not agree on why the archduke's assassination led to the outbreak of a global war in a matter of weeks. However, three schools of thought have developed. The first argues that it was wholly Germany's fault, the second that the war was a calculated risk that Germany was forced into taking in late July 1914, and the third that all of the European powers had some responsibility.

In the case of Germany, it has been suggested, correctly, that by 1914 it was Europe's leading economic and political power. However, its prestige as a truly world power was undermined by its lack of international status, chiefly access to colonies and world trade.

Germany's response to this issue, which came to dominate the thinking of Emperor Wilhelm II, leading industrialists, and the military, was threefold. First, the German Navy was vastly expanded under Admiral Alfred von Tirpitz, causing concern in Britain. Second, the German Army underwent a similar program, which alarmed France and Russia. Third, both the emperor and his military planned for a preemptive war in December

1912, but postponed any firm decision for 18 months—until the summer of 1914. It has been argued that the archduke's assassination in June of that year was a suitable pretext for Germany to go to war.

The second view of the war's origins is that Germany did not intend to go to war following the assassination of Archduke Ferdinand, but only desired to offer political support to Austria-Hungary during its attempts in

early July to gain some recompense from Serbia over the archduke's assassination at the hands of Serbian nationalists. Germany's leaders believed they could support Austro-Hungarian military action but that any conflict would be confined to the Balkans. Effectively, according to this view, they were taking a diplomatic risk.

However, it is further argued that German policy changed in the latter part of July as the

▲ *Germany's Emperor Wilhelm II (right) greets Austria-Hungary's emperor, Franz Joseph.*

likelihood of the conflict spreading beyond the Balkans grew, and the German military pressed for immediate war. Simply, if the war was going to spread, as was increasingly likely, then Germany had to strike first to avoid defeat at the hands of France and Russia. The German leadership may also have had other reasons for going to war. Historians have also suggested that Germany was becoming increasingly politically unstable. The old order was being threatened, as it was to some extent in other European countries, by burgeoning democratic movements calling for social change. A short, successful war, it was argued, would reunite the German people behind the emperor and reduce the likelihood of greater political unrest.

The third position is that all of those involved in the outbreak of World War I held some responsibility, chiefly because the various leaders and their

publics viewed the Balkan crisis with certain preconceived ideas, thereby allowing it to lead to world war. It is accepted that Germany had embarked on a course that made Europe more and more unstable, but other states also contributed to the outbreak of war by fatally misunderstanding the nature of the issues involved. Events moved far too quickly, chiefly because of military necessities, for diplomats to put a brake on the rapid drive to war.

Several illusions were prevalent in Europe in the weeks immediately before the outbreak of war. Among them was the belief that diplomacy could contain the crisis; that war was far too risky to be entered into by regimes that were politically unstable; that any conflict could somehow be managed and contained, and would be short; and that conflict would revitalize the nations involved. As World War I revealed, all of these beliefs were wholly unfounded.

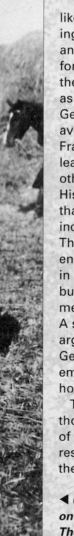

◄ *German officers photographed on maneuvers before the war. Their superiors held sway over much of the country's politics.*

The July Crisis, 1914

The assassination of Austria-Hungary's Archduke Franz Ferdinand set in chain a course of events that would lead to the outbreak of World War I in just a few weeks.

Many of the details about the plot to kill Austria-Hungary's Archduke Franz Ferdinand in June 1914 are still disputed, but the Serbian Army's head of intelligence, Colonel Dragutin Dmitrijevic, also seems to have been involved. Apart from his military duties, Dmitrijevic was the head of the extremist Serbian nationalist society popularly known as the Black Hand. There is no proof that the Serbian government knew of his involvement with the group, but it is likely that it did and preferred to turn a blind eye.

In June 1914 Franz Ferdinand was to pay an official visit to Bosnia's capital, Sarajevo. Bosnia was a Slavic territory that had been annexed by the Austro-Hungarian Empire, but was regarded by Serbian nationalists as a key component of what they hoped would become what they termed Greater Serbia, potentially the dominant state in the Balkans. Franz Ferdinand was the nephew and

◀ *Archduke Franz Ferdinand and his wife Sophie in the Bosnian capital Sarajevo on June 28, 1914, just a few hours before they were assassinated.*

POLITICAL WORLD

THE BLACK HAND

The Black Hand was a popular name for the Serbian Union or Death society. It was devoted to the creation of a Greater Serbia by adding to the existing independent state those areas it considered to be Serbian but which were administered by other Balkan countries.

Chief among these areas were Bosnia, a province ruled by the Austro-Hungarian Empire, and areas in the Balkans controlled by Turkey. The society was founded by the Serbian Army intelligence officer Dragutin Dmitrijevic, but it had antecedents in other societies. In Bosnia the Black Hand organized anti-Austro-Hungarian activity and is chiefly remembered for its involvement in the assassination of Archduke Franz Ferdinand in June 1914. Dominant in Serbian Army intelligence, it also often defied the country's legitimate government.

After 1914 the Serbian Army was driven from Serbia and the government was established on the island of Corfu, where the Black Hand continued to operate. In December 1916 the exiled Serbian government, headed by Prince Alexander, felt strong enough to deal with the society. Some charges were concocted against its leadership and a dubious trial took place. In June, Dmitrijevic and two other members were executed, and the Black Hand fell apart.

▲ *Gavrilo Princip, the Serbian nationalist who shot Archduke Franz Ferdinand and his wife, Sophie, when their car stopped outside a cafe in Sarajevo.*

heir to the Austro-Hungarian throne of Emperor Franz Joseph, and an obvious target for a radical society seeking to achieve its aims through violence.

There was an expectation among less radical Serbians that when Franz Ferdinand came to the throne he would try to ease the position of the Serbs and other Slavs in the empire, probably by creating a state for them with a measure of self-government. This vision of the Austro-Hungarian Dual Monarchy reorganized into an Austro-Hungarian-Slavic Triple Monarchy was a nightmare for extreme Serbian nationalists. They feared any moderate political reform that would satisfy the political demands of Slavic peoples within the Austro-Hungarian Empire, as it would fall short of their aim of full independence.

One senior member of the Black Hand, Major Voja Tankosic, was approached by a Bosnian-born Serb, Gavrilo Princip, at some point in the first half of 1914, and asked to provide six bombs and a number of revolvers.

Princip, a student and ardent nationalist, enlisted two other Bosnian students in Belgrade. He also asked a friend in Sarajevo, Danilo Ilic, to recruit three more conspirators. Aided by Tankosic, Princip and his two colleagues were able to cross into Bosnia and meet up with Ilic's recruits.

Meanwhile the Serbian prime minister, Nikola Pasic, had learned of the plot. He realized that if he kept quiet the murder might well take place and set off an unprecedented diplomatic crisis or even a war. On the other hand, if he warned the Austro-Hungarian government, the latter would assuredly take it as proof that Serbia had connections with radical nationalist societies inside Bosnia. Moreover, such an act would incur the wrath and maybe the violence of the Black Hand against the Serbian authorities, because its members would see it as a betrayal.

Pasic instructed the Serbian ambassador in Vienna to advise the Austro-Hungarian minister of finance, Leon von Bilinski, who also ran the empire's civil administration in Bosnia, that there might be trouble during Franz Ferdinand's visit to Sarajevo, which was scheduled for June 28. This was a significant date for both Princip and the archduke. It was the day of St. Vitus, the patron saint of Serbia, and was also the day on which Franz Ferdinand had married his wife, Sophie Chotek, in 1900. Bilinski, who was on poor terms with Franz Ferdinand and also had little real diplomatic responsibility in Bosnia, did not pass on the warning.

When on June 28 Franz Ferdinand and his wife drove into Sarajevo in a convoy of six cars, there were no special security precautions, the visit being entrusted to the city's police force. The route of the royal couple had been well publicized, to allow the population to greet them, and the six conspirators were stationed separately at points along the route. The first conspirator, on seeing the approach of the royal motor vehicles, feared arrest and did nothing. The second felt sorry that he might have to kill Franz Ferdinand's wife and also did nothing.

However, the third, Cabrinovic, took careful aim and lobbed his bomb. It bounced off the back of the archduke's automobile and exploded under the following vehicle, causing a dozen injuries, but the archduke and his wife, though shaken, were unhurt. After a brief halt the cavalcade continued. The fourth conspirator, Gavrilo Princip, investigated the explosion and saw the arrest of Cabrinovic. Believing the assassination had failed, Princip entered a nearby cafe. The fifth conspirator, who was too shortsighted to identify Franz Ferdinand, lost his nerve. The final member of the party also did nothing.

The archduke proceeded to the official reception at the city hall, where the mayor gave a speech that emphasized the warm welcome that the Sarajevans had prepared for their royal visitors, much to the annoyance of Franz Ferdinand. The archduke expressed his concerns to General Oskar Potiorek, the Austro-Hungarian military governor of Bosnia and Herzegovina, asking, "Do you think other attempts will be made?" Potiorek replied, "Go at ease. I accept all responsibility." In view of the obvious peril, it was decided to change the scheduled route for the rest of the day. However, nobody told the archduke's driver, so when the imperial automobile left the city hall it initially proceeded along the original return route.

His revolver still loaded, conspirator Gavrilo Princip was still sitting in the cafe, convinced that the plot had failed. At the same time, the driver of the imperial automobile was being told that he was driving down the wrong road, which happened to be the sidestreet where Princip was loitering. The chauffeur stopped to back up, placing the

▼ *A photograph purporting to show the arrest of Gavrilo Princip (second from right) by Bosnian police officers immediately after the assassination in Sarajevo on June 28. It is more likely to show the arrest of one of the other suspects involved in the events at Sarajevo.*

royal couple directly in Princip's line of fire. Princip promptly fired two shots from a range of probably no more than a few feet, a distance at which it was difficult for him to miss. Sophie, sitting in the back of the automobile and apparently unaware that she herself had been hit, asked her consort, "Whatever's happened to you?" as she died. The archduke, sitting in the front with Potiorek, was also fatally wounded. In words that were repeated around the world in the next few days and would help raise the international tension, the archduke's last words were, "Sophie dear! Don't die! Stay alive for our children!" Princip was arrested at the scene.

In Russia, Czar Nicholas II ordered a memorial service for the archduke, but Russian supporters of a Greater Serbia made it clear they thought this was a pathetic gesture in honor of a man who, after all, had been killed in the name of Serbian nationalism, a cause that Russia was bound to support. In Vienna, the Austro-Hungarian capital, a private funeral was arranged for the archduke and his wife, but it was far less grand than might have been expected. Traditionalist circles in Vienna had not liked his liberal tendencies, and they had liked his wife, Sophie, even less because she was considered by some to have been of insufficiently high royal rank to warrant such a senior place in the Hapsburgs. However, there was much popular support in Austria-Hungary for direct action against Serbia, not least to repair the empire's damaged reputation and prestige.

▼ *The Sarajevo conspirators (front row) stand trial for the assassination. Cabrinovic is seated second from left and Princip third—both would die in prison from natural causes.*

Of the six conspirators, Cabrinovic and Princip were arrested on the day of the assassination, and three more shortly after. The five were put on trial long after the war had started and were eventually found guilty. Being only teenagers, they were not liable to the death penalty, but Cabrinovic, Princip, and one other died in prison. The other two conspirators were released after the war. Dmitrijevic, head of Serbian Army intelligence, was never publicly implicated in the assassination. Perhaps this turn of events gave him excessive self-confidence because he continued to plot in support of aggressive Serbian nationalism. However, he went too far even for his own leaders and in 1917 the Serbian government-in-exile in Corfu had him executed.

The response to Sarajevo

The death of Franz Ferdinand evoked considerable sympathy, not least among other crowned heads of Europe because he was the empire's heir apparent and "one of their own." If Austria-Hungary had struck back immediately at Serbia, while world opinion was still broadly sympathetic, the war might have been localized, but there were delays. Emperor Franz Joseph was against hostilities. Equally, the Austro-Hungarian general staff, headed by Field Marshal Franz Conrad von Hötzendorf, said that it had made no plans that allowed for a quick campaign against Serbia, so a war could not be started for at least two weeks—and would involve full mobilization of the country's armed forces, a move that Russia would view as provocative.

The Austro-Hungarian government, under Prime Minister Karl von Sturgkh, decided to postpone war until two matters were settled. First, could Austria-Hungary rely on German help if its attack against Serbia resulted in a wider conflict with Russia? Second, would it be possible to find real evidence implicating the Serbian government in the murders? It took a week to discover how Germany would react. A letter composed by the Austro-Hungarian foreign minister, Leopold von Berchtold, was addressed to Emperor Wilhelm II of Germany. It suggested that "Serbia must be eliminated as a power factor in the Balkans" if Austria-Hungary was to regain its former prestige. What would Germany do if Austria acted accordingly? The note reached the German emperor on July 5.

Franz Ferdinand had been a close friend of Wilhelm II, so emotion rather than thoughtful deliberation played a large part in the emperor's immediate response. He said that if Austria-Hungary did act, and Russia came in to help Serbia, then Germany would aid Austria-Hungary. The German emperor also believed that Austria-Hungary

▲ *Istvan Tisza, the Austro-Hungarian prime minister, was initially very reluctant to go to war against Serbia.*

should act immediately to prevent the crisis dragging on. In this he was probably right, and it is possible that he mistakenly believed that Austria-Hungary could act quickly, in which case his advice would have been less dangerous than it turned out to be. Wilhelm's backing for action against Serbia and offers of possible German military support if the crisis drew in Russia was termed a blank check—one effectively giving Austria-Hungary a free hand in Serbia with German support.

Later on July 5, Wilhelm talked to members of his government. However, his foreign minister, Gottlieb von Jagow, was away on honeymoon. His chancellor, Theobald von Bethmann Hollweg, was the only major adviser available. Bethmann Hollweg fully realized, even if Wilhelm did not, that the assurance of German help could lead to an all-Europe war. The chancellor had tried to restrain Wilhelm's more bellicose demands with a certain amount of success in the past, but by July 1914 Bethmann Hollweg was convinced that it was in Germany's best interests to support Austria-Hungary. He believed that Russia would protest strongly over any attack on Serbia, but would eventually back down. Consequently, he backed Wilhelm's initial response.

Germany's favorable response to action against Serbia encouraged a more belligerent position in sections of the Austro-Hungarian government. Leopold von Berchtold, the foreign minister, had been accused of indecision in the past and this time he was determined to act strongly. He wanted an immediate war and was against any delay. However, he discovered that the empire's Hungarian prime minister, Istvan Tisza, was not only against an immediate war in principle, but also dreaded victory against Serbia for fear that it would bring a territory populated by Serbs into the empire.

It was only after a week of argument, and a promise that no Serbs would be added to Hungary's population, that Tisza changed his mind and accepted the idea of war against Serbia. This delay, which made any immediate response to the Sarajevo assassination even more remote, affected Berchtold badly, and he became convinced that the war should be postponed.

Nevertheless, it appeared on the surface that all the obstacles to an immediate war were disappearing. Austro-Hungarian leaders were saying to each other that if they did not take a strong line against Serbia they would lose German respect and consequently Germany would not regard its alliance with the empire as worth preserving. Simultaneously, German leaders were telling each other that if they did not back Austria-Hungary the latter would not regard its alliance with Germany as worth preserving. By this point the move toward war seemed to be fired more by the wish to preserve the Austro-German alliance than to avenge the archduke's recent murder.

However, with the passing days wider sympathy for Austria-Hungary was diminishing. This made it more likely that Russia would intervene if Austro-Hungarian forces marched against Serbia. Germany had promised to help Austria-Hungary in that eventuality, and since France had an alliance with Russia, a Europe-wide war might well result. Everybody except the Serbs and some Russians saw a need to localize the conflict, so that it could be a matter of Austria-Hungary punishing Serbia. To regain international sympathy the Austro-Hungarian government decided to wait until it could publish its report into the Serbian government's supposed complicity in the plot.

However, the search for Serbian connivance in the plot was not as successful as had been expected. The foreign ministry official sent to Belgrade, the Serbian capital, discovered that neither in Serbia nor in Bosnia had police investigations uncovered any evidence directly implicating the Serbian government. Those who had been arrested had revealed no clear-cut links, and the police investigations had been ineffectively pursued. It had been established that the conspirators had been in Belgrade and that the bomb was made in Serbia. It was also discovered that a Serbian railroad official and major had also been involved, but that was all, which was hardly enough to indict the Serbian government and declare war.

Having promised damaging revelations, the Austro-Hungarian government was disappointed by this report. Despite this humiliating lack of evidence, Berchtold and the advocates of war pushed ahead regardless. Serbia was a menace, they believed, and this was a suitable occasion to resort to force. An ultimatum was composed, one offering Serbia a chance to avoid war provided certain conditions were met. These conditions were so tough that nobody in Vienna really thought that the Serbian government, which was in effect being asked to surrender its authority and Serbia's independence, would accept them. The ultimatum was ready by July 14.

▼ *Crowds gather on the streets of Vienna to demonstrate their support for an Austro-Hungarian war declaration against Serbia in late July 1914.*

Austria-Hungary's fatal ultimatum

The preparation of Austria-Hungary's ultimatum proceeded under great secrecy, but hints of what was in process soon leaked out. Secrecy was desirable because the longer Russia was kept in ignorance, the more likely it was that its government would acquiesce to the ultimatum, not having been given the chance to prepare for Serbia's rejection. The Austro-Hungarians also kept the German government in the dark, because Berchtold feared that the Germans might advise caution and thereby arouse within Austria-Hungary itself significant objections to what was going on. Emperor Franz Joseph was known to be half-hearted in his support for an aggressive policy, and he was by no means alone, although the empire's general staff, led by Field Marshal Hötzendorf, was still urging war.

The hope was that Russia would not intervene in the crisis, and that hope was largely based on another hope, that France would not declare war to help Russia fight Austria-Hungary, given that Austria-Hungary would be attacking Serbia in the role of outraged victim rather than aggressor.

The crisis that intensified as July progressed was exacerbated (and dragged out) by the absence of influential figures at important times. The German foreign minister, Gottlieb von Jagow, had been away on honeymoon when Wilhelm II needed his advice at the beginning of July. General Helmuth von Moltke, the German chief of staff, was vacationing at a spa at another critical stage. Indeed, Wilhelm II himself enjoyed a yachting holiday when he should perhaps have been in Berlin.

Equally, at the very end of the July crisis, as Britain was deciding whether to declare war or not, most of the members of the British government retired to their various weekend retreats, with only the foreign secretary, Edward Grey, acknowledging the gravity of the situation by delaying departure to his country cottage by a few hours. Meanwhile, the Russian representative in Serbia, N. E. de Hartvig, died suddenly on July 10, thereby making the flow of information between Russia and Serbia difficult.

The most significant absence was that of the French president, Raymond Poincaré, and his prime minister, René

▼ Austria-Hungary's Franz Joseph (left) was only reluctantly persuaded to sign the orders to mobilize against Serbia.

▲ **President Poincaré of France was sailing home from Russia at the height of the crisis and was not kept informed of vital developments.**

Sazonov was known to be smarting from criticisms of Russia's apparent weakness in previous Balkan crises. Austria-Hungary hoped that he would show weakness again, but in fact he was determined to show how strong he was. Like many other senior Russian figures, he feared any Austro-Hungarian take-over of Serbia, believing that it would allow Germany to spread its influence southward through the Balkans toward the Turkish-controlled Bosporus and Dardanelles seaway, which was Russia's only means of communication between the Black Sea and the outside world.

Austria-Hungary's ultimatum to Serbia was delivered on July 23 by its ambassador, Wladimar Giesl von Gieslingen, just one hour after Poincaré and his entourage left Russia. It was blunt and made ten sweeping demands in all. The Serbian government was to stop all subversive activities by its nationals in Austria-Hungary, and all anti-Austro-Hungarian propaganda in Serbia. All people involved in the Sarajevo assassination were to be put on trial, with Austro-Hungarian representatives taking part in the court proceedings. The Serbian government was to take effective measures to prevent arms passing over the Serbian-Bosnian frontier, and those Serbian frontier officials who had helped the conspirators infiltrate Bosnia had to be punished. The Serbian government was given 48 hours to reply, the deadline being 6:00 P.M. on July 25. The Austro-Hungarian Army, believing that Serbia would reject these demands, was to begin mobilizing on the morning of the following day.

In terms of accepted diplomatic language and procedures the Austro-Hungarian ultimatum was a brutal document, one requiring the Serbian government to humiliate itself or face a war. In the world at large, sympathy generated by the archduke's murder four weeks previously was replaced by a growing feeling of disquiet at what was perceived as Austria-Hungary's bullying of Serbia.

Viviani, who was also handling foreign affairs. Their crucial absence was due to a long-planned state visit to Russia, a visit that just happened to coincide with the deepening crisis. The two French leaders were due to sail home from Russia on July 23. In choosing this date for the delivery of their ultimatum to Serbia, the Austro-Hungarians ensured that Poincaré and Viviani would not be able to hold immediate face-to-face talks with their Russian counterparts to plan a coordinated response to it.

However, during the French state visit to Russia, Poincaré pointedly reminded the Austro-Hungarian ambassador in the Russian capital that France was Russia's ally. At about the same time Serge Sazonov, the Russian foreign minister, told the same ambassador that Russia "would not allow" Austria-Hungary to use threatening language or military force against Serbia. Thus the Austro-Hungarian government had been left with no reason to doubt that an attack on Serbia would almost certainly lead to a European conflict.

The drift to war

On learning the terms of the Austro-Hungarian ultimatum the Russian government decided that, if necessary, it would partially mobilize its armed forces close to its border with Austria-Hungary to protect Serbia against possible aggression. It believed that partial mobilization would send a signal to Germany that Russia's quarrel was with Austria-Hungary alone. However, the Russian government had not first spoken to the chief of staff, N. N. Janushkevich, and was unaware that partial mobilization was not practical.

Two minutes before the expiry of the Austro-Hungarian ultimatum on July 25, the Serbian government handed over its reply. To most people's surprise, and to Berchtold's annoyance, it was conciliatory. Serbia agreed to the various demands except in two instances. It could not locate, and therefore could

▼ *Edward Grey, the British foreign secretary, realized that a Europe-wide conflict would swiftly follow an Austro-Hungarian attack on Serbia and made last-minute efforts for peace.*

not arrest, the Serbian railroad worker who had helped get the conspirators across the border into Bosnia. More importantly, Serbia could not agree to Austro-Hungarian representatives taking part in its investigative and judicial processes. Much of the diplomatic world agreed that this would be a breach of Serbia's sovereignty.

The Serbian government had bent as far as it could without being rejected by its own people, and most diplomats thought that the crisis was now ready for final mediation. However, they were already behind events. The Serbian reply had been handed to the Austro-Hungarian government's representative in Belgrade, Giesl von Gieslingen, at 5:48 P.M. During the next 30 minutes he glanced through it and sent back a preprepared letter informing the Serbian government that its response was considered insufficient and that Austria-Hungary was therefore breaking off relations. The ambassador then arranged for the burning of the Austro-Hungarian legation's secret documents and caught the 6:30 P.M. train back to Vienna. Later that day, foreign minister Leopold von Berchtold encouraged a reluctant Emperor Franz Joseph to sign the order confirming the mobilization of Austria-Hungary's armed forces.

The following day, July 26, the European powers realized that they were facing a growing crisis, possibly war, and some tried to limit it to Austria-Hungary and Serbia. While the British government ordered its warships, which had been assembled for a review in home waters, to remain on station, the foreign secretary, Edward Grey, suggested a meeting with the foreign ministers of Italy, France, and Germany. Germany's chancellor, Theobald von Bethmann Hollweg, initially refused Grey's suggestion, believing that an Austro-Hungarian victory over Serbia in a localized and short-lived war would be politically beneficial to both Austria-Hungary and Germany.

However, Emperor Wilhelm II, who arrived back in Berlin later in the day, was less belligerent. Suddenly convinced that Germany was in great danger of supporting not a localized conflict but engaging in war with Russia and France, and maybe Britain, he advised Austria-Hungary to negotiate. Yet, on July 28, without consulting Germany, Austria-Hungary declared war on Serbia even though its forces would not be able to invade Serbia before August 12. Was there still time to reach a negotiated solution?

Also on July 28, Wilhelm II suggested that the Austro-Hungarians, once their forces had reached Belgrade, should declare a period of peace during which Serbia might be persuaded to give additional satisfaction. However, Leopold von Berchtold, the Austro-Hungarian foreign minister, having come so far, was not willing to listen. He wished for the total occupation of Serbia. Next day,

July 29, the German emperor had another idea and sent a telegram to his Russian cousin, Nicholas II, assuring him that he, the German emperor, was doing what he could to restrain Austria-Hungary, and would Nicholas also help to prevent a European war? At about the same time, Nicholas was sending Wilhelm a similar telegram. However, Wilhelm also learned that, five days previously, Nicholas had consented to Russia's partial mobilization against Austria-Hungary, and also to the issue of secret orders initiating the "period preparatory to mobilization." Wilhelm felt betrayed, and his negotiations with Nicholas came to an aggrieved end.

Also on July 28, Sazonov, the Russian foreign minister, decided it was finally time to use the czar's earlier consent to partial mobilization against Austria-Hungary. He had been encouraged by French assurances of support. These assurances were really the creation of

▲ Reservists of the recently mobilized Austro-Hungarian Army receive their pay in 1914. The empire's decision to mobilize was supported by Germany, although such a development was likely to lead to the outbreak of a Europe-wide war.

▲ *King Albert of Belgium, whose announcement that his country would defend the neutrality it had held since 1839 led Germany to declare war on Belgium as a necessary prelude to the invasion of France.*

mobilization of the Russian Army would take some time, thereby leaving a breathing space for further negotiation.

Declarations of war

Russia's decision to mobilize fully was followed by a prompt German reaction, chiefly instigated by the military. On July 31 the chief of the German general staff, Field Marshal Helmuth von Moltke, telegraphed his Austro-Hungarian counterpart, Field Marshal Franz Conrad von Hötzendorf. The message read, "Mobilize at once against Russia." Two ultimata were also sent out from Berlin. The first, to St. Petersburg, requested an end to Russian mobilization, failing which Germany would itself mobilize its forces. In fact, Germany had no expectation of Russia halting its mobilization and was attempting to portray itself as being dragged reluctantly into the conflict due to Russian war threats. The second ultimatum required France, Russia's ally, to give an assurance of total neutrality should Germany and Russia be at war. As a pledge of good faith France was also to hand over the strategically vital fortified towns of Toul and Verdun.

Germany had already decided to order full mobilization and go to war. The first ultimatum was used as a pretext. The second, which Germany knew the French would not accept, was an attempt to get the French government to declare war. Germany's plan for war was based on the belief that it would have to fight France and Russia. France was likely to mobilize quicker and had to be defeated first, then German forces could crush Russia. By August 1 it was clear that neither ultimatum would be accepted, and Germany ordered full mobilization.

In Britain there were fears of Germany and there was the understanding with France. However, why Britain should go to war for Serbia would be hard to explain to the British people. There was a question over the

Paléologue, the French ambassador in St. Petersburg, the Russian capital. Paléologue was very much in favor of war. With the French president and prime minister still at sea, he was virtually making French policy and not keeping his government informed.

Having decided on mobilization against Austria-Hungary only, Sazonov was finally made aware that the Russian Army had no plan for such a mobilization, only plans for full mobilization against both Austria-Hungary and Germany. The leadership was split on the matter. Russia's war minister, General Vladimir Sukhomlinov, argued that Russia was ill prepared for war, while Nikolai Maklahov, the Russian minister of the interior, believed that such a conflict would lead to revolution in Russia. On the morning of July 29 the czar signed two orders, one for full and one for partial mobilization, but the issue of which to implement remained unresolved. Next day, July 30, persuaded by his foreign minister and his generals, Nicholas changed his mind more than once. Finally, at 4:00 P.M, the order for full mobilization was sent out. Nicholas hoped that full mobilization could be used as a threat only. Full

neutrality of Belgium, guaranteed since 1839 by Britain, France, and Germany, to address. On July 31 the British foreign secretary, Edward Grey, asked for assurances from both France and Germany over Belgium's status. France agreed to maintain the status quo, but Germany refused to reveal its intentions. A day later the Belgian government and Belgium's monarch, King Albert, announced their decision to defend their neutrality.

Germany's ultimatum to Russia expired on August 1. The German ambassador in the Russian capital delivered the declaration of war to foreign minister Sazonov. Two hours previously, France had ordered its own mobilization. During the evening of August 2, Germany handed over its ultimatum to Belgium, demanding passage for the German Army across Belgian territory. Belgium rejected the ultimatum and on August 3, having declared war on France, Germany invaded Belgium, still hoping that Britain would not go to war to protect it. Although a handful of British government members resigned on the issue, Britain now felt it necessary to declare war on Germany on August 4. Austria-Hungary declared war on Russia on August 6. On August 12, both Britain and France declared war on Austria-Hungary.

The outbreak of war was greeted favorably by most people. Indeed, war fever gripped many. The war was seen as an opportunity to settle old scores, for people to revel in patriotism, and as an adventure. However, not everyone was so enthused. The British foreign secretary, Edward Grey, was much more pessimistic and was heard to say, "The lamps are going out all over Europe and we shall not see them lit again in our lifetimes."

Some political groups and individuals, notably left-wingers and radicals, had tried to prevent war. Efforts to forestall war centered on the various

KEY FIGURES

JEAN JAURÈS

The French socialist leader Jean Jaurès (1859–1914) was a notable victim of the war fever that gripped the whole of Europe in July 1914. A former lecturer at the university of Toulouse and the author of several books, he was primarily a socialist politician who had succeeded in uniting the various French socialist organizations.

Jaurès co-founded the socialist newspaper *l'Humanité* (*Mankind*) and was a member of the French parliament. His support for the French Army officer Alfred Dreyfus, who was imprisoned in 1894 on false charges of spying for Germany, cost him the 1898 election. He was strongly in favor of Franco-German friendship, and distrusted the alliances with Britain and Russia.

During the summer of 1914 Jaurès was busy with attempts to calm the prevailing prowar mood, and for this and his sympathy for Germany he was assassinated on July 31. His death had a depressing effect on those socialists who, in several countries, were trying to organize opposition to the war.

socialist groups who attempted to organize a conference. One of the leading lights in the movement was French radical Jean Jaurès, considered by many the best hope for peace. However, his views outraged many and he was assassinated in Paris on July 31.

Global War Declarations

The outbreak of war in Europe in 1914 was just the first step toward a worldwide conflict. Few corners of the globe remained untouched by the fighting, and many independent countries outside Europe were sucked into the confrontation.

World War I was sparked by what should have possibly remained a localized squabble in the Balkans between the Austro-Hungarian Empire and Serbia following the assassination of the heir to the empire's throne, Archduke Franz Ferdinand, in Sarajevo on June 28. However, by the first days of August the conflict had spread to include virtually all of the leading

▲ *Turkish troops on the march. Around the world, young men of many different nationalities were called on to fight.*

European powers. As many of these had colonies, it was likely that many of these territories and their peoples would become involved in the war to a greater or lesser degree, thereby making the conflict truly global.

This list indicates all those countries that declared war between 1914 and 1918, or severed relations with either the Allies or Central Powers:

1914
July 28: Austria-Hungary declares war on Serbia.
August 1: Germany declares war on Russia.
August 3: Germany declares war on France.
August 3: Germany declares war on Belgium.
August 4: Britain declares war on Germany.
August 5: Montenegro declares war on Austria-Hungary.
August 6: Austria-Hungary declares war on Russia.
August 6: Serbia declares war on Germany.
August 8: Montenegro declares war on Germany.
August 12: France declares war on Austria-Hungary.
August 12: Britain declares war on Austria-Hungary.
August 23: Japan declares war on Germany.
August 25: Japan declares war on Austria-Hungary.
August 28: Austria-Hungary declares war on Belgium.
October 29: Turkey declares war on Russia, France and Britain.
November 2: Russia declares war on Turkey.
November 2: Serbia declares war on Turkey.
November 5: France declares war on Turkey.
November 5: Britain declares war on Turkey.

1915
May 23: Italy declares war on Austria-Hungary.
June 3: San Marino declares war on Austria-Hungary.

August 21: Italy declares war on Turkey.
October 14: Bulgaria declares war on Serbia.
October 15: Russia declares war on Bulgaria.
October 15: Montenegro declares war on Bulgaria.
October 16: France declares war on Bulgaria.
October 16: Britain declares war on Bulgaria.
October 20: Italy declares war on Bulgaria.

1916
March 9: Germany declares war on Portugal.
March 15: Austria-Hungary declares war on Portugal.
August 27: Romania declares war on Austria-Hungary.
August 28: Italy declares war on Germany.
August 30: Turkey declares war on Romania.
September 1: Bulgaria declares war on Romania.

1917
March 14: China severs relations with Germany.

April 6: United States declares war on Germany.
April 7: Cuba declares war on Germany.
April 7: Panama declares war on Germany.
April 11: Brazil severs relations with Germany.
April 13: Bolivia severs relations with Germany.
April 18: Nicaragua severs relations with Germany.
April 23: Turkey severs relations with United States.
April 27: Guatemala severs relations with Germany.
May 8: Nicaragua declares war on Germany.
June 27: Greece declares war on Austria-Hungary, Bulgaria, Germany, and Turkey.
July 22: Siam (now Thailand) declares war on Austria-Hungary and Germany.
August 4: Liberia declares war on Germany.
August 14: China goes to war on Austria-Hungary and Germany.
September 21: Costa Rica severs relations with Germany.
October 6: Peru severs relations with Germany.

▲ *Bulgarian troops take up their positions in mountainside trenches on the Macedonian front in 1915. Bulgaria was the last country to side with the Central Powers during the war. The decision was made in secret during September 1915, and war was declared on Serbia the following month.*

October 7: Uruguay severs relations with Germany.
October 26: Brazil declares war on Germany.
December 7: United States declares war on Austria-Hungary.
December 8: Ecuador severs relations with Germany.
December 10: Panama declares war on Austria-Hungary.

1918
May 8: Nicaragua declares war on Austria-Hungary and Germany.
May 23: Costa Rica declares war on Germany.
July 12: Haiti declares war on Germany.
July 19: Honduras declares war on Germany.

The World Response

Before World War I ended in 1918, 18 states joined the original Allies, while two, Turkey and Bulgaria, sided with the Central Powers. Several other nations in Europe remained close to the scene of hostilities but without being involved in the conflict. The Netherlands, squeezed between Germany and the North Sea, was perhaps the most remarkable of these, but Spain, traditionally neutral Switzerland, and the Scandinavian countries also remained at peace. In Latin America, the states divided between those remaining neutral, those severing diplomatic ties with the Central Powers, and the handful that declared war on the Allied side.

World War I confronted many countries not directly involved with a dilemma. Their governments had to decide between neutrality and joining one side or the other in the conflict.

In the summer of 1914 much speculation surrounded countries that were expected to join the war but had not made an immediate decision. Turkey watched from the sidelines during the summer of 1914, but soon made its intentions clear by joining the Central Powers in late October. Several Balkan states were supposedly neutral, but many had pro-German rulers. Italy was known to have made alliances with both sides, but how its government would react to the war caused concern among both the Allies and the Central Powers. Japan, allied with Britain and with ambitions to be a Pacific power, was likely to declare against the Central Powers. Portugal, a colonial power (though not of the first rank), was Britain's oldest ally in Europe. It was not expected to declare war in solidarity with Britain, but might come into the conflict later.

Turkey and the Middle East

For much of the nineteenth century Britain had regarded itself as Turkey's protector, chiefly against Russia, but by 1914 events had moved on. Russia, Turkey's traditional regional enemy, was now an ally of Britain. The Young Turks, members of the nationalist and expansionist Union and Progress Party who took overall charge of Turkey's government in January 1913, were establishing closer links with Germany. Smarting from Turkey's recent humiliations in

▶ *Talaat Pasha, one of the ruling body of the Young Turks who sought to modernize Turkey after 1913 and also established close links with Germany.*

the Balkan Wars (1912–1913), the Young Turks seemed dedicated to restoring the empire's prestige, which had been gradually eroded during the nineteenth century. Britain, for example, had taken effective control of the Turkish province of Egypt.

The ruling body of the Young Turks was led by three men: Enver Pasha, Mehmed Talaat Pasha, and Ahmed Djemal Pasha. These men embarked on a process of modernization involving industrialization, military expansion, and the reestablishment of Turkish authority and culture throughout the empire. They also attempted to secure an alliance with either of the European power blocs, chiefly Britain and France or Germany. Germany, increasingly involved in Turkey's economy, was becoming dominant in Turkish affairs. Indeed, Germany's Emperor Wilhelm II paid an official visit to the country.

Britain's interest in Turkey was increasingly focused on the latter's role as a power in the Middle East. Whereas Turkey's Balkan possessions were diminishing rapidly, its hold on Mesopotamia (now Iraq) was still strong. This territory had significance for the British because it provided one possible invasion route toward India, and Britain was extremely sensitive about India, its prize imperial possession. The availability of oil in the region was also known and, although in 1914 it did not have the strategic importance it would later acquire, the British Admiralty in 1914 was already building oil-fired battleships, and the British government had prudently acquired an interest in an Anglo-Persian oil company.

In 1914 Britain did not relish the prospect of German penetration into the Middle East by way of Turkey. When in 1902 the Turkish government asked for German assistance in extending an existing Turkish railroad into Mesopotamia and then out toward the Persian Gulf, the British government

POLITICAL WORLD

PORTUGAL

Although it was beset by internal political problems throughout World War I, Portugal offered military support to the Allies. However, its commitment to the war against the Central Powers left the country deeply in debt, and political upheavals in Portugal continued after 1918.

In 1910 the Portuguese monarchy of King Manoel II was overthrown and a republic proclaimed. However, the country was destabilized by political infighting between republicans and monarchists. Political violence was widespread in the country on the eve of World War I (and beyond), which was probably one reason why the British advised Portugal to remain neutral, even though Portugal had declared its support for Britain on August 7, 1914.

However, military incursions from Germany's African colonies into Portugal's adjacent territories of Angola and Mozambique in the first weeks of the conflict drew Portugal into the war, although far from officially. Portuguese troops were sent to Africa to protect the colonies in September. Ultimately, 40,000 Portuguese troops would operate in Africa.

In February 1916, at Britain's request, Portugal seized 36 German merchant ships interned in Portuguese waters, and this led to a German declaration of war on March 9. Then on March 15 Austria-Hungary declared war on Portugal. The various political factions in Portugal fully supported going to war against the Central Powers, and Portugal sent an expeditionary force under General Fernando Tamagnini to the western front in 1917. In total, Portugal mobilized 100,000 troops and suffered some 21,000 casualties, of whom 7,000 were fatalities.

Portuguese troops hold trenches on the western front.

the Balkan Wars. However, Sanders was much more than an adviser, as he was expected actually to command Turkish troops in wartime. This development suggested the beginning of German interference in Turkish military affairs and was especially alarming to Russia. In reality, Russia's concern was not so much the German participation but the likelihood that Sanders would actually succeed in creating an effective Turkish Army. In a concessionary move, Germany acted swiftly. Sanders was promoted to Acting Field Marshal, a rank that according to military tradition never takes personal command of troops in the field. This seemed to satisfy Britain, although there were still grumbles from leading politicians in Russia.

There had long been tension between Russia and Turkey, with the Russian government making no secret of its support for the Slavs within the Turkish

was alarmed but had no convincing reason for protest. The route, which became known as the Berlin-Baghdad Railroad, brought a German presence alarmingly close to India. However, on the eve of World War I an agreement was reached by which the most sensitive part of the route, its southern tip, would be transferred to British control.

A second sign of seemingly improving relations was the settlement of a problem revolving around a German officer, General Otto Liman von Sanders, who had been sent to reconstruct the Turkish Army after its defeats during

▲ *German General Otto Liman von Sanders was given the task of rebuilding the Turkish Army after its defeats in the Balkan Wars.*

Empire who were hoping to win independence, and the influential pro-Slavists in Russia constantly declaring that Constantinople, the Turkish capital, should be Russian. Both countries had been at war with each other-recently, not least in the Crimean War (1853–1856) and the Russo-Turkish War (1877–1878). Equally, the right of passage for Russian warships from the Black Sea into the Mediterranean Sea by way of the Dardanelles seaway, which was Turkish-controlled, was denied by international treaties. This remained a sore point in St. Petersburg and could only be securely obtained by Russian occupation of the area. Another point of friction was the Russo-Turkish frontier in the Caucasus.

However, Germany could offer Turkey something that the British and French could not as allies of Russia—the possibility of territorial gains from Russia. Such an offer was attractive to the Young Turks. Not only would victory as a German ally expand the empire at the expense of Russia, war would also allow Turkey the opportunity to regain control of former regions of the empire that had been taken over by Britain and France. Any hopes that the Allies had of persuading Turkey to join their side were to be disappointed. In July 1914 Turkey signed a secret defense treaty with Germany. Although the Allies continued to court the Young Turks after this period, the die had been cast.

The Balkan perspective

Bulgaria, a Slavic nation whose language is very close to Russian, had won a degree of independence from Turkey with Russian support in 1878, but relations between the two had deteriorated since then, mainly because of Russian interference in its affairs. The country finally won full independence from Turkey in 1908, and its ruler, Czar

▼ *This contemporary lithograph depicts the annihilation of Turkish troops by Russian troops near the town of Bajatsid in 1877, during the Russo-Turkish War.*

Ferdinand I, who had been born in Austria-Hungary, embarked on a campaign to expand the new country's borders. However, this plan backfired and Bulgaria suffered territorial losses at the end of the Balkan Wars, including the surrender of the Black Sea province of Dobrudja to neighboring Romania.

Shortly before World War I, Bulgaria's resentment at Russian involvement in its affairs led to a gradual realignment with the Central Powers, a repositioning that was chiefly engineered by its pro-Austro-Hungarian and pro-German prime minister, Vasil Radoslavov, who enjoyed the support of Ferdinand. Economic ties with Austria-Hungary and Germany strengthened. On the eve of war, predominantly agricultural Bulgaria took 55 percent of its imported manufactured goods, metals, and raw materials from the two Central Powers.

After August 1914, both the Allies and the Central Powers strove to bring Bulgaria into the war. Both offered territorial gains: the Allies suggested

▶ *Czar Ferdinand I of Bulgaria tried to expand his country's borders after it won independence from Turkey in 1908, but Bulgaria lost territory in the Balkan Wars.*

Turkish territory, while the Central Powers indicated parts of Macedonia that had been Bulgarian lands taken over by Serbia at the end of the Balkan Wars. The Bulgarians made no immediate decisions, but Allied defeats on the eastern front and the failure of their Gallipoli campaign in 1915 pushed the country toward support for the Central Powers. Matters were settled at the Pless Convention in Germany on September 6. This document, and a second document signed in Sofia, the Bulgarian capital, on the same day, confirmed a military alliance between Bulgaria and the Central Powers. The country was contracted to support a German-led invasion of Serbia within 35 days, and to declare war on Greece or Romania if they joined with the Allies. In return, Bulgaria would be granted parts of Macedonia and Greece, and also the province of Dobrudja. Bulgarian forces duly attacked Serbia on October 5, although it did not actually declare war until October 12.

Like Bulgaria, Romania had gained its independence from Turkey in 1878, being formed out of the empire's provinces of Moldavia and Wallachia. Although democratic, its National Assembly was subordinate to the Crown Council that reported directly to the country's monarch, who on the eve of World War I was Carol I, a relative of Emperor Wilhelm II. Romania had mixed relations with the Central Powers. Austria-Hungary and Germany were major trading partners (Romanian oil was much valued by them both) and they had invested heavily in the country, but the fact that Austria-Hungary's empire contained some three million Romanians in its province of Transylvania was a source of discord between Austria-Hungary and Romania.

Romania had signed a formal treaty with the two Central Powers in 1883, but at the outbreak of World War I it refused to abide by its provisions, citing the ongoing friction over Transylvania.

Although Carol tried to dissuade the government, it formally declared its neutrality on August 3, 1914. Carol died on October 14 and was succeeded by his nephew, Ferdinand I, who was mildly pro-Germany and pro-Austria-Hungary. Germany's Emperor Wilhelm II was his cousin, Austria-Hungary's Emperor Franz Joseph was a close friend, and, at that time, two of his brothers were serving in the German Army. Ferdinand's

▲ *Romania's King Carol I was a relative of Emperor Wilhelm I of Germany but had mixed relations with the Central Powers because Austria-Hungary controlled Transylvania.*

wife, Princess Marie, was a granddaughter of Britain's Queen Victoria and a supporter of the Allies. Equally, the country's prime minister, Ion Bratianu, was sympathetic to the Allied cause and not to the Central Powers.

During 1915 and 1916, Romania moved toward outright support of the Allies, a large British loan in January 1915 and Russian successes on the eastern front in mid-1916 deciding the matter. In exchange for military supplies, support from Allied troops, and the future acquisition of Transylvania, Romania declared war on the Central Powers on August 26, 1916. The decision proved an immediate disaster for Romania, which was overrun by the Central Powers in a matter of months.

Greece, like Bulgaria and Romania, had won its independence from the Turkish Empire in the nineteenth century, but somewhat earlier, in 1829, after a popular uprising. Greece had done very well out of the Balkan Wars,

gaining further territory from Turkey, chiefly Macedonia and Thrace. On the eve of World War I, Greece was divided politically. The ruling Greek monarch, Constantine I, was strongly pro-German (his wife was Emperor Wilhelm II's sister), but his prime minister, Eleuthérios Vénizelos, was determinedly pro-Allied.

However, both the Allies and the Central Powers were concerned over Bulgarian and Turkish territorial ambitions toward Greece and, until their true allegiances were revealed, both Constantine and Vénizelos agreed to adopt a policy of neutrality, despite pressure from both Germany and the Allies to join their respective alliances. This accord between the two men was not to last. Vénizelos resigned in March 1915, after Constantine had blocked his plans to join the Allies. The ex-prime minister's break from power did not last long. The following June he won a huge electoral victory, one that undermined King Constantine's position. Vénizelos

▼ The Greek prime minister, Eléutherios Vénizelos, reviews a regiment of Greek troops in Salonika before they march out to engage Bulgarian forces. Because of Greek political instability, he was only able to side with the Allies in June 1917.

mobilized Greece's forces as a precaution against the Austro-Hungarian, Bulgarian, and German invasion of neighboring Serbia, and also offered the Allies the Greek province of Salonika as a base from which to launch their military operations.

Vénizelos's stance was undermined by the king in turn. Constantine was not in a position to block the Allied occupation of Salonika, but was able to force the prime minister's second resignation in October 1915. However, once again the issue was far from clear cut. Constantine increasingly ruled with the support of pro-German elements in the government, but opposition to his rule began to center on Vénizelos. In the fall of 1916, Bulgarian troops occupied parts of Macedonia as a block to the Allied forces in Salonika. This affront to Greece's neutrality fatally wounded Constantine. Vénizelos proclaimed an alternative government in Corfu during September, and the Allies flexed their

▲ *King Constantine I, who was strongly pro-German, was forced to stand down from the Greek throne in 1917 by an Allied blockade. He returned after the war in 1920 but abdicated in 1922.*

military muscle against the king by operating a naval blockade of Greece. The Allies demanded that Constantine be removed from power on June 11, 1917. This occurred the next day and the throne of Greece was assumed by his second son, Alexander. Vénizelos returned to Athens, the capital, and his government declared war on the Central Powers on June 29, 1917.

Italy and war

On the eve of World War I, Italy was a country rent by political upheaval and social unrest. Indeed, King Umberto I, the father of the Italian ruler during the war, King Victor Emmanuel II, had himself been assassinated by an anarchist in 1900. Since Umberto's violent death there had been attempts to extend democracy within Italy. The vote had

been extended to all literate males over 21 and all illiterate males over 30. An effort had also been made to reduce the use of troops and police on the side of employers in disputes with their workers. However, the extension of the right to vote did not necessarily bring about stable government. Many of the new voters were attracted to the more extreme elements of both right-wing and left-wing parties.

On the right, Italian nationalism became a big vote winner and in 1911 the prime minister, Giovanni Giolitti, much against his will, launched an invasion of Libya, a province of the Turkish Empire. The war ended successfully, with Italy gaining not only Libya but also Rhodes and the Dodecanese Islands. However, the brief war drained the Italian treasury and revealed major

shortcomings in the Italian Army. Giolitti resigned in March 1914 and was replaced by Antonio Salandra.

Salandra had just taken office when his administration had to face an outbreak of domestic political violence. It occurred in June and became known as Red Week. It began when police killed three demonstrators in Ancona after a peaceful antimilitarist meeting was held on June 7. A socialist newspaper edited by Benito Mussolini urged a general strike. This was wildly successful for a couple of days but then petered out, partly because the government intercepted most of the telegrams from the organizers to the local strike leaders. The failure of the short strike only increased general bitterness against the regime, against the Catholic church, which seemed to support it,

▲ *Italian and Turkish troops clash in Libya during the brief war between the two during 1911 and 1912. Although the Italians were victorious, the war highlighted several shortcomings in their armed forces and also brought the country close to financial ruin.*

and against the Italian Army, which had been used to suppress the strike. Clearly Italy was not a nation ready to take part in a world war. When the war did start, Italy, which had been part of the Triple Alliance with Austria-Hungary and Germany since 1882, argued it was not a purely defensive war, because Austria-Hungary had marched against Serbia. Therefore, argued Italy, the conditions of the alliance had not been met.

However, the politicians and the wider population of Italy were split on Italian intervention in the war. As Europe slid toward war in July 1914, Italian pacifist and socialist groups demanded that the country remain neutral. Nationalists argued that Italy should side with the Allies, a move that would offer the chance of regaining Italian-speaking areas of the Austro-Hungarian Empire. Partly bowing to public pressure, the government announced Italy's neutrality on August 2. However, Salandra's government slowly moved toward support for the Allies, chiefly over fears concerning Austria-Hungary's territorial ambitions in the region. The latter's renewed invasion of Serbia in December provoked protests from the Italian government.

Over the following months, both the Central Powers and the Allies offered Italy inducements in the form of territorial gains to maintain or end its neutral stance. In December, for example, a German mission to Italy met Giolitti as well as other neutralist politicians. Its aim was to keep Italy out of the war. If the Central Powers were given a free hand in the Balkans, Italy would be allowed to occupy Albania and the Austro-Hungarian Trentino. However, Italian nationalists wanted more, chiefly Trieste, the Austro-Hungarian port on

▼ *Italian crowds cheer their royal family on hearing of their country's declaration of war against the Central Powers in 1915.*

Latin America and the War

At the beginning of World War I many Latin American countries were occupied by quarrels with their neighbors or faced internal unrest. However, the conflict began to impinge on their affairs, and each had to make a decision on its political position.

In the end Argentina and Chile, as well as Mexico, Colombia, Venezuela, Salvador, and Paraguay maintained their neutrality in World War I, but Bolivia, Ecuador, Peru, and Uruguay severed their relations with Germany. Brazil, Costa Rica, Honduras, and Guatemala declared themselves for the Allies after the United States entered the war in April 1917. Cuba, Haiti, Panama, and Nicaragua, whose foreign policies at that time were effectively determined by the United States, also declared war.

In the years before 1914, Latin America's relations were changing. The United States was emerging as a replacement for the weakening British connection, and there were also strong cultural links with France and Italy. Immigration from Europe was high, and although French, Italian, and British immigrants were numerous, there was also a flow of Germans and Austro-Hungarians. Germans seemed to favor Chile, whereas Argentina was still very much in the British sphere of influence.

The big three, the "ABC powers" of Argentina, Brazil, and Chile, were in general agreement over their foreign policies, although this unity would be strained by World War I. Neutral or not, most of the bigger Latin American countries would benefit from the war, chiefly through trade. For example, Chile saw a surge of copper and nitrate exports, and Mexico became a big petroleum exporter.

◀ *The interior of a German U-boat. The loss of shipping to these submarines turned many Latin American states against Germany.*

Brazil, despite its strong economic ties with Germany, was predisposed to be sympathetic toward the Allies in August 1914. However, it initially maintained strict neutrality. However, attacks on Brazilian vessels by German warships gradually moved Brazil to declare war. On April 4, 1917, the steamship *Paraná* was sunk off the northern coast of France, an unprovoked attack that sparked anti-German riots in Rio de Janeiro, the capital of Brazil. The country's foreign minister, Dr. Lauro Müller, refused to meet the German ambassador, who was to have offered an explanation. The Brazilian government, led by Dr. Wencesláo Braz, severed diplomatic ties on April 11.

Other incidents followed. In May the *Tijuca* was sunk, an event that lead to the seizure of German ships that had already been interned in Brazilian waters. The final straw was the sinking of the *Macao*, which led to a declaration of war on October 26, 1917. Brazil's most tangible contribution to the Allied War effort was in supplying various trade items, not least frozen and preserved meats.

Brazil was also able to take a more active part in the war. Conscription raised some 54,000 troops, a force that was not

▲ *Cargo is unloaded at a British port. Britain imported many vital goods from Latin America and the attempted severing of this trade threatened its war effort.*

used. However, Brazilian doctors and airmen did serve on the western front. Also, two Brazilian cruisers and some destroyers were earmarked for service with British forces stationed at Gibraltar for operations in the Mediterranean. However, British and U.S. commanders spent so much time discussing who should have overall control of these vessels that they did not arrive in Gibraltar until after the end of hostilities.

the coast of the northern Adriatic Sea. This was far more than Austria-Hungary could accept, and the Central Powers publicly rejected Italy's demands on April 8, 1915.

The Italian foreign minister, Giorgio Sonnino, announced that the Central Powers would not accede to all of Italy's territorial demands. In the meantime, the Allies had been offering Italy such territorial concessions. On April 26, the secret Treaty of London was signed. Italy would be permitted all of its territorial demands in Europe and in North Africa, and the Allies would also furnish considerable economic and military support. Italy declared war on the Austro-Hungarian Empire on May 23, 1915, Bulgaria on October 20, 1915, and Germany on August 28, 1916.

The Far East

Japan declared war promptly against Germany, on August 23, 1914, although Japan was not directly threatened at the outbreak of World War I. However, Japan did have some legitimacy for its declaration of war against Germany, having signed or reconfirmed treaties with Britain in 1902, 1905, and 1911— these stated that Japan would go to war against Germany if Britain's Far Eastern possessions, chiefly Hong Kong and Weihaiwei (in China), were threatened.

▼ *A parade of Chinese workers at Boulogne in August 1917. Some 300,000 Chinese served as laborers for the Allies in World War I.*

In fact Germany had stated that it would not attack these British possessions, but only if Japan remained neutral.

However, Japan's overriding preoccupation was not honoring its treaties with Britain but strengthening its position in China, which it saw as a potentially valuable territorial acquisition, one offering economic resources, trading rights, and an opportunity for Japan to join the front ranks of the world's great powers. Japan was already militarily strong. It had inflicted a defeat on China in the Sino-Japanese War (1894–1895), a victory that had allowed it to annex southern Manchuria, Korea, Taiwan, and various islands in the Pacific. Japan had also confirmed its position as the dominant military power in the region, one capable of defeating an acknowledged world power, by inflicting a catastrophic defeat on Russia during the Russo-Japanese War (1904–1905).

In 1914 Japan had an emperor, Yoshihito, as its head of state, but he was essentially a figurehead. The emperor's closest advisers and his government, headed by Prime Minister Okuma, were convinced by the country's foreign minister, Takaaki Kato, that a declaration of war against Germany would be in the country's national interests. Japanese forces rapidly overran Germany's colonies in the Pacific. The Marshall Islands, the Caroline Islands, and the Mariana Islands all fell in October, and Germany's chief possession on mainland China, the port of Tsingtao, surrendered to an Anglo-Japanese invasion force in November.

Japan's colonial ambitions alarmed Britain and the United States, both of which saw them as a prelude to further colonial expansion in China and the Pacific. This view was fully confirmed in 1915, when the Japanese presented the Chinese government with their 21 Demands. Much to the irritation of the British and U.S. governments, these effectively demanded that China surrender a large part of its economic and

POLITICAL WORLD

LANSING-ISHII AGREEMENT

This understanding between U.S. Secretary of State Robert Lansing and Japanese envoy Ishii Kikujiro was made in November 1917. At its core was an attempt to normalize the relationship between the two Pacific powers in regard to the conduct of their political and economic relationships with China.

Much of China had been carved up among the world's leading powers before 1914, although Japan's involvement was comparatively recent. However, Japan attempted to strengthen its already sizable influence over the country during World War I, when all of the European colonial powers were at war with each other and their positions in distant China were of secondary importance. The United States had always favored what was called an open door policy toward China. Chinese political integrity was to be respected, and all foreign trade and commerce was to be conducted on an equal footing.

In the event, the United States accepted Japan's special position in China, while Japan appeared to pay respect to the guiding policy of equitable access to China. In reality, the Japanese authorities read far more into the agreement than it actually contained, believing that it allowed them to increase their political and economic involvement in China dramatically. Japan's adoption of this stance led to increasing resentment in the United States, a feeling that would intensify after World War I.

political independence to the Japanese. Attempts to reach an international understanding over the status of China eventually centered on an understanding signed by the U.S. Secretary of State, Robert Lansing, and Japan's special envoy, Ishii Kikujiro, in December 1917. For its part, China declared war on the Central Powers on August 14, 1917. However, the country was beset by internal instability and its military commitment was negligible. Nevertheless, some 300,000 Chinese served as laborers on the western front, in East Africa, and in Mesopotamia.

The Central Powers' Forces

Germany was the strongest of the Central Powers in August 1914 but was backed by Austria-Hungary and Turkey.

The strongest, although not the biggest, of the armies that entered World War I, was that of Germany. Its peacetime strength in 1914 was about 860,000 men supported by around 5,500 pieces of artillery of all calibers. This force was considerably smaller than the combined forces of Germany's two main opponents, Russia and France, which totaled almost 2.5 million men in peacetime and more than 10,000 artillery pieces. Germany's military equipment was on a par with those of its potential opponents, but it did have an advantage in machine guns and the artillery needed to pulverize fortifications, mainly due to the armaments produced in the large factories of Gustav Krupp.

The German Army of World War I had its roots in the Napoleonic Wars of the late eighteenth and early nineteenth centuries, when a new Prussian Army was created following its predecessor's destruction by Napoleon. The Prussian Army was carefully developed during the first half of the nineteenth century, adopting and refining modern theories of war. Prussia's armed forces, which became the core of the subsequent German Army, reached their peak during the Franco-Prussian War (1870–1871). Dominated by Prussia, the German Army comprised the armed forces of all of the previously independent German states. Only Bavaria's forces enjoyed a modicum of independence.

KEY FIGURES

GUSTAV KRUPP

By 1914 Krupp was Germany's major arms producer. It had begun as a steel producer and then turned to arms production, but the company also owned coal and iron ore mines, as well as a number of shipbuilding facilities.

Friedrich Krupp, the first owner, committed suicide in 1902, having been implicated in a scandal, and his daughter, Bertha, inherited the business. The idea of a woman heading a vital arms producer alarmed Germany's generals, and Kaiser Wilhelm II helped to arrange Bertha's marriage to a suitable and competent man, Gustav von Bohlen und Halbach (1870–1950), a Prussian diplomat.

He took the name Krupp and managed the enterprise until 1943. Among Krupp products prior to World War I were the first U-boats and the heavy howitzers that were to devastate Belgium's great fortified city defenses in 1914. Germany's defeat in 1918 was not the end of Gustav Krupp's career. He managed the Krupp concern when it engaged in Germany's secret rearmament in the 1920s, and he later became an ardent supporter of Adolf Hitler's Nazi Party.

◀ *Gustav von Bohlen und Halbach was born in The Hague in 1870 and died in Salzburg in 1950. Known by the name of Krupp after his marriage into the family, he ran the industrial concern up until World War II.*

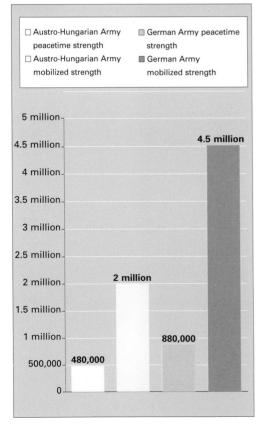

The respective strengths, both peacetime and mobilized, of the Central Powers' land forces in August 1914.

▲ *A German infantry company in 1914 wearing the distinctive spiked helmets that were worn in battle until 1916.*

Universal conscription

The basis of Germany's military might lay with universal mass conscription. Every able-bodied male was liable for military service. The authorities called up the number of men aged 20 they required each year. These recruits were trained for two years in the infantry or three years in the horse artillery and cavalry, and then released back into civilian life. After this, they formed the First Class of the Landwehr (National Guard), where most remained for five (and the horse arms for four) years. Next came 12 years in the Second Class of the Landwehr, and finally six years in the Landsturm, a reserve for the Landwehr. By that time a man who had been conscripted at 20 was 45 years old, and free from further military obligation. Regular periods of training kept German males ready for war service in case of emergency during these years.

Those who had not been called up as young men, possibly due to family commitments or minor disabilities, were placed in the so-called Ersatz Reserve, where they received some training that would enable them to be used on basic, probably noncombatant, military tasks in the event of a grave emergency. After 12 years in the Ersatz Reserve, these men also became part of the Landsturm. In the years preceding 1914 only about 250,000 conscripts were taken each year, considerably fewer than the young men available, as this was the maximum number of recruits that the training facilities could process. This enabled the German Army to select the best of the available conscripts, and also saved money for other purposes, notably artillery procurement. Most pre-1914 recruits were taken from rural areas, with just 5 percent drawn from urbanized industrial workers.

Although other European powers had imitated this system of short compulsory regular service followed by a long reserve period, thereby maintaining a small peacetime force while building up huge reserves, they had not done it as thoroughly as Germany. The German First and Second Reserves were not second-grade troops, as some outsiders considered them, but were maintained in a state of readiness that would allow them to move directly from civilian activities into frontline military service.

The heart of the German military machine was the body of wholly professional regular and noncommissioned officers. These men, responsible for the training of conscripts in peace and for leading them during war, were highly motivated and superbly trained.

Both the regulars and conscripts had the additional military virtue of belief in their country. Foreigners of the time often described the Germans as arrogant, but this confidence was largely an outward sign of the population's patriotic conviction that they were citizens of a nation destined for greatness. This was not the short-term ardor of soldiers enthusiastically going to war, but a deep, long-held feeling that had been instilled in them when they were schoolchildren. Germany, they were taught, was a country destined for greatness, and the German Army, which was held in high esteem, was the instrument that would bring about that greatness.

Supervising this vast war machine was the German general staff, a body consisting of hard-working, highly specialized officers whose task it was to plan both the peacetime life of the German Army and its wartime deployment down to the minutest detail. In the decades preceding 1914 a large portion of the general staff had been engaged in the

▼ German recruits in Hamburg undergoing their compulsory military training after being conscripted. Most continued to have a military role until their mid-40s.

The German General Staff

The German general staff was a coordination body that created the various plans that its members thought would give Germany a quick and resounding victory in a matter of a few weeks.

With wars becoming more complex and the forces available with which to fight them much larger in the nineteenth century, the creation of strategies for future war in peacetime and the working out of means to put them into operation during war could mean the difference between victory and defeat. In the middle of the century, Prussia's Field Marshal Helmuth von Moltke (the uncle of his World War I namesake) recognized the need for forward planning, and he provided the Prussian Army with a central body of officers, known as the general staff, that contained specialists in every aspect of modern war, not least railroads and telegraphy. The working out of mobilization plans would, eventually, be the staff's most important work but in fact there were countless tasks which its members could perform in evolving standards, rules, and procedures for the whole of the country's armed forces.

Moltke's general staff proved itself in the brief war against Austria-Hungary in 1866, particularly in the use of rail transport to take troops to places where the enemy did not expect them. The great Prussian victory over France during the Franco-Prussian War (1870–1871), again masterminded by Moltke, confirmed the importance of the system, which other countries soon began to imitate.

One innovation devised by the general staff had a lasting effect on the German conduct of war.

▼ *Kaiser Wilhelm II, together with Field Marshal Helmuth von Moltke and other commanding officers, attend maneuvers before 1914.*

This was the "general directive system." It was realized that officers in the rear, however advantageous their general overall view might be, could not know the details of action at the front. So officers at the front were given general directives, for example, to capture a particular town by a certain day, and then allowed to use their own initiative in carrying them out. This system worked well, although in 1914 there were already signs that officers at the front were making decisions and carrying out acts without telling their overall commanders.

The general staff was divided into sections, and the most important of these was the railroad section. Apart from devising successive mobilization plans for the railroads, this section kept an eye on what the railroad managements were doing in peacetime.

In 1914 the German general staff was unmatched in its professionalism, but defects were already apparent. The tendency of experts to reject advice and information that did not conform with their own ideas was one such. Any officer who questioned the staff's way of doing things might well find himself posted to a remote garrison.

The other problem was that, whereas the elder Moltke had insisted, with some success, on recruiting only the most intelligent and capable men for his staff, this was an ideal hard to maintain. Moltke's nephew of the same name, who was chief of staff from 1906 until 1914, was not really fit for the job, but his promotion had been more

▲ Field Marshal Helmuth von Moltke was the driving force behind Germany's scheme to avoid fighting a war on two fronts.

rapid than he deserved because of his illustrious forebear. As several commentators pointed out after the war, a more competent chief of staff might just have made Germany's war-winning strategy for 1914, the Schlieffen Plan, work.

The younger Moltke had his virtues, however. He was not afraid to tell Kaiser Wilhelm II, constitutional head of the Army, that his ideas were overambitious, and he insisted that in annual maneuvers the practice of allowing the emperor's side to win should cease.

highly detailed and absolutely vital plan of mobilization and deployment in the event of war. No other planning body had such mastery of railroads and timetables, which were vital for moving huge numbers of reservists to their unit depots and then to the various theaters of operations. Within a week of mobilization being ordered, some 3.8 million Germans were under arms.

Although everyone accepted that the German Army was the world's best, the general staff was somewhat frustrated in its attempts to make it even larger and better. One reason for the discontent was that conscription was only universal in theory. In reality, only about half of the available men were called up each year. While the Reichstag (German Parliament) had little real authority, it did have some power over the country's budget, and it was reluctant to spend more money than necessary on maintaining the army. The political parties that were coming to dominate the Reichstag, those representing socialists and Catholics, regarded the general staff, which was chiefly drawn from the upper class of Protestant landowners, with distrust, seeing it as a force that might one day suppress their respective parties. The ever-growing demand for resources to expand the German Navy also meant that there was less money available for other services.

The pressure for pre-emptive warfare

The result of under-conscription was that, although the German population was bigger than that of France, and included a greater proportion of young men, it brought no advantage in terms

---

KEY FIGURES

HELMUTH VON MOLTKE

Nephew of his illustrious namesake, who had perhaps done more than anybody else to create the victorious Prussian Army of the second half of the nineteenth century, Field Marshal Helmuth von Moltke (1848–1916) was tasked with putting Germany's war plans into operation in 1914.

He served as adjutant for his uncle in 1882 and gradually rose to hold the same position. In 1906 he succeeded Alfred von Schlieffen as Germany's chief of the general staff. From 1906 until 1914, Moltke tinkered with his predecessors war-winning strategy, fatally weakening its key elements. When the crisis that led to World War I developed in June 1914, Moltke, who should have advised Kaiser Wilhelm II on military matters, was absent because he was taking the waters at a spa town. Moltke's chief intervention during the period was to advise the emperor that a decision to initiate the Schlieffen Plan could not be reversed.

Once the Schlieffen Plan began, Moltke further modified some of its key elements, chiefly diverting forces from the key sector in northern France and sending them either to eastern France or the eastern front. The Allied victory at the First Battle of the Marne in September, partly won because of Moltke's failure to control his generals, sealed his fate. He was sacked on September 14, although he remained the nominal head of the general staff until early November. His final role was as the deputy chief of staff. However, he was based in Germany, far from any action, and the post was little more than an honorary one.

of numbers. In 1914 Germany had five million men ready for war, but France was very close behind, simply because the French Army had been conscripting every available man each year, exempting only the physically or mentally unfit. This meant conscripting 85 percent of each year group as it came of military age, compared to barely 50 percent in Germany. Although the Reichstag was compelled to relax its financial grip on military spending with a new law in 1913, it did not change the immediate manpower situation. The general staff believed that, since things would not get any better, and war seemed inevitable, it would be better to have it sooner rather than later.

In the minds of the German general staff, and most notably in that of Field Marshal Helmuth von Moltke, its head from 1906, the ability of the German Army to carry out its war plan was deteriorating year by year. The German plan was named after Moltke's predecessor, Count Alfred von Schlieffen, and was first formulated in the late 1890s. It was dominated by the need for Germany to avoid fighting a war on two fronts. Specifically, this meant inflicting a quick defeat on France, which was

▲ *German troops pictured in a civilian train pressed into service during the country's rapid and well-planned mobilization in August 1914.*

believed to be capable of mobilizing rapidly, during the six weeks that Russia was expected to need for its slower mobilization, and then transporting the victorious Germany Army eastward to deal with Russia. However, more recent evidence suggested ever-faster Russian mobilization due to an improvement in the country's railroad facilities. In 1910 Russia could mobilize at the rate of 250 train-loads of troops per day, but by 1914 this had risen to 360, and the plan being drawn up for 1917 envisaged 560. By 1917 Russian mobilization, far from taking the six weeks initially anticipated by the German generals, would need less than three. The logic was seemingly inescapable—if it were to avoid fighting actions on two fronts simultaneously, Germany had to go to war sooner rather than later, while the differing rates of mobilization still stood in its favor.

The Austro-Hungarian Army

This strategic situation in Europe made the Austro-Hungarian Army all the more important in Germany's plans. Having a common frontier with the Russian Empire, Austria-Hungary could use its forces to supplement the German Army on the eastern front.

KEY FIGURES

FRANZ CONRAD VON HÖTZENDORF

On the recommendation of Archduke Franz Ferdinand, Field Marshal Conrad von Hötzendorf (1852–1925) was appointed chief of staff of the Austro-Hungarian Army in 1906. An ardent and aggressive militarist, he fully backed the empire's declaration of war on Serbia in 1914.

As chief of staff he attempted, unsuccessfully, to expand the Austro-Hungarian Army. He did, however, have some success in modernizing its artillery arm. In 1911 Conrad von Hötzendorf had wanted a preventive war against Italy, nominally an ally of Austria-Hungary, and for his outspokenness he was demoted until December 1912.

When he finally launched the attack on Serbia in 1914, it failed, and only German assistance rescued the situation. Although the German general staff was steadily taking control of Austria-Hungary's war policy, it was he who planned their joint offensive against Russia in 1915, which was successful. However, when Emperor Franz Joseph I died in 1916, his position became increasingly untenable. He was finally dismissed on March 1, 1917, but took up an active field command on the Italian front. Further military disasters followed and Conrad von Hötzendorf was sacked again on July 15, 1918.

Although the Austro-Hungarian Army had been beaten during the Seven Weeks War against Prussia in 1866, it had been subsequently modernized along German lines, and was expected to perform a valuable role in support of the Germany Army.

However, the Austro-Hungarian Army was by no means a wholly efficient fighting machine on the eve of World War I. Remarkably, its nominal commander was the same man who had led it in 1866, Franz Joseph I, although effective command resided with Field Marshal Franz Conrad von Hötzendorf, its chief of staff. The empire's forces, though, had not been tested in war since 1866, so there was no evidence of how thorough the subsequent reforms had been. Although not initially evident, the Army was unprepared to fight a long war and the replacement of weapons would become increasingly problematic.

◄ *Austro-Hungarian soldiers assembled in Jaroslav in the province of Galicia, bordering Russia. These men were drawn from all corners of the empire and many were Slav in origin. Their loyalty to the empire could not be taken for granted.*

Equally, the term Austro-Hungarian Army was something of a misnomer. There was such a force, the Common or Active Army, with some 325,000 men drawn from all corners of the empire and owing their allegiance to Emperor Franz Joseph I. However, both Austria and Hungary also had their own forces. The military was dominated by Austrian officers and politicians, a fact resented by Hungary, which had attempted to block plans for further expansion of the country's armed forces. Also, many of the empire's other ethnic groups were less than whole-hearted in their support of those in power.

Evidence of the polyglot nature of the country's armed forces was abundant. Some 80 percent of officers spoke German, as opposed to just 30 percent of ordinary soldiers. Some 75 percent of all infantrymen were Slavs, not ethnic Germans or Hungarians. In July 1914 mobilization posters had to be produced in 15 different languages. Many high-ranking German-speaking officers had grave doubts about the loyalty of soldiers from different ethnic groups, and some early evidence suggested they might be correct. In April 1915, for example, one Czech unit surrendered wholesale to the Russians.

The peacetime Austro-Hungarian Army had a strength of about 450,000 men, and mobilization would bring it to around three million men, of whom nearly two million would form the effective fighting force. About 2,500 artillery pieces were in service, including an impressive heavy howitzer nicknamed "Schlanke Emma" (Skinny Emma), a number of which were loaned to Germany for its opening operations on the western front in 1914. However, the quality of the average soldier was lower than his German counterpart, and there was the additional handicap that Austria-Hungary had a long, often mountainous frontier to defend against several possible aggressors.

The empire's war plans reflected this problem. Unsure as to who the actual enemy might be in any future war, Hötzendorf had divided his forces in three. One part was to mobilize along the Russian border, while a second was earmarked for action in the south, probably against Serbia or possibly Italy. The final third was deemed a mobile reserve and was to be deployed wherever was appropriate. In the event, this caused chaos. The reserve was initially sent to Serbia after mobilization, but a late change of heart brought about by a speedier Russian mobilization than anticipated led to it being redeployed. Due to the chaotic state of the Austro-Hungarian railroad system, the reserve arrived too late to prevent the Russians gaining the early initiative in 1914.

Turkey's military strength

In the summer of 1914 Germany had the aim of winning Turkey over to the side of the Central Powers, an ambition that was finally achieved in October of that year. The Turkish Army was not as strong as those of Austria-Hungary or Germany, either in terms of numbers or training, but it would be a useful means of drawing some of Russia's forces away from the eastern front to defend the country's mountainous border with Turkey in the Caucasus.

The Turkish Army consisted of about 200,000 men in peacetime, a figure that was expected to double in wartime, and it had about 600 artillery pieces. An estimated 250,000 conscripts were eligible for service each year, but some 75 percent usually avoided military service. The recruits were drawn from various ethnic groups contained within the Ottoman Empire. Arabs, Armenians, Kurds, and Syrians, most of whom

▼ *Turkish infantry drilling near Constantinople. Germany had well-established historic links with the rulers of Ottoman Turkey and was helping to modernize the country's armed forces.*

◄ *Enver Pasha, Turkey's Minister of War and a leading member of the Young Turks.*

entertained thoughts of independence, were considered unreliable though, and only ethnic Turks were expected to fight wholeheartedly for the empire.

The Turkish Army had experienced humiliation during the Balkan Wars (1912–1913), which had highlighted its shortages of modern equipment and poor training at all levels. The country's newly installed ruling body, the General Council of the Union and Progress Party, headed by Enver Pasha and commonly known as the Young Turks, had initiated a reform program in 1913. Among the measures taken was the use of the skills of a military mission under German General Otto Liman von Sanders, who arrived in Turkey during December 1913 and became inspector general of the Turkish Army in January 1914. However, the reforms were far from complete by the time Turkey sided with the Central Powers, and the Turkish leadership gradually grew more resentful of Germany's interference in their country as the war progressed.

The Anglo-German naval contest

At the end of the nineteenth century Germany, already the major military power in Europe and an industrial giant, was also intent on becoming a great naval power. Prior to the 1890s, its small navy was designed for the defense of German waters or for supporting the army in its operations. It was not designed to take on the might of Britain's Royal Navy, nor could it effectively protect Germany's few overseas colonies. However, at the end of the

◀ *A sign of Germany's naval power—a Zeppelin airship passes over one of the country's warships during an exercise in the Baltic Sea shortly before the outbreak of war.*

decade Germany's naval minister, Admiral Alfred von Tirpitz, initiated major modernizing and building programs through the enactment of the Navy Laws of 1898 and 1900, the latter called for a doubling of German naval strength—a plan the British viewed with alarm. Tirpitz was supported by Kaiser Wilhelm II, who had been suitably impressed by Britain's naval might on several ceremonial occasions. Tirpitz's decision sparked an all-out naval race with Britain that intensified the underlying frictions between the two powers.

After battleship design had been revolutionized by the launching of the British *Dreadnought* in 1906, the naval contest between Germany and Britain, the world's foremost naval power, settled down to a shipbuilding race that was won by Britain.

Thus in August 1914 Germany had only five dreadnoughts under construction compared to Britain's eight, and its existing dreadnought fleet comprised 16 vessels against Britain's force of 22. In the faster and lighter-armed battlecruiser category, Britain had nine plus one ship building, whereas Germany possessed six and was building one. Because Britain was setting the pace, it also led in certain design developments. At any given point, the British dreadnoughts under construction were bigger and also had heavier guns than the German battleships being built.

Dreadnoughts carried ten 12-inch (30 cm) guns, but the first German dreadnoughts, which appeared three years later, mounted 11-inch (28 cm) guns. The German ships under construction in 1913 marked a move up to 12-inch guns, but Britain was then building ships with 15-inch (38 cm) guns. A bigger technical lag concerned engine power—whereas the *Dreadnought* had introduced turbine propulsion, only in 1911 had Germany laid down its first turbine battleships.

However, Germany had technical leads in other areas that tended to cancel out any lags in propulsion and gun caliber. The British superiority in armament was largely compensated for by German superiority in range-finding and fire-control. Moreover, British shells tended to break up on impact and had less penetrating power than German shells. Thanks perhaps to Germany's excellence in industrial chemistry, its navy's propellant charges for shells were more stable (that is, less liable to ignite prematurely) than those of the British. German armor protection, on the whole, was probably also superior, and its underwater compartmentation of ships to prevent sinking was more thorough.

German marine designers had the advantage of wider permissible widths of vessel (British designers were constrained by narrow docking dimensions) and a smaller requirement for fuel stowage, because German ships were generally only required to operate over the short distances of the North Sea. German torpedoes were marginally superior to British ones, while their mines were plainly better, so much so that in due course the British copied the German mine design. Germany was also more advanced in certain aspects of naval aviation. In the airship, highly flammable but capable of heavy lifting and long ranges, it had a revolutionary and possibly crucial means of undertaking reconnaissance missions. In 1914 Germany was working with both the Zeppelin and Schütte-Lanz designs.

In smaller warships Germany lagged behind Britain. Although the armored cruiser had been outmoded by the battlecruiser, Britain's superiority in this class (48 vessels against 15) was significant. In lighter cruisers there was a similar German inferiority (71 British ships to 33 German ones). The Royal Navy had roughly twice as many destroyers. Surprisingly, in view of what happened subsequently, in 1914 Germany had only 30 submarines against Britain's 75. Although the British superiority, particularly in cruisers, was partly thanks to obsolete warships still in service, such vessels did have their uses in maintaining a naval blockade of Germany and protecting Britain's colonial outposts.

Whereas British bases, traditionally oriented for a war against France, were poorly situated for conducting a war against Germany, Germany's naval bases were ideally located for operations in the North Sea and were well protected from any surprise attack. The island of Helgoland off Germany's northern coast provided offshore protection. The Kiel Canal, which was opened in 1895 and later widened, gave safe passage for German warships between the North Sea and the Baltic. In the Baltic Sea there was only the weak Russian Navy to contend with, and it provided a good location for training.

Training, however, was a weak point of the German Navy. Tirpitz had praised the German conscription system, which in theory would enable him to find crews for more ships than the Royal Navy, which relied on volunteers. However, the short-term conscript did not make the ideal sailor. With a three-year conscription period, there was at any time a high proportion of men who were still not properly trained and who did not feel part of naval life. Although naval training methods, with repeated drilling and practice, followed routines that worked well in the German Army, the average German sailor was not the equal of his British counterpart.

When World War I began, the German naval commanders opened their orders to discover that there were no strategic surprises. The grand plan was gradually to wear down the British warships blockading Germany by using mines, submarines, and torpedo-boats, and the submarine and mining campaign might even be stretched as far as the British coast. Eventually, when enough damage had been done to the

British to reduce their numbers, the main German force, the High Seas Fleet, would seek an opportunity to attack and defeat Britain's Home Fleet.

This was a sensible plan for a naval power that was numerically inferior to an enemy fleet maintaining a close blockade of its coast. The problem was that, just as the land war did not turn out as the German general staff expected, neither did the sea war. The British had decided that they would not institute a close blockade of Germany; it was felt to be too dangerous in view of the enemy's naval strength. Instead, the British established a distant blockade which, with their numerous cruisers, they were well able to do. Tirpitz had not planned for this eventuality, and the battleships of the High Seas Fleet were left searching for a role, while other German ships, chiefly smaller warships and submarines, bore the everyday burden of Germany's maritime campaign.

Central Powers in the Mediterranean

Germany's allies in 1914, Austria-Hungary and Ottoman Turkey, were

essentially land-based powers. The two had limited naval resources at the outbreak of World War I, although both had zones in which they deployed their maritime resources. Turkey was primarily concerned with the Black Sea and the Dardanelles, the seaway that linked the Black Sea and the Mediterranean. The chief rival was Russia.

Austria-Hungary was concerned with two areas. First, the Danube River, which flowed into the Black Sea by way of several Balkan countries and was a major economic artery, and the Adriatic Sea, which was the empire's direct route into the Mediterranean and the world beyond. Austro-Hungarian monitor vessels patrolled the Danube waterway.

In the Adriatic, Austria-Hungary's naval rival was Italy, as it would be in 1915 following the latter's declaration of war. Before 1914 Austria-Hungary's naval chief of staff, Montecuccoli, had initiated an expansion program with the support of Archduke Franz Ferdinand that had shown some promise by 1914, and offered the opportunity for Austria-Hungary to become a major

▼ *Shallow-drafted Austro-Hungarian monitors were deployed to protect the empire's control of the Danube River, a vital economic highway that runs through the Balkans to the Black Sea.*

naval power not only in the Adriatic but also in the Mediterranean, where its main rivals at the outbreak of war were Britain and France. The main base for the fleet was at Pola in the northern Adriatic, with subsidiary bases along the eastern coast, chiefly at Cattaro.

The Adriatic, a narrow sea bordered by Italy in the west, made it difficult for Austro-Hungarian warships to enter the Mediterranean proper. It was necessary for them to pass through the Straits of Otranto, which were heavily defended in the wake of Italy's declaration of war. Consequently the Austro-Hungarian Navy's surface ships operated mostly in the Adriatic. However, its submarines, operating from Cattaro, did break out and enjoyed some successes. For example, the French dreadnought battleship *Jean Bart* was damaged in the Straits of Otranto on December 21, 1914, and the French cruiser *Leon Gambetta* was sunk on April 26, 1915.

Turkey's navy was undergoing expansion during the years prior to World War I. Warships were ordered from British, French, Italian, and German shipyards to offset the shipbuilding programs of Greece and Russia. Two key vessels, the dreadnoughts *Sultan Osman I* and *Reshadieh*, had been completed in Britain by August 1914, but both were taken over by the British, an act that caused an outcry in Turkey. Germany countered by sending two modern warships, the *Breslau* and *Goeben*, to Turkey in the middle of the month, a calculated diplomatic act that encouraged the country to side with the Central Powers in late October.

The Turkish Navy was effectively confined to the Black Sea, where Russia was the main opponent, particularly after the Allies blockaded the Dardanelles at the beginning of 1915. Generally short of modern warships and trained crews, Turkey's small fleet played a limited role in the conflict, with many of its vessels being lost to British submarines and Russian surface warships.

The Allied Forces

The Russian Army was by far the largest in the world in 1914, with a peacetime strength of some 1.4 million men, expandable to 5.3 million on full war mobilization. With a potential pool of some 25 million men of military age to draw on, Russia's rivals, Germany in particular, saw the country as a military monster. However, such a view was ill-judged, as Russia's armed forces had many weaknesses.

In August 1914 the armed forces of six countries—Belgium, Britain, France, Montenegro, Russia, and Serbia—were mobilized to oppose the Central Powers.

In 1905 the Russian conscript's length of full-time service had been reduced to three years for infantry and artillery (four years for other arms), followed by 14 or 15 years in the reserve, and a final five years in the second reserve. There were so many exemptions that only small proportions of successive age groups were called up for service. Even by the end of the war, when more than 15 million had been called up, it represented only 9 percent of the population (the corresponding figure for Germany was 20 percent).

Socially, the average soldier was a peasant, and treated poorly. He was not allowed to enter restaurants apart from second-class railroad buffets. If he went to the theater, he was not allowed to sit in the stalls. If he defended his wife against a predatory officer, he could be guilty of a crime. He lived mainly on black bread, soup, and tea. Pay was poor and not always forthcoming. Many necessities, such as heating and shelter, were of an unacceptable standard.

▼ Russian soldiers massing to form an advance guard in a Polish town, fall 1914. Life for the ordinary soldier was very tough.

Russian military leadership

Unlike the German Army, the Russian Army did not draw all its officers from the ranks of the well-born. In fact, a surprising proportion of officers were originally peasants or sons of peasants. Without these men it would have been impossible to officer such a huge force, for the Russian middle class was small and an officer's career was not as prized as it was in Germany. Among the top ranks, however, there was an overwhelming proportion of upper class and aristocratic officers. There were serious conflicts among officers of different backgrounds. There were the traditionalists who not only disliked the military reforms that had been made necessary by the Russo-Japanese War (1904–1905), in which Russia's forces had been humiliated, but who actively or passively opposed them.

A Russian general staff had been set up after 1905 to provide a body of experts that could determine broad military policy and strategy, but its work was so obstructed that it soon lost influence. Instead, the war ministry, always headed by a general and officially in charge of merely routine matters, acquired more influence. From 1909, the war minister was General Vladimir Sukhomlinov, and he attempted to transform the armed forces. His proposals incited the hatred of traditionalists.

Upper and middle officers split into pro-minister and anti-minister groups and cliques—very often a commander might not be on speaking terms with his chief of staff. One reason why the Russian offensive into German-held East Prussia failed so miserably in 1914 was that the various Russian generals disliked each other so heartily that they failed to inform each other of what they were doing. Opposition to the war minister centered around Grand Duke Nicholas, the czar's uncle, who was inspector-general of cavalry. The grand duke was dedicated to expanding the country's cavalry forces and building

---

KEY FIGURES

GRAND DUKE NICHOLAS

Russia's Grand Duke Nicholas (1859–1929) was Czar Nicholas II's uncle. He was a traditionalist, who strongly opposed many measures that would have modernized the Russian Army.

It was around the grand duke that the opposition to the progressive war minister, General Vladimir Sukhomlinov, gathered. War ministers were expected to take command of the Russian Army in wartime, but Sukhomlinov refused this privilege. In August 1914 Nicholas was given the position instead, but appears to have been a figurehead.

After the Russian defeats of 1915, the grand duke's military position was taken over by the czar himself. Nicholas was placed in command of the Caucasus front, where his troops were successful against the Turks. However, much of the credit should have gone to his field commander, General Nikolai Yudenich. In 1917 the grand duke supported calls for the abdication of the czar. After the Russian Revolution he emigrated to France where, at his funeral, the former Allies accorded him full military honors.

▲ *Czar Nicholas II in the Crimea, May 1916. His weak leadership contributed to the ineffective performance of Russia's armed forces between 1914 and 1917.*

costly fortresses—plans totally at odds with those of Sukhomlinov, who was eventually made a scapegoat for the army's early defeats and dismissed in July 1915. One of his assistants was even shot as an alleged German spy.

Czar Nicholas II did not help matters. He appointed incompetent officers to responsible posts and was especially weak in his distribution of key positions to the grand dukes. It was largely because he placed the general staff directly under him, so the war ministry did not know what was being discussed, that the general staff became ineffective. He also loved the superficial rules and rituals of military life, but, in fact, he had no military experience.

On the eve of World War I some substantial improvements were being introduced, entirely thanks to the efforts of

Sukhomlinov. The war minister had set up a special commission to examine the competence of generals and dismiss those found wanting. Equally, the Great Program, first discussed in 1913 and introduced in July 1914, planned a huge increase in military spending, and an even bigger force of two million men in peacetime, with 8,358 field guns. Railroad improvements were to reduce the mobilization and deployment time of the Russian Army to just three weeks. To the German military, these seemed very ominous developments, but the reforms were far from wholly successful.

When the war started, key shortages soon developed. There were cases of recruits sent to the front without boots, and others who were unarmed until they were given the rifle of a killed or wounded soldier. Plans for increasing war production were either nonexistent or faulty, and unofficial committees of industrialists and others set themselves up spontaneously to do the work where government departments were obviously failing. This created tension as the traditional elite saw itself threatened by these more efficient spontaneous initiatives. So, in the war economy as in the Russian Army, internal divisions and quarrels diluted the effort.

The French Army

Having a population only two-thirds that of Germany, France faced problems in creating an army strong enough to cope with Germany's in the years before World War I. By calling up every available male who was physically and mentally fit for three years of full-time service, plus 11 years in the first reserve, seven years in the second reserve, and ultimately seven years in the final reserve, France could produce an army of nearly four million trained men on mobilization—just a million less than Germany and alarming to the latter's military leaders.

The French general staff, the body tasked with directing France's military strategy, was a thoughtful collection of officers, some of whose members produced notable works of military theory before the war. However, much of this work, which became accepted military policy in France, grew out of the country's poor performance during the Franco-Prussian War (1870–1871), in which Prussia had inflicted a swift series of defeats on the French. Failure in that war was ascribed to several factors, not least the reliance on defensive tactics against a fast-moving enemy. After the war, the French adopted a new code of war, one based on all-out attack, or *offense à l'outrance* (attack to the utmost). This was how they fought in the opening period of World War I.

▼ French horse-drawn artillery in the marketplace at the town of Stenay. Field guns such as these would be dug in behind the lines to provide a barrage of concentrated fire on enemy trenches which were about to be attacked.

Mobilization

The rapid expansion of the Allies' peacetime forces to their full war strength, a process known as mobilization, was to be a critical factor in August 1914.

The continental European powers relied on rail mobilizations, for which very detailed advance plans were made. The process was divided into mobilization proper, during which reservists reported to their regimental depots using ordinary trains or sometimes special trains added to regular schedules, and the actual deployment. During deployment, special military trains carried units to the sectors of the front that had been allocated to them.

The speed of mobilization was crucial for Germany, and its mobilization plan was the most detailed of all the combatant nations, right down to the last carrier-pigeon. The plans of France and Russia, however, were almost as dense. In France, each year officers from the general staff's 4th Section (which dealt with transport matters) visited the Eastern Railroad, the one that was to carry French troops to the front in any war against Germany, in order to acquaint themselves with its facilities and layout.

The railroad also had a special relationship with the government, which subsidized double-tracking and improved signaling so as to increase the line capacity and hence the overall speed of mobilization. The French government also guaranteed Russian railroad loans, which were largely used for improving strategic lines. Railway districts and their officials were generally acquainted with their wartime duties but their precise part in the plan remained secret until actual mobilization was declared by the authorities.

The French plan covered the first 16 days after mobilization was declared. For the first 11 days the most urgent combatants and their supplies were shipped. These included the *transports de couverture*, which carried troops to cover the deployment areas. After those initial 11 days there was a 12-hour break, to allow any lateness to be recouped,

▼ *Colorfully uniformed French troops assemble in the streets of Paris, where they wait to depart for the Belgian front on August 3, 1914.*

▲ Troops of the British Expeditionary Force (BEF) board French trains for the front in 1914. Boulogne, Le Havre, and Rouen were the three designated staging points for the transportation of British troops.

movement because the time of arrival of the British troops was subject to political factors as well as the weather. However, it had been decided that the British, if and when they came, would move through Le Havre, Rouen, and Boulogne and then by two railroads to their positions on the Franco-Belgian frontier. Because each ship brought different numbers of men, standard-length trains could not be used. Despite the uncertainties, the French railroads coped well, running 361 trains to deliver 115,000 British troops and 46,000 horses to the front in time to meet the Germany invasion forces in mid-August.

followed by five days of planned activity, by which time plans for the subsequent days would have been elaborated. In the event, full French mobilization took just 20 days—one million men and 400,000 horses being conveyed to the front. At Troyes, an important junction, there were days when trains passed every four minutes. Some 42 corps were deployed in these days, a typical corps requiring 80 trains.

In Britain, which did not have reserves to mobilize or frontiers to defend, mobilization implied the manning of the Royal Navy's reserve vessels and their taking up of war stations. Luckily, there had been a naval review on the eve of the war, so it was merely necessary to keep the reservists aboard their ships. The military mobilization involved the dispatch of the British Expeditionary Force (BEF) to France, and the railway companies had no difficulty in running the extra trains to the ports.

Deployment of the BEF, in fact, was more a problem for the French than for the British. The French could not pre-plan this

▼ A poster of the French notification of the first day of mobilization on August 2, 1914. Reservists rushed to join their units.

ORDRE DE MOBILISATION GÉNÉRALE

Par décret du Président de la République, la mobilisation des armées de terre et de mer est ordonnée, ainsi que la réquisition des animaux, voitures et harnais nécessaires au complément de ces armées.

Le premier jour de la mobilisation est le *dimanche deux août*

Tout Français soumis aux obligations militaires doit, sous peine d'être puni avec toute la rigueur des lois, obéir aux prescriptions du **FASCICULE DE MOBILISATION** (pages coloriées placées dans son livret).

Sont visés par le présent ordre **TOUS LES HOMMES** non présents sous les Drapeaux et appartenant :

1° à l'**ARMÉE DE TERRE** y compris les **TROUPES COLONIALES** et les hommes des **SERVICES AUXILIAIRES**;

2° à l'**ARMÉE DE MER** y compris les **INSCRITS MARITIMES** et les **ARMURIERS** de la **MARINE**.

All-out attack

The strategy relied on massed infantry and cavalry attacks, rapid movement, and a smaller artillery piece that could keep up with mobile infantry and cavalry units. Constant attacks, it was believed, would shatter an enemy's morale and its will to resist. Elements of warfare that clearly became important during World War I, not least the machine gun and heavy artillery, and their impact on the battlefield were neglected. Although these were charges that could be equally applied to most of the combatants in 1914, with the exception of Germany, they had the greatest initial impact on France when its forces recorded huge casualties.

In 1914 French losses, proportionately based on the number of men committed to the war each year, were three times higher than they were for each subsequent year until 1918. Partly this also reflected French decisions regarding uniforms. Alone among the nations going to war in 1914, its troops wore brightly colored uniforms—colors that were supposed to create the necessary unit cohesion, and possibly even intimidate the enemy.

General Joseph Joffre, the chief of the general staff, was to command the French Army in wartime. A veteran of several colonial wars, his appointment was largely due to his acceptability to French politicians of all hues. Joffre was wedded to the concept of all-out attack, and France's war strategy, Plan 17, which envisaged mass offensives into Germany, was his brainchild.

Another general, Joseph Galliéni, an officer of equal stature, had refused the appointment and retired in 1914, although he quickly returned to active service once the war had broken out, becoming a key figure in saving the French capital, Paris, from capture by the Germans during August and September. Another talented officer, General Henri-Philippe Pétain, was confined to the command of a division,

probably as he was one of the few senior officers who expressed skepticism about the strategy of attack and instead stressed the importance of firepower. His views were out of step with the then prevailing ethos of the French Army.

Like the other belligerents, France was to experience an acute shell shortage within a few weeks of war being declared, but it was quickly able to organize increased production. With the Allies in command of the sea,

France was also able to tap the resources of the United States, which soon found itself playing the role of the "arsenal of democracy." Most of the locomotives for the all-important supply railroads would come from the United States. However, in some technologies, France had a lead. Notable among these were the aviation and the motor vehicle industries, both of which would gain considerable importance during the course of the war.

Neutral Belgium's forces

In contrast, the Belgian Army was small, and destined to spend most of the war fighting outside its own country. An international treaty signed in the 1830s ensured that Belgium had to remain neutral and its forces, totaling around 150,000 troops on full mobilization, were for home defense. Command during World War I rested with the country's ruler, King Albert I. In Belgium's strategy, heavy reliance had been placed

▼ *General Joseph Joffre (below, far left) in consultation with French and Italian officers. Joffre and the other leaders of the French Army were considered to be a highly capable and gifted group of military men.*

▼ **Belgian troops formed up behind a barricade on a road outside Louvain on August 20, 1914, during the Allied retreat to Antwerp. The Belgian Army was small and lacked many items of the most modern equipment.**

on very strong fortresses surrounding Antwerp, Liège, and Namur. These had been constructed during the 1880s, according to the most advanced military design of the time, but had not been modernized to withstand the heavy artillery that had been developed over the following decades. They would succumb in a matter of days to Germany's heavy guns–Liège and Namur in August and Antwerp in October. Military service in Belgium was not popular and the morale of officers and men was never high. Because of the neutrality requirement, a third of the Belgian Army was initially positioned to block a possible British attack, a third to fight France, and just a third was earmarked to meet any German threat.

The British Army
Unlike the continental powers, Britain did not have a conscript army. It relied on volunteers, and limited its army to a size just sufficient to defend the country's empire. Britain was somewhat isolated from European affairs, and relied on its navy, the world's largest, to protect it from invasion and secure its links

with the rest of its vast domains. In peacetime the British Army's total strength was less than 250,000 men, and that included the somewhat small reserve. A body of some 120,000 home-based troops, known as the British Expeditionary Force (BEF), was earmarked for service overseas, with the remainder stationed throughout the empire. There was also a pool of reservists in Britain, some 250,000 men. The country also possessed the 164,000-strong British-officered Indian Army. To some extent, the Indian Army could support the British Army in wartime, but its chief role prior to 1914 was to prevent unrest in India and foreign subversion along its borders.

The small size of the British Army in part reflected its recent history. It had not fought a major war in Europe for some 100 years, and its only recent overseas war was against Russia during the Crimean War (1853–1856). For the most part the British Army had been engaged in expanding the empire or squashing local revolts. Against such forces it had the edge in technology, and had generally been successful.

However, the British had learned a recent valuable lesson during the Second Anglo-Boer War (1899–1902). The Boers, settlers of Dutch origin in southern Africa, had attempted to resist British attempts to incorporate their lands into the British Empire. Although few in number, they had certain advantages. They knew the local terrain, were top-class marksmen, and used hit-and-run tactics that baffled the British. The war was eventually won by Britain, but it was a painful experience. Casualties were high, and the whole ethos of the Army was questioned, from training to the competence of its officers.

There was a conscious effort to learn from the war, although the lessons were not necessarily of value for a large-scale conflict involving the world's leading powers. However, the fact that British infantrymen by 1914 were far better marksmen than their continental contemporaries was one exceptionally useful result of the lessons learned.

However, the official body set up to examine the Second Anglo-Boer War heard witnesses who, in retrospect, seem shortsighted. General Douglas Haig, who would command the BEF in France from December 1915 onward and had been a staff officer during the Second Anglo-Boer War, testified that cavalry would be of even greater value in a future war and that artillery was of little use except against panicky or poorly trained troops.

Haig was, of course, a cavalry officer and the British Army, like others, had many such men in high places who simply could not believe that the cavalry was becoming irrelevant. The evidence that modern technology was vastly increasing firepower and not only threatening the whole concept of the cavalry sweep, but also traditional infantry tactics as well, was there to be seen, but most chose to avert their eyes. An exception to this was General Ian Hamilton, later to distinguish himself in

▲ *British soldiers led by their mounted officers march out of London at the beginning of their move to northern France, September 1914. Railroads and ships transported them to their final destination.*

125

the Gallipoli campaign (1915–1916), who pointed out the problems that firepower was posing. He argued, prophetically, that infantry should be provided with steel shields on wheels.

When approaching problems about which he had no prejudices, Haig could make sensible decisions. In the prewar decade he helped Secretary of War Robert Haldane to introduce a number of useful measures. One of these was the setting up of the Territorial Army, providing spare-time training for volunteers and thereby creating a small reserve force of 270,000 men, which, in the event, proved far more effective than its critics had predicted. At the same time the regular units stationed in Britain were organized into the BEF, suited for fast transfer overseas, either to meet a colonial crisis or to help a continental ally. The decision regarding where and when to deploy the BEF ultimately rested with the government of Prime Minister Herbert Asquith and his secretary of war, who from August 3, 1914, was Field Marshal Kitchener.

Anglo-French staff talks were taking place and the two general staffs had made plans for the BEF to take over the northern part of the French frontier (facing Belgium) in time of war. This arrangement was not cemented as a formal treaty but it was instrumental in ensuring that when World War I did break out the bulk of the British Army would be sent to France directly and without delay. It went equipped for a war of mobility and lacked the heavy artillery pieces, mortars, grenades, and machine guns that would become so essential in the static trench warfare that was to come.

The Balkan allies

Two other European countries provided forces to fight against the Central Powers in 1914—the Balkan states of Serbia and Montenegro. The Serbian Army was undergoing reorganization when war broke out, but it had a full strength of some 360,000 men. Frontline troops were reasonably well provided for with modern weapons, but

▼ *Field Marshal Douglas Haig congratulating Canadian troops near Domart in the wake of the Battle of Amiens in August 1918.*

reservists had to make do with older equipment. Despite the country's poor roads and railways, mobilization in August 1914 went smoothly, mainly thanks to the organizational skills of the country's chief of staff, the impressive Field Marshal Radomir Putnik.

Although outnumbered, the Serbian Army proved able to defeat a series of Austro-Hungarian invasions. However, it was finally forced to abandon its homeland after a joint invasion in October 1914 by Austro-Hungarian, Bulgarian, and German troops. What followed, in November and December, became known as the Great Retreat. Putnik led his forces across mountainous terrain to Albania, from where the remnants—around 150,000 troops and refugees—were evacuated to Corfu. An estimated 200,000 people had perished on the long march and Serbian troops would not return home until fall 1918.

In 1914 Montenegro was a tiny state of some 500,000 people, a country ruled by the autocratic King Nicholas I. It had very close ties with neighboring Serbia and chose to follow Serbia's lead

---

KEY FIGURES

FIELD MARSHAL HERBERT KITCHENER

Horatio Herbert Kitchener (1850–1916) was one of the most famous British generals in the period before 1914, and he played a significant, if controversial role, in directing Britain's military operations during much of World War I.

He began his career in 1871 as a military engineer, and became a major general in 1896 while leading a successful campaign in the Sudan. He took over Britain's faltering campaign against the Boers in South Africa during the Second Anglo-Boer War (1899–1902) and brought it to a successful conclusion. He was military governor of Egypt between 1911 and 1914, but happened to be in Britain when World War I began.

Very much a British popular hero, he was appointed as secretary of war on August 3, 1914. Kitchener undoubtedly lacked detailed knowledge of many modern military matters, and he was often ill at ease with politicians and other military figures. He was regarded by many as difficult to work with. However, he had the rare perception that this was not going to be a short war, and that the British Army would need to be vastly strengthened to endure it. He succeeded in raising and equipping three million volunteers, helped by a celebrated poster that featured himself.

Kitchener generally supported the view that the war would be won or lost on the western front, yet he agreed to the launching of the disastrous attack on the Turkish-held Gallipoli Peninsula in 1915. Its failure damaged his already tarnished reputation. He offered to resign in 1916, but was refused. However, the growing problem of Kitchener, as many saw it, was resolved on June 5. On his way to visit Czar Nicholas II of Russia, to discuss the progress of the war, the vessel transporting him, the *Hampshire*, struck a mine and sank. Kitchener was not among the survivors.

The mesmerizing recruiting poster by Alfred Leeze depicting Kitchener as Britain's war minister.

by declaring war in August 1914. The Montenegrin armed forces, some 40,000 troops, fought alongside the Serbians, but did not take part in the Great Retreat of late 1915, preferring instead to fight on until it was forced to surrender in January 1916, when Montenegro itself was overrun by Austro-Hungarian forces. Sporadic guerrilla warfare then followed, which was characterized by frequent atrocities against civilians. Serbian forces finally liberated the country in 1918 and on November 26, Montenegro agreed to a union with Serbia.

Allied naval forces

In 1914, in the all-important dreadnought battleship class, Britain's Royal Navy had a 22 to 15 superiority over Germany, its nearest rival, and this superiority extended to the lesser categories of ships. This naval power was supplemented by the world's biggest merchant fleet, and many ocean liners would be fitted with guns to enable them to perform military roles in the event of war. The threat posed to the battleships' preeminence by submarines was acknowledged, but was seen as a future factor rather than an existing one. The fact

▼ *Soldiers from the army of the Balkan state of Montenegro. Although small, it showed tremendous fighting spirit.*

that the Royal Navy was prepared for war was due to the reforms carried out by Admiral John Fisher.

A belief that they were the best gave British sailors and their officers a self-confidence that at times fully compensated for other defects, which certainly became evident under the stresses of war. Officers were not promoted for initiative but for following procedures; this was not necessarily a mistake, because the command of ships when visibility might be poor and communications by either flag or lamp signals relied on such procedures being followed.

KEY FIGURES

ADMIRAL JOHN FISHER

John Arbuthnot Fisher (1841–1920) was the outstanding figure in Britain's Royal Navy in the decade before World War I. An acute analyst of trends in naval warfare, he was responsible for transforming the country's naval forces.

Fisher became First Sea Lord, the head of the Royal Navy, in 1903 and initiated a wide-ranging review of the navy. Outdated training techniques were modernized and poor officers ruthlessly removed from their positions. With regard to equipment, he promoted maritime aviation, which was then in its infancy, and backed an expansion of the submarine fleet. His greatest achievement was the development of the dreadnought, the world's first true battleship, which made the older battleships of all the world's navies obsolete. This event, some have argued, sparked a renewed naval armaments race.

Fisher retired in 1910 but remained an influential, if not always popular, figure in British naval circles. In October 1914 he was brought out of retirement and again assumed the role of First Sea Lord. Initially, Fisher enjoyed a harmonious relationship with his political opposite number, Winston Churchill, the naval minister. However, Fisher strongly disagreed with Churchill's plans for naval operations against Turkey in the Dardanelles in 1915 and resigned in May that year. Despite calls for him to return to his post, Fisher declined.

As for matériel, Britain's record was patchy. For example, weapons' design was not entirely satisfactory. Apart from its lack of a reliable mine, the Royal Navy's torpedo design needed improvement, and its shells had less penetrating power than those of Germany. There had been a successful campaign to improve gunnery, but there were still faults. With the longer gun ranges, with opposing ships on converging courses, plotting the aiming point for guns to fire was extremely complicated.

While the "director" system (where guns were under the control of an elevated fire-control center) had been

▲ An Allied troop transport heads for a French battleship during operations in the Dardanelles. This area was heavily mined by the Turks in 1915 as it was the key to control of the Gallipoli peninsula to the north and the Turkish coast to the south.

evolved in the navy, and proved to be highly successful, in 1914 it was available in only a few ships. Meanwhile, a promising plotting gear for range-determination had been designed by British industry but was rejected by the Admiralty, the body responsible for the Royal Navy. This was headed by two men, the First Sea Lord (an experienced naval officer) and the First Lord of the Admiralty (a political figure). At the outbreak of war these posts were filled by Prince Louis of Battenberg and Winston Churchill. Prior to the war other senior navy officers had devised their own plotting system and exploited their influential contacts within the navy to get it accepted. This adoption of the second-best, together with German superiority in optical range-finders, gave Germany an advantage.

The British did have one enormous advantage over the German Navy, partly due to a stroke of luck early in the war. A German warship was wrecked in the Baltic Sea and boarded by the Russians, who discovered that the crew had not removed or destroyed their naval codes. These were passed to the Admiralty's intelligence department, known as

Room 40, headed by Sir Alfred Ewing and Commander James. Room 40, aided by radio listening posts dotted across southern England and the capture of later codes, was able to furnish the Royal Navy with detailed intelligence from December 1914 onward.

The French Navy suffered decades of neglect prior to the war, chiefly because the country concentrated on building up its land forces to oppose the expansion of the German Army. In 1909 the minister of marine, Admiral Auguste Boué de Lapeyrère, began a program of modernization and expansion. Naval expenditure almost doubled between 1910 and 1914, although few of the 14 planned battleships were completed by 1914. Due to an agreement with Britain signed in 1912, the French Navy was entrusted with the defence of the Mediterranean Sea, while the British concentrated on the North Sea and English Channel. Its first task in World War I was the convoying of French colonial troops to Europe from North Africa. Subsequent French Navy operations included the Gallipoli Campaign and the evacuation of Serbia's Army from Albania in late 1915.

The Russian Navy was decimated as a force during the Russo-Japanese War, and a massive rebuilding program was initiated soon after. However, it was not due for completion until 1917. Some 105 new warships were ordered before 1914 but only one was in service by the outbreak of war. The delays were due to bureaucracy, shortages of funds, and poor shipbuilding facilities. Although the Russian Navy had responsibilities in the Pacific and Black Sea, its major theater of operations was in the Baltic, where the Baltic Fleet under Admiral Nikolai von Essen was active. Although Essen argued for an aggressive strategy, for much of the war the fleet was used to protect the Russian coastline from German operations. The Black Sea Fleet was primarily tasked with blockading Turkey, a role it performed effectively. The remaining Allies—Belgium, Montenegro, and Serbia—had either negligible or no naval forces.

Allied air forces

Both land-based and naval aviation were in their infancy in 1914, and few senior officers were convinced of its worth. Britain's William Nicholson, the chief of staff between 1908 and 1912, remarked, "Aviation is a useless and expensive fad advocated by a few individuals whose ideas are unworthy of attention."

The Allied air forces were recent creations. Russia's was founded in 1912, the same year as Britain's Royal Flying Corps, while the French Aéronatique Militaire (Military Aviation) dated back to 1910. The Allies had few aircraft at their disposal in 1914. Russia had some 300 fit for service, France around 150, and Britain just 60. (By 1918 the French had more than 3,200 aircraft in frontline service and the British some 4,000.)

The aircraft that were available were initially envisioned as having no role beyond reconnaissance for ground forces, and even here many believed that cavalry units could perform the role to a higher standard. Fighters and bombers, later to become so important, were rare in 1914. The Allies could also call on a variety of airships, but again these were often used for reconnaissance for most of the war.

Naval aviation was also limited in 1914. There had, however, been some attempts to develop warships capable of carrying aircraft. Initially, these were known as tenders. Aircraft did not take off or land on them, but, fitted with floats, were lowered into the water for take-off and then hauled back on board after landing. The first true aircraft carrier was Britain's *Argus*, but the ship did not enter service until October 1918 and saw no action.

▼ *A French biplane pictured in 1914. Military aviation was in its infancy at the outbreak of war in August 1914. Early air operations were carried out by single aircraft, flying over enemy lines to observe and report troop movements. They were vulnerable to ground fire and pilots would arm themselves with pistols, rifles, and the occasional machine gun tied to the fuselage.*

Dein ist mein Herz!

Dein ist mein Herz!
   In seligem Verzücken
Möcht ich Dich fest
   in meine Arme schließen.
Ich fühl' das Glück
   in Deiner Nähe sprießen
Und lese es in
   Deinem Strahlenblick.

The Western Front, 1914–1915

In 1914 many people believed that the war would be short. However, by the end of the year it was stalemated, and all sides were digging deep lines of trenches.

◀ *A romantic German postcard showing a young soldier taking leave of his girlfriend on the eve of the war.*

▼ *British troops come under accurate German artillery fire in northern France, August 1914.*

Germany's generals had long feared fighting a war on two fronts—against Russia and France. Led by the chief of the general staff, Alfred von Schlieffen, they developed a strategy to defeat France quickly and then deal with Russia. Germany's concern about fighting any future war on two fronts dated back to the latter part of the nineteenth century.

In the 1890s the French and Russians had signed an alliance that worried Germany's Schlieffen. He was sensitive to the dangers of Germany having to fight both France and Russia and saw France as the chief threat in any conflict involving the three. He therefore developed a plan to knock France out of any war in a matter of weeks, before Russia could mobilize its huge forces.

The Schlieffen Plan recognized that France's border defenses with Germany were far too strong to be taken quickly and that rapid movement through Switzerland's mountainous terrain was impossible. Schlieffen decided to violate the neutrality of Belgium, the Netherlands, and Luxembourg by sending a huge force, some 90 percent of the German Army, through these countries and south to capture Paris. Only 5 percent of his forces would defend the German provinces of Alsace and Lorraine, which Schlieffen expected—and wanted—the French to attack. The provinces' fortresses, backed by a strong defense, would tie up a large part of the French Army. France was to be defeated in a matter of 42 days.

The remaining 5 percent of the German Army was to be deployed in East Prussia to hold the Russians until other German forces, fresh from their rapid victory over France, could be rushed east to crush Russia. Essential to the strategy were rapid mobilization and the speedy movement of troops by rail to their various theaters of war.

The Schlieffen Plan amended

Schlieffen retired in 1906, and his successor, General Helmuth von Moltke, modified the original plan. He believed

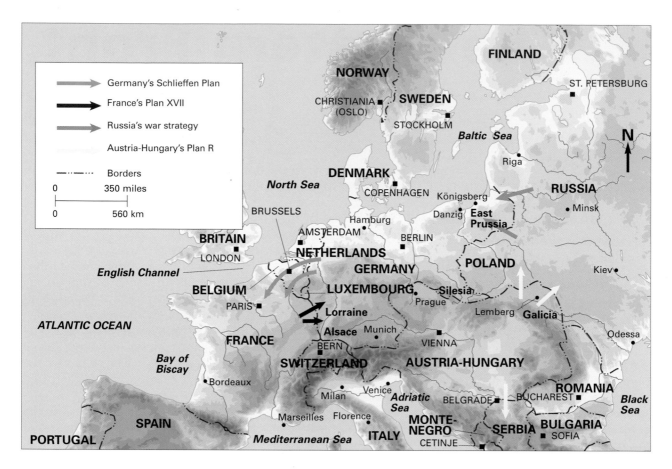

that the Russians would mobilize more quickly than originally thought and therefore earmarked 15 percent of his forces to defend East Prussia. Moltke also did not want to lose any part of Alsace or Lorraine, however temporarily, and he was determined to protect the adjacent industrial center of the Rhineland. He increased the forces in this key region to 25 percent of the total. Because of this change only 60 percent of the German Army was therefore available for the decisive sweep into northern France through Belgium.

Finally, Moltke decided not to move through the Netherlands, believing (mistakenly, as events proved) that Britain might not go to war to protect Belgium if Dutch neutrality was honored. Consequently, the planned attack had to take place on a narrower front than that envisaged by Schlieffen. It also forced the Germans to neutralize the

◀ *The various rival strategic plans of the major nations involved at the outset of World War I. For a review of the Austro-Hungarian, Russian, and Serbian strategies, see page 152.*

◀ *Count Alfred von Schlieffen was the architect of Germany's scheme to avoid fighting both France and Russia at the same time.*

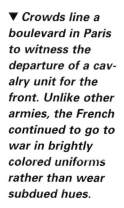

▼ *Crowds line a boulevard in Paris to witness the departure of a cavalry unit for the front. Unlike other armies, the French continued to go to war in brightly colored uniforms rather than wear subdued hues.*

massive defenses of Liège, Belgium, which stood directly in the path of the advancing German forces.

France's Plan XVII

France's war planning before World War I was dominated by the desire to erase the humiliations that had been inflicted on the country following its defeat in the Franco-Prussian War (1870–1871), chiefly the loss of the provinces of Alsace and Lorraine on its eastern border. France expected to go to war with Germany again at some time in the near future, and its generals became obsessed with devising a strategy to win back the two provinces. Between 1911 and 1914 General Joseph Joffre, France's commander in chief, created Plan XVII. It called for the various French armies to assemble along the Franco-German border, from Switzerland in the south to Belgium in

▲ *German troops cheer their departure for the western front by railroad on the "Paris Express." Similar enthusiasm was found in most of the European countries going to war in 1914.*

the north, on the eve of war. On the outbreak of any fighting, these armies were to launch an all-out attack in great strength into Alsace and Lorraine.

Joffre saw that the Germans might violate Belgium's neutrality in any attack on France but believed that they would be unable to advance past the Meuse River in northeast France without becoming too overextended. The French also had an arrangement with the British government, which had pledged to use its small army to plug gaps on the Franco-Belgian border.

However, Plan XVII had two weaknesses. First, Joffre underestimated the quality of the German Army and the speed with which it could mobilize and move. In the advent of war, this speed would allow the Germans to have a greater frontline strength than the French and permit an advance that would not leave the various German armies overextended.

The second weakness was that the French believed in the idea of constant attack. They thought that a resolute attack could fight its way through any defenses. All that was needed was the willpower of the ordinary French soldier to carry out what was termed *offense à l'outrance* (offense at the utmost).

French training concentrated on attack and neglected defense. For their part, the Germans trained to both attack and defend, and their infantry units were equipped with a greater proportion of machine guns. As the French discovered in 1914, resolute attacks in the face of heavy defensive fire simply led to enormous casualties.

Opening moves against France

Once World War I became a political certainty, the German Army began to mobilize for war on August 1. As a prelude to attacking France through Belgium, Luxembourg was occupied by the 3rd. Next day, in accordance with the Schlieffen Plan and following an official declaration of war, four German armies (some 960,000 men) invaded Belgium, which was defended by fewer than 150,000 Belgian troops. Three other German armies, some 565,000 men, were in various positions to protect the German provinces of Alsace and Lorraine on the Franco-German border or support the main advance to the north. The fighting that took place over the next month later became known as the Battles of the Frontiers.

Of the four German armies arrayed against Belgium, the key to victory lay with the two in the north. These armies were to sweep through central Belgium in a wide loop, enter France, and then swing south in the direction of Paris. The First Army, some 320,000 troops under General Alexander von Kluck, was based around Aachen. It had the farthest to advance—more than 200 miles (320 km), a route that would see it move through Brussels, the Belgian capital, before entering France near the frontier fortress of Maubeuge. From there it was to cross the Somme River and advance directly on Paris.

Kluck was expected to maintain a blistering march rate of up to 25 miles (40 km) a day—this in the heat of summer with most troops having to move on foot and many having to fight for much of the way. Kluck's advance into Belgium began on the 16th. The initial attacks went well, and Brussels was occupied four days later. Most of the Belgian Army withdrew, basing itself for the moment at the heavily fortified port of Antwerp to the north.

While pushing steadily through southern Belgium over the following days, Kluck's forces fought a sharp engagement against the newly arrived British Expeditionary Force (BEF), some 120,000 men under Field Marshal John French, at Mons on the 23rd. Although the German emperor, Kaiser Wilhelm II, dismissed the BEF as "that contemptible little army," it was highly experienced. Its ranks were filled with long-serving volunteers, instead of the conscripts who served with all of the other forces, and many had seen action within the British Empire.

At Mons, French's men used rapid and accurate rifle fire to inflict a bloody nose on the First Army, despite being outnumbered. Mocking the German emperor, French's veterans began calling themselves the Old Contemptibles. Similar actions followed over the next days, chiefly at Le Cateau, France, from the 25th to the 27th. The British were being pushed back slowly but surely, but their actions were disrupting the Schlieffen Plan, albeit at a high price in killed and wounded.

To the south of the German First Army in Belgium lay General Karl von Bülow's Second Army, some 260,000 men. It was to follow a course roughly paralleling the First Army's, but it was blocked by the large forts circling

▼ *British troops and their equipment are unloaded at a port in northern France before moving to the Belgian frontier, where the force would plug the gap between the French armies and the English Channel.*

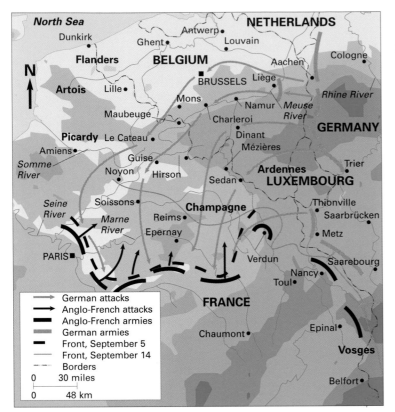

▲ The German attack in the summer of 1914 and the course of the fighting on the western front until the end of the French-led counterattack along the Marne River in early September.

▼ British forces race to the Marne River to prepare for the battle with the German invaders in 1914.

they both pressed south. Kluck believed that the BEF was no longer an effective fighting force and that there were no other enemy forces positioned to threaten his vulnerable right flank. On both accounts he was wrong. The BEF was battered but still capable of action, and a new French force, the Sixth Army under General Charles Manoury, was assembling to the east of Paris and was ideally placed to attack his flank. Equally, a move to help the Second Army would take Kluck away from Paris, the key objective of the Schlieffen Plan.

To make matters worse, Kluck could not easily or quickly get in contact with the chief of the general staff, General Helmuth von Moltke, the officer who should have made any decision relating to further modifications of the Schlieffen Plan. Moltke was at his headquarters in Luxembourg, some 150 miles (240 km) from the ever-changing military situation. By September 2 Kluck had switched his advance to the east of Paris on his own initiative, and the left flank of his First Army had reached the banks of the Marne River.

Liège. The city was surrounded on August 5, and its forts were pounded into submission by massive German howitzers on the 11th. Meanwhile, Bülow continued his march, crossing into France southwest of Charleroi and running into the hastily positioned French Fifth Army under General Louis Franchet d'Esperey at Guise on August 29. French attacks temporarily halted Bülow, who, shaken by events, called on Kluck to the north to come to his aid the following day. The various actions that followed proved decisive.

Kluck decided to answer the call for help, chiefly to plug the increasingly wide gap that was opening between his troops and Bülow's Second Army as

French attacks thwarted

As events had been unfolding in Belgium and northeast France, there had been equally critical and wide-ranging actions elsewhere, chiefly along France's border with Germany. In accordance with their war strategy, Plan XVII, the French forces entered Alsace and Lorraine, as well as the wooded

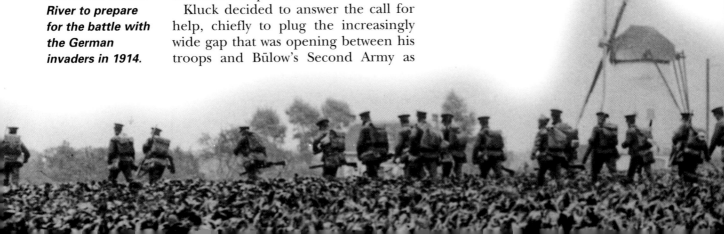

Ardennes region of southern Belgium and along the Meuse River. The Germans expected these movements and, through most of August, fought successfully to halt them. French casualties in these sprawling battles were enormous, with some 300,000 men killed, wounded, missing, or taken prisoner. Both the morale of the various French forces and the nerve of their senior commanders held, however.

The Germans overestimated the scale of their victories in these areas. The chief of the general staff, Helmuth von Moltke, believed the French Army was almost finished as a fighting force and that there was a chance to surround a considerable part of it. To this end he moved forces from the north (the key area of operations in the Schlieffen Plan) to support further attacks from Lorraine into France. He also further reduced the strength of the First Army and Second Army by moving units to the east, where Russia's mobilization

had been speedier than expected. Thus, as the most critical moment of the 1914 campaign on the western front arrived, Moltke, who had virtually abandoned the key features of the Schlieffen Plan, was somewhat deluded as to the state of the various enemy armies opposing him, and unsure of the position of his own forces in key sectors.

As Moltke was struggling to see clearly through the fog of war, his French counterpart, General Joseph Joffre, was more accurately informed, in part thanks to excellent air reconnaissance (a first in modern warfare). Acting quickly, Joffre reorganized his forces, transferring some units from the far right of his defensive line to the left and continuing to build up the Sixth Army, which was monitoring the exposed German right flank east of Paris. Joffre was planning a major counteroffensive and ordered his various armies to stand fast along the line of the Marne River and prepare to attack.

▲ *A German field artillery unit moves southward heading for the Marne River. Although there were some motorized vehicles in 1914, all armies relied on horses to move their heavy equipment.*

KEY FIGURES

MARSHAL JOSEPH JOFFRE

A veteran of the Franco-Prussian War (1870–1871) and also of numerous colonial campaigns, Joffre (1852–1931) was appointed the French Army's chief of the general staff in 1911 and also formulated Plan XVII, his country's strategy for any future war with Germany.

With the outbreak of the fighting in 1914, Plan XVII failed miserably, and France came close to defeat as the Germans were within a stroke of capturing Paris, the capital. That they failed was in large part due to Joffre, who was able to keep the retreating French field armies from collapsing during the opening weeks of the fighting and then launch a successful counterattack during the First Battle of the Marne.

At the end of 1914 the war of maneuver on the western front ended, and both sides settled down to build trench systems. In 1915 Joffre went over to the offensive to recapture French territory, but his forces suffered huge casualties for little gain, and his reputation suffered.

His fortunes declined further in 1916, when he was surprised by the German attack on the fortress city of Verdun, from where he had recently moved much of the defending artillery. The long list of French casualties during the battle sealed Joffre's fate. He was removed from office on December 13 but was promoted to the rank of marshal a few days later. In 1917 he was made head of a military mission to the United States.

Joffre's attack began on September 5. The First Battle of the Marne, a series of engagements, continued until the 10th. However, the key events occurred east of Paris. The French Sixth Army struck at Kluck's exposed right flank, one created by his rush to the aid of Bülow. Kluck faced a dilemma. If he moved to counter the French east of Paris, he would have to turn his army through 90 degrees. Kluck would widen the gap between himself and Bülow's Second Army, inviting the French and British to move through the gap and strike both of them in the flank.

On September 8, one of Moltke's staff officers, Colonel Richard Hentsch, was visiting Bülow's headquarters. Hentsch's actual role and authority remain

unclear, but he concurred with Bülow that his Second Army should withdraw. This move, though, would leave Kluck's army open to attacks from front, flank, and rear. Kluck had no option but to follow suit. Moltke, belatedly appraised of the situation, agreed with the move. The decision was a turning point. The Schlieffen Plan was in tatters. Blame for its failure was placed on Moltke's shoulders, and he was replaced by General Erich von Falkenhayn, Germany's minister of war, on September 14.

The First Battle of the Marne did not end 1914's war of maneuver. The French and British set off in pursuit of the withdrawing Germans, who were attempting to hold a line between Noyon and Verdun in Champagne. The

▲ *Germans are escorted into captivity during the First Battle of the Marne.*

▶ *The Race to the Sea was a series of battles that ended the fighting in 1914 and heralded the beginning of trench warfare.*

▼ *German troops move northward during the Race to the Sea.*

most likely place for the French and British to win a victory was along the exposed German right flank. For their part the Germans attempted to swing around the French and British left.

The final battles of 1914

What followed, from September until late November, was a series of mutual flank attacks that developed through the northern French regions of Picardy and Artois and in Flanders, where the remnants of the Belgian Army were assembling along the coast. This group of inconclusive battles across northern France and Belgium became known as the Race to the Sea, as every attempt to

Atrocities and Propaganda

All sides used their media to portray their enemies as inhuman. While most stories of atrocities were untrue, some incidents against civilians did occur, chiefly as German forces advanced through Belgium.

The German invasion and occupation of Belgium and northern France in 1914 led to the imposition of a policy known as *Schrecklichkeit* (frightfulness) on the local populations. Through it the Germans attempted to prevent any resistance movements from developing by acting forcefully to nip any local unrest in the bud.

The origins of the policy dated back to German experiences in the Franco-Prussian War (1870–1871). Although the German Army was successful in battle against the French regular forces, irregular units of *franc-tireurs* (armed civilians) made hit-and-run guerrilla raids in German-occupied areas of France, particularly against supply lines and isolated military posts. It became German policy that any attack by *franc-tireurs* would be answered in full meaure. First, the area or building from where the shot or shots were fired would be burned to the ground. Second, civilians in the vicinity of the attack would be executed in reprisal.

▼ *A Belgian church damaged by German artillery. Often reported as acts of vandalism, such incidents were usually inadvertent.*

▲ *A French poster depicting an alleged German atrocity in Belgium. Stories of such mutilations against women and children were common, yet there was never any hard evidence to support them.*

▲ *A French propaganda poster showing Germany as a warmongering specter.*

It is undeniable that incidents of *Schrecklichkeit* occurred in 1914 (and later), particularly in Belgium, where 5,000 civilians died during the German invasion. Some events were no more than the execution of a single Belgian civilian proved to be firing on German troops, but others were on a much greater scale and were often unjustified. Two examples stand out. In the town of Dinant some 639 civilians, one-sixth of whom were women and children, were shot in cold blood between August 21 and 23. A similar event occurred at Louvain after the German military governor of Brussels ordered his troops to raze the ancient town to the ground on the 25th following reports of resistance activity. During a five-day period, around 12 percent of the city was destroyed, along with its world-renowned library, and a number of civilians were executed.

The propaganda agencies of those fighting Germany were quick to capitalize on such atrocities. In fact, they had initiated a virtual hate campaign against Germany in the first days of the war. Pamphlets and newspapers were full of stories of German soldiers murdering priests and nuns, killing babies, violating women, and destroying works of art. Posters and public meetings reinforced the message.

These reports were designed to convince the wider public of the "beastliness" of the German

▲ *Belgian civilians are stopped and searched by the German troops.*

enemy and justify the "righteousness" of the war. However, the majority were usually either unsubstantiated or false. One British newspaper, *The Times*, misleadingly declared: "Louvain has ceased to exist. A town of 40,000 inhabitants has been completely wiped out."

One other example of such an event in 1914 was the German shelling of the magnificent cathedral in the French city of Reims. Anti-German accounts raged against such desecration; virtually every commentator neglected to mention the fact that French troops had probably been using the building's tall spires as artillery observation posts, making the cathedral a legitimate—if unfortunate—target for German artillery attack.

The hysteria whipped up by such stories did work in the short term, helping to silence any critical public debate over the outbreak of the conflict, but they became less successful as the war and its many real agonies continued.

EYEWITNESS

SERGEANT J. F. BELL

Bell, serving with the British Expeditionary Force, was seriously wounded by a German shell during the First Battle of Ypres, Belgium, just a few months after war had been declared. It marked the end of his life as a frontline soldier:

"I bade farewell to my right leg, and to my career as a soldier, outside a trench on October 29, 1914. If we could not be driven out of the trench, it seemed certain that we would be blown out of it. Shells kept landing near enough, in front of, or behind the trench to shake us almost out of it. A message was then sent to me to retire and join a platoon entrenched near us. I had only gone about six yards when I received what in the regiment was called the 'dull thud.' I thought I had been violently knocked on the head but, feeling I was not running properly, I looked down and discovered that my right foot was missing.

"I then put on a field dressing and a shirt from my pack over my stump. There would be about 60 badly wounded British soldiers of all ranks. The soldier nearest me was a sergeant who was severely wounded in both arms and both legs.

"Judge my surprise when two German infantrymen jumped into the trench. One of them got quite excited, raised his rifle and leveled it within a yard of me, but the other knocked his mate's rifle up and asked me when and where I was wounded. I asked them to do something for the wounded, but they seemed in great haste as they jumped out of the trench. It was then 12 noon. So ended one morning in Flanders."

From Everyman at War, *1930, an anthology of soldiers' war experiences.*

▲ *A scene to be played out many times during the war—prisoners are marched to the rear. In this case they are Germans taken at the First Battle of Ypres.*

◄ *A battery of German howitzers moves up to the front in Belgium shortly before the opening of the First Battle of Ypres in late October 1914.*

find the enemy's flank brought the rival armies ever closer to the barriers of the English Channel and the North Sea.

The climax of the Race to the Sea came at the end of October, around the Belgian town of Ypres. All sides had run out of ground to maneuver. Beyond Ypres lay low-lying land, much of which had been flooded by the Belgians to make it impassable. The First Battle of Ypres was initiated by General Erich von Falkenhayn in late October in a last-ditch attempt to win victory in 1914 by breaching the front to capture the ports through which the British moved troops and supplies, but it ended in a German defeat. Victory went to the BEF, albeit at a terrible cost. The force that had gone to war in August 1914 was no more—50,000 had been killed or wounded.

PEOPLE AND WAR

CHRISTMAS TRUCE

The fighting between August and December 1914 shattered many illusions, not least the one that the war would be brief, but traces of humanity remained among ordinary soldiers.

As winter bit harder, all sides settled down to hold their positions, digging and strengthening their trenches. For the front-line soldiers, it was a miserable time. They were exhausted, often cold and hungry, grieving for lost comrades, and slowly recognizing that they would not be at home for Christmas.

There was considerable fellow feeling between the soldiers in the trenches—they had all witnessed the same horrors. At dawn on December 25 the British around Ypres, Belgium, heard carols ringing out from the German lines. Peering over the parapet, they saw Christmas trees appearing on top of the German trenches. Slowly groups of German soldiers left their trenches and advanced into no man's land, from where they called on the British to join them.

The British soldiers moved into no man's land. The erstwhile foes talked, exchanged gifts, and played games of soccer. Similar events were reported along the lines where British and German troops opposed each other and continued for up to a week until the military authorities gave orders for it to desist. Occasional artillery shells were lobbed into no man's land to deter fraternization. There were similar incidents on the eastern front between German and Russian troops. However, no such truces occurred where French and German soldiers were in opposition. The French saw the Germans as ruthless invaders of their country and were not willing to fraternize.

British and German troops during the Christmas truce.

EYEWITNESS

J. HALCOTT GLOVER

U.S. citizens volunteered for the American Ambulance Field Service. Glover recorded French casualties arriving at his aid post:

"Many of the former [walking wounded] have come down on foot from the trenches; one sees them arrive in the street at Montauville looking around—perhaps a little lost—for the *poste de secours* [aid post] appointed for this particular regiment or company. Sometimes they help one another; often they walk with an arm thrown around a friendly shoulder. I have seen men come in, where I have stood waiting in the *poste de secours*, and throw themselves down exhausted, with blood trickling from their loose bandages into the straw. They have all the mud and sunburn of their trench life upon them—a bundle of heavy, shapeless clothes—always the faded blue of their current uniform—and a pair of hobnailed boots, very expressive of fatigue. They smell of sweat, camp-fire smoke, leather, and tobacco—all the same, whether the man be a peasant or a professor of mathematics. Sometimes, perhaps from loss of blood, or nervous shock, their teeth chatter. They are all very subdued in manner."

Personal letter published for private distribution in With the American Ambulance Field Service in France.

The First Battle of Ypres finally ended on November 24, and all of the combatants, their illusions of a short war shattered over the preceding months, settled down to dig the trenches that would come to dominate the remainder of the war on the western front. Soon, these defenses would stretch from the North Sea to the Swiss border. In some areas the rival lines would be separated by just a few yards of heavily shell-cratered ground. Crossing these bleak yards of whatever depth—no man's land—in the face of barbed wire, and machine-gun and artillery fire would come to dominate the thinking of French and British planners in 1915 and beyond. However, for the moment Germany's generals were content to hold what territory they had taken in 1914, including most of Belgium and a large part of France's main industrial region, and to look for signal victories elsewhere, chiefly on the eastern front.

A brief British success

Joffre, still committed to evicting German forces from France, continued with the First Battle of Champagne, which had begun in late 1914 and stretched into the first three months of 1915. The French attacks centered on

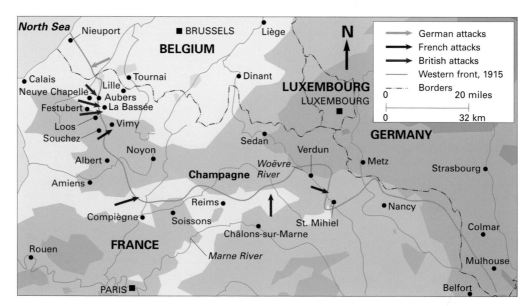

▶ *The fighting on the western front in 1915 was dominated by British and French offensives to drive the Germans from the territory they had occupied in 1914. The attacks gained little ground and human losses were enormous.*

two main areas—the western face of the salient (bulge in the line) around Noyon and in the vicinity of Reims and Verdun. The offensives were beaten back by the Germans, who launched local counterattacks of their own, chiefly around La Bassée and Soissons in January and early February.

The French attacks continued during March, with the British making their own contribution at Neuve Chapelle on the 10th. The attack was designed to capture the high ground of Aubers Ridge and threaten Lille. The BEF's commander, Field Marshal John French, had assembled four divisions for the attack, moving them into position in considerable secrecy. The British advance was preceded by a short but intense artillery bombardment, which caught the Germans off guard. Early progress in the battle was good. The village of Neuve Chapelle was overrun, and it seemed for a moment as if the German line might be broken.

However, the British were plagued by the severe problems that would confront many attackers until the last year of the war. It proved difficult to move reserves across the muddy, shell-blasted no man's land; those units committed to the initial assault had lost heavily and were incapable of making any further attacks; and the senior generals were

unsure of the situation because of severe communications difficulties.

Rapid German counterattacks prevented any further major exploitation of the initial onslaught, and the fighting petered out after three days. Both sides had suffered around 13,000 casualties; the British had used a considerable portion of their stock of shells, and further supplies were limited. Such shortages would become a highly public scandal over the next months and contribute to the dismissal of the British commander, Field Marshal John French.

In the first part of April, the French launched the Battle of the Woëvre River, an attempt to capture the northern face of the St. Mihiel salient to the south of the fortress city of Verdun in the east of the country. The attacks were easily repulsed by the Germans. Indeed, despite several attempts to capture the salient, it was not taken until 1918.

The Germans were next to launch an offensive. It was designed to capture the Channel ports through which British troops and equipment arrived in France and Belgium. Between April 22 and May 25 they battered away against the British holding the Ypres salient. The Second Battle of Ypres saw the British line buckle but not break. Again, early German attacks, supported for the first time on the western front by poison gas,

▲ *A French casualty is taken to an aid post by two of his comrades during the fighting in the Champagne region of France in early 1915.*

U.S. Food Aid

At the outbreak of the war one of the British government's first acts was to impose a rigorous naval blockade on the Central Powers. Merchant ships of any neutral nation suspected of trading with the Central Powers were likely to be stopped, boarded, searched, and have their cargoes confiscated.

The blockade, which became increasingly effective, had major consequences. It had a disastrous impact on German-occupied Belgium, which could not produce enough food to feed its civilians. As the supply of food dried up, the Belgian people began to suffer hunger.

However, a group based in London, the Commission for Relief in Belgium (CRB), negotiated an agreement with Germany. The Germans agreed not to confiscate for their own use food earmarked by the CRB for Belgium and also guaranteed that German submarines would not attack CRB ships.

The CRB board, chaired by future U.S. president Herbert Hoover and enjoying the backing of the U.S. government, was also able to win safe passage for its ships from Germany's foes. The plan was far from universally popular in the United States, however. One of its

strongest critics was former president Theodore Roosevelt, who was an outspoken supporter of Britain and France. He argued that the German authorities would simply grab the food aid once it had arrived in Belgium and use it to feed their own people. Despite Roosevelt's misgivings, the CRB operation in Europe continued.

The shipments to Belgium began in October 1914, and they took place throughout the war. Around 2,300 CRB-sponsored

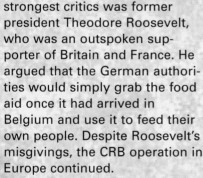

◄ *Herbert Hoover, who had spent much of his life overseas before World War I, was one of the major figures responsible for bringing aid to war-ravaged Europe through the efforts of the Commission for Relief in Belgium.*

◄ The German grip on Belgium was absolute. Here, a class is given lessons by German instructors.

ships were able to dock in the country's ports during this period. Once the supplies had been landed in Belgium, they were distributed by the local *Comité National de Secours et d'Alimentation* (The National Committee for Aid and Food). The operation proved such a success that the CRB was able to extend its efforts. In April 1915 it began operating in German-occupied parts of northern France. Aid was distributed by the local *Comité d'Alimentation* (Committee for Food). However, the CRB's work was not without risk; in 1917, for example, 12 CRB ships were sunk in error.

▼ Belgian refugees escape the German invaders in 1914. However, many were unable to escape.

were successful. However, difficult ground, lack of reserves, and stubborn British defense combined to deny the Germans a decisive victory.

In May and June the British and French launched the Second Battle of Artois (the first had been joined in the previous year's Race to the Sea). The British made limited gains around Festubert, while the French, advancing near Souchez, were slightly more successful, capturing parts of the key Vimy Ridge. This low ridge dominated the local terrain. However, both sides were exhausted and spent the next few months reorganizing, resting, and building their strength in the sector.

On September 25 the French and British again attacked in Artois and Champagne. None of the advances achieved much. In the Second Battle of Champagne the French bore more than 100,000 casualties, the Germans 75,000. At the same time, the Third Battle of Artois was being fought. The French again attacked toward Vimy Ridge between September 25 and October 30. For their part the British moved against Loos. The attackers suffered the greater of the casualties: some 60,000 British and 100,000 French as against some 65,000 German losses. The fighting ebbed away in early November.

Stalemate on the western front

The year 1915 brought home the realities of trench warfare. Casualties had been huge. The French had suffered losses of 1.2 million men, the British some 279,000, and the Germans 612,000. The French and British, whose gains could be measured in hundreds of yards at best, had begun the year firmly believing that they could crash through the German trench systems on the western front, but they had singularly failed to do so.

The Allied generals had been committed to offensive operations above all else, almost as a matter of national pride, and had attacked repeatedly, despite growing evidence that they did not have the tactics to achieve the breakthrough they craved. The generals were hampered by personal friction and a lack of coordination between the British and French senior commands, a dearth of heavy artillery and the huge number of shells needed to overwhelm the German defenses, and the growing depth and sophistication of the German fortifications. These increasingly consisted of three or more lines of trenches, one behind the other, and each protected by dense belts of barbed wire, machine guns, and artillery.

The British and French might capture one or two of the trench lines but would be halted, usually after suffering appalling casualties, by the third. Rapid counterattacks by fresh German troops would often evict them from the ground they had won. The German chief of the general staff, General Erich von Falkenhayn, believed that he had won the strategic initiative on the western front in 1915. For 1916 he planned to abandon his defensive strategy and

▲ *This painting,* **The Return of the Patrol** *by French artist Devambez, shows Germans captured around Vimy in late 1915.*

◄ *British troops are pinned down by German fire during the Battle of Loos.*

go over to the offensive. His principal target was to be the French Army around the fortress city of Verdun.

There had been changes in the British high command in France in late 1915. Field Marshal John French was removed as head of the BEF, partly because of the lack of success of his attack at Loos and also for his public criticism of the shortage of artillery shells. His replacement was General Douglas Haig, who was committed to attack and believed that he would have the means to win victory in 1916.

Haig was planning to launch a major offensive along the Somme sector using the so-called New Army, which was being formed and undergoing training in both England and France. Many of its enthusiastic volunteers were lifelong friends from close-knit communities, who had enlisted together, and were serving in the same regiments. Their baptism of fire on the western front would be along the Somme River during the early summer of 1916.

KEY FIGURES

GENERAL ERICH VON FALKENHAYN

Falkenhayn (1861–1922) was Germany's chief of the general staff from September 14, following the dismissal of General Helmuth von Moltke.

For the remainder of 1914 Falkenhayn exercised overall control of the fighting on the western front, which became increasingly trench-bound. In 1915 Falkenhayn agreed to stay on the defensive on the western front while concentrating Germany's efforts against Russia. Victories were won, but Falkenhayn was convinced that it was only on the western front that final victory could really be achieved.

In 1916 he attempted to break the stalemate on the western front during the Battle of Verdun. The fighting resulted in huge German casualties, but the long battle was nothing like Falkenhayn's total victory. He was dismissed and for the remainder of the war Falkenhayn held lesser military posts in Romania, Mesopotamia, Palestine, and Lithuania.

The Eastern Front, 1914–1916

The strategies of both the Austro-Hungarians and the Russians were shaped to fall in line with Germany's plans. Austria-Hungary had two strategies. First, there was Plan B to fight across the Balkans against Serbia; second, there was Plan R, which envisaged a conflict on two fronts against Serbia and Russia. In the latter, more likely, scenario it was proposed that Austro-Hungarian troops would support their German allies, forces which would be mainly based in East Prussia. The greater part of the Austro-Hungarian element was to launch an attack into Russian-controlled Poland in the south to divert numbers of Russians away from the German units holding East Prussia. Other Austro-Hungarian forces were to move directly against Serbia in the south, which had a much smaller army than its larger neighbor could field.

Russia also had two war plans, both of which depended on the military actions of Germany. First, if Germany attacked Russia directly at the outbreak of war, the Russians would fight a defensive war. Second, if Germany chose to invade France first, then Russian troops would attack, advancing into East Prussia as quickly as possible.

Smaller Serbia's strategy was essentially defined by the weakness of its comparatively small armed forces. Its commanders could realistically only fight a defensive war, thereby hoping to delay any aggressor for long enough until events on other war fronts would force the enemy to pull some of its troops out of Serbia.

Fighting on the eastern front was characterized by large maneuvers over long distances rather than trench warfare. Austria-Hungary, Germany, and Russia did not have enough troops to hold trenches from the Baltic Sea to the Balkans.

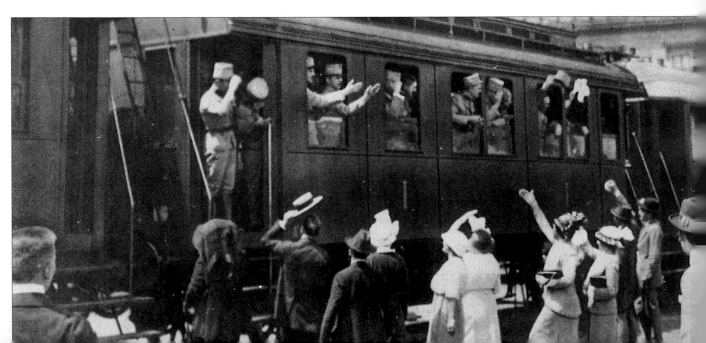

Opening moves in the Balkans

The opening phase of the fighting on the eastern front—and of the whole war—took place in the Balkans. On July 29, 1914, gunboats of Austria-Hungary operating on the Danube River attacked Belgrade, the Serbian capital. Their short and largely ineffective bombardment heralded what would become a world war in a matter of days.

The shelling of Belgrade, though, was just a prelude to a large Austro-Hungarian offensive against Serbia. This attack began on August 12, when more than 200,000 troops commanded by General Oskar Potiorek invaded Serbia from the west and northwest, crossing the Sava and Drina rivers in a major push toward Belgrade. However, the Serbian commander in chief, Marshal Radomir Putnik, quickly responded to the threat. His counterattack began on the 16th, and in the Battle of the Jadar River his forces threw the Austro-Hungarians back across the Drina River in confusion.

The Austro-Hungarians struck back in early September and managed to make a breakthrough by the 18th after ten days of hard fighting along the Drina River, forcing the Serbians to abandon Belgrade and then slowly retreat over the following weeks into the country's

▲ German troops hold a defensive position around the Masurian Lakes in East Prussia at the outbreak of war.

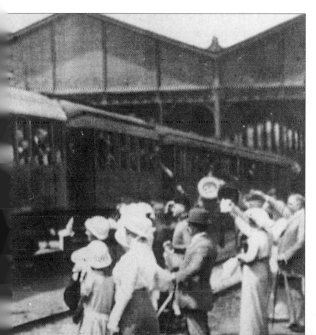

◀ Civilians cheer the men aboard an Austro-Hungarian troop train as they leave for the Balkan front, August 1914.

mountainous interior. The invading Austro-Hungarian forces finally entered Belgrade on December 2.

Putnik was far from finished. He realized that the Austro-Hungarian troops were overstretched and very probably exhausted, and he had received much-needed supplies of ammunition from France. Putnik's counterattack began on December 3, and the action, the Battle of the Kolubara River, was decisive. The Austro-Hungarians, with their backs to the river, collapsed, allowing the Serbians to reoccupy Belgrade on December 15. In just a few months of fighting, Austro-Hungarian casualties totaled 227,000 out of an initial force of 450,000 men. Serbia lost 170,000 men out of 400,000. Potiorek was sacked and replaced by Archduke Eugene.

While Austria-Hungary was singularly failing to knock Serbia out of the war, fighting had erupted elsewhere on the eastern front. Immediately after Germany declared war on August 1 with Austria-Hungary following suit five days later, Russia began to organize for the invasion of East Prussia. Two armies were committed to the enterprise. The First Army under General Pavel Rennenkampf was to enter the German province directly from the east, and

East Versus West

The Central Powers, whose grand strategy was dominated by Germany's senior generals, and those nations arrayed against them, both faced a core military dilemma during the conflict: where was the war most likely to be won?

▲ *Russian prisoners captured in 1915. Content to defend ground gained on the western front, Germany launched a series of successful attacks in the east during the year.*

The dilemma was most acute for Germany's military leadership, particularly following the failure of the Schlieffen Plan (see pages 132–141) in 1914. One consequence of this development was that Germany was condemned to fight a war on two fronts—against Britain and France (and later the United States) on the western front and against Russia in the east.

Germany's senior commanders were divided over the issue. The chief of the general staff, Erich von Falkenhayn, was an avowed "westerner." Field Marshal Paul von Hindenburg and General Erich Ludendorff, the men who would come to dominate Germany's military and political establishments from the summer of 1916 onward, were "easterners."

Germany's war strategy from 1915 through 1918 switched between the two fronts, partly due to changes in the balance of power between the two camps and partly due to more pressing military necessities—chiefly enemy action or the need to bolster a weaker ally, mainly Austria-Hungary.

In 1915 the focus of attention was on the eastern front. Germany launched offensives that had considerable success but did not knock Russia out of the war as intended. On the western front the Germans defended the ground they had won during 1914 in Belgium and northern France against British and French attacks.

In 1916 the strategy changed— the western front was seen as the key theater. Falkenhayn launched the attritional Battle of Verdun designed to destroy the French Army. The fighting lasted most of the year, but the French stood firm—and Falkenhayn was sacked. On the eastern front the Germans and their increasingly weak Austro-Hungarian allies adopted a defensive posture against Russia and used only limited resources in their conquest of Romania.

▶ *The British begin to leave the Turkish-held Gallipoli Peninsula, December 1915. The failed campaign was an attempt to knock one of Germany's weaker allies out of the war.*

In 1917 Germany was very much on the defensive on the western front as the British and French launched offensives. In the east a Russian attack was defeated, and only limited counterattacks launched. However, the Russian Revolution and the collapse of the Russian Army effectively ended the strategic dilemma. The revolutionaries wanted to take Russia out of the war, thereby freeing the bulk of the German forces on the eastern front for action in the west.

The final year of fighting revealed the truth: the war would be won or lost on the western front. German offensives from spring through midsummer came close to success—but the German Army was finally beaten in the fall.

British and French strategies

Britain's leadership also debated war strategy. Most senior generals saw the western front as the decisive theater, but many politicians, appalled by the growing casualties, sought to knock out one of Germany's allies, chiefly Turkey, to bring about a swift and less bloody end to the war. Troops were sent to Mesopotamia (modern Iraq) between 1914 and 1918, as well as to Palestine (1915–1918) and the Gallipoli Peninsula (1915–1916); others were committed to campaigns in Greece and the Balkans (1915–1918).

None of these large-scale efforts brought about an early victory—all of the Central Powers fought on until the later part of 1918. However, they did produce their own heavy toll of casualties, and they tied up substantial numbers of troops that might have been of much more use on the western front.

The French had a more fixed view of the war. With Germany occupying territory in northeast and eastern France, it was a matter of national pride to defeat the invader on the western front and regain the lost ground. Some French troops were sent overseas, principally to Gallipoli and the Balkans, but in comparatively small numbers. Only the defeat of the German Army on the western front would salvage France's damaged national pride.

◀ *A German soldier shelters in a former French trench at Verdun in 1916, a year in which Germany's military efforts focused on the western front.*

Erich Ludendorff, who just a few days before his appointment had won fame in capturing the Belgian fortress city of Liège on the western front.

Hindenburg and Ludendorff acted decisively. Noting that the two slowly advancing Russian armies were effectively isolated from one another by thick forests and the Masurian Lakes and thus could not offer support if either was attacked, they decided to destroy each in turn, beginning with Samsonov's command. A single cavalry division was positioned to delay Rennenkampf in the east, while the bulk of the German Eighth Army moved by road and rail to concentrate against Samsonov in the south. On August 24 Samsonov's advance was slowed, giving time for Hindenburg and Ludendorff to prepare. The Germans, who knew the Russian plans because they had intercepted Samsonov's messages, attacked on the 26th.

The decisive battle that followed, Tannenberg, was a victory for the Germans. Samsonov's army, its troops exhausted and short of food and key equipment, blundered into the German Eighth Army. The Russian troops were

General Alexander Samsonov's Second Army was positioned to strike from the south. Opposing the two Russian forces was the smaller German Eighth Army, commanded by General Max von Prittwitz. Prittwitz, in accordance with the Schlieffen Plan, was under strict orders to delay any Russian advance into East Prussia for as long as possible until troops from the western front could be transferred to the east by rail after supposedly defeating France.

The war in East Prussia
The first battle took place just inside East Prussia, at Stallupönen, on August 17. The result was a German victory. Rennenkampf's force was temporarily flung back to the border, but then he recommenced its advance, reaching Gumbinnen on the 20th. The German attack there delayed the Russians, but Prittwitz feared being crushed between the two larger Russian armies, and he panicked. The general demanded of his superiors that he be allowed to withdraw over the Vistula River in a move that would have meant abandoning both East and West Prussia.

Prittwitz's superiors could not agree to a surrender of German territory at such a critical juncture of the war. Prittwitz was instantly replaced by General Paul von Hindenburg, who was called out of retirement, and General

▲ *Huge columns of Russian prisoners, just some of the tens of thousands captured during the Battle of Tannenberg in August 1914, wait for the Germans to distribute rations.*

▶ *German troops move through the thick forests of East Prussia during the opening phase of the war against Russia on the eastern front. Although outnumbered, the Germans used swift movement to concentrate their forces against the widely dispersed Russian armies and defeat each of them in turn.*

virtually surrounded and destroyed—the Germans captured more than 100,000 Russians and 500 artillery pieces. Samsonov wandered off into the local forests and committed suicide. German casualties were 15,000 men.

The battle ended on August 31, and the Germans next turned north to deal with Rennenkampf, whose forces had been advancing very slowly. Again it was intended to surround the Russians, and the Germans came close to doing so during the First Battle of the Masurian Lakes fought between September 9 and 14. Only a Russian counterattack saved the day. Nevertheless, Rennenkampf's command had been mauled—a further 125,000 Russians had been killed, wounded, captured, or posted missing. German casualties totaled 10,000 men. The Russian invasion of East Prussia had been crushed in a matter of days.

To the south, the Austro-Hungarians were also battling against the Russians, but with considerably less success. Austria-Hungary's war plan, which was overseen by their chief of the general staff, Franz Conrad von Hötzendorf, was to drive into Russian Poland from the province of Galicia. The operation

EYEWITNESS

OCTAVIAN TASLAUANU

Romanian-born Taslauanu was an officer in the Austro-Hungarian Army. In the early winter of 1914–1915 he had to endure the freezing winter conditions of the Austro-Hungarian province of Galicia. His diary entries record one of the most common problems of troops living in unhygienic conditions—lice, parasitic insects that thrive on human body heat, live in the seams of clothing, and suck blood from their host:

"The men, despite the cold, lost no time in undressing to change their linen. I then saw human bodies which were nothing but one great sore from the neck to the waist. For the first time I really understood the popular phrase, 'May the lice eat you!' One of the men, when he pulled off his shirt, tore away crusts of dried blood, and the vermin were swarming in filthy layers in the garment. The poor peasant had grown thin on this. His projecting jaws and sunken eyes were the most conspicuous features of him. Even we officers were regular hives. Fothi [a fellow officer] yesterday counted 50. He pulled them one by one from the folds of his shirt collar. He counted them, threw them in the fire, and while we drank our tea and smoked, we scratched ourselves and laughed. Oh, those days—and nights. We often smoked 100 cigarettes a day and drank as many as 25 cups of tea. It was our only means of distraction."

Extract from Taslauanu's With the Austrian Army in Galicia.

---

began well. Three Austro-Hungarian armies advanced on a 200-mile (320 km) front from the vicinity of the border fortress of Lemberg. Opposing them was the Russian Southwestern Army Group, four armies under General Nikolai Ivanov stationed around the Pripet Marshes.

The series of battles that followed, fought between late August and mid-September, was highlighted by Austro-Hungarian defeats, principally at Rava Russkaya in Galicia (September 3–11). The Austro-Hungarians were forced to fall back in confusion some 100 miles (160 km) to the Carpathian Mountains, abandoning their base at Lemberg. Most of Galicia was now in Russian hands; only the fortress city of Przemysl was holding out. The offensive had cost the Austro-Hungarians more than 350,000 casualties. Russian losses during the brief campaign were most likely to have been on a similar scale.

Germany could not stand by and see its weakened ally crushed, particularly as Silesia, a key German industrial area, was now being threatened by the Russians after their recent victories in Galicia. Swift movement by rail from East Prussia to the north of Russian Poland was the key factor in its ability to react. A new force, the Ninth Army, under Hindenburg's direct command, was assembled in late September. A limited offensive delayed the Russians until the end of October, but the main action began on November 11, following a redeployment of German forces. The focus of the attack, led by the Ninth Army now under General August von Mackensen, was the Polish city of Lódz.

▶ Russian gunners pose beside their siege howitzer outside the Austro-Hungarian fortress city of Przemysl. It finally fell to the Russians on March 22, 1915, but the defenders destroyed its forts with explosive charges before they raised the flag of surrender.

▼ German troops push deeper into the Russian province of Poland during the spring of 1915, while Russian prisoners are taken into captivity. All of Poland would be captured by the Germans by the end of the year.

Both sides fought hard, but the battle was a draw. However, the Germans had saved Silesia from invasion.

For winter 1914–1915 Hindenburg planned a huge double envelopment of the Russian forces in Poland. Toward this end, in the south three Austro-Hungarian armies were to advance

across the Carpathian Mountains, striking for Lemberg and the besieged fortress of Przemysl. To the north two German armies were to move eastward from the Masurian Lakes. The offensive began on January 31 with a feint attack by the German Ninth Army at Bolimov in Poland, where gas was used for the first time in the war. (Its impact went virtually unnoticed by the Russians—in part because of the cold weather, which effectively stopped the gas from dispersing) The main attack, known as the Second Battle of the Masurian Lakes, opened on February 7. The Russians just managed to escape encirclement but were forced to retreat some 70 miles (112 km) after suffering approximately 200,000 casualties.

Pincer attack on Poland

To the south the Austro-Hungarian advance into Galicia was much less successful. The highlight was the capture of Czernowitz on February 17 by General Karl von Pflanzer-Baltin's Seventh Army. However, the attempt by the Third Army under General Svetozar Boroevic von Bojna to break the siege of Przemysl made little progress. The fortress, with no hope of relief, surrendered on March 22. Some 110,000 Austro-Hungarian troops surrendered after a siege of 194 days.

By the spring of 1915 the Germans had gone over to the defensive on the western front, and their chief of the general staff, General Erich von Falkenhayn, transferred units to the eastern front, looking for a decisive victory. His proposed new offensive had two elements. In the north, Hindenburg's forces were to feint in the direction of Warsaw to keep the Russians around the Polish capital occupied. The main attack was to be in the south. This was to be on a 30-mile (48 km) front in the direction of the towns of Gorlice and Tarnow and was led by General August von Mackensen's new command, the Eleventh Army. The

offensive began on May 2, preceded by a four-hour bombardment of the Russian positions. Progress was rapid, and Mackensen recaptured Przemysl on June 3 and Lemberg on the 22nd.

As the Russian forces in the south were being pushed back, the Germans struck again in the north, with General Max von Gallwitz's Twelfth Army leading the way. The Russians were forced to abandon Warsaw in early August and had to make a headlong retreat of some 300 miles (480 km), which only ended

▲ *The eastern front, 1914–1915. The Russians gained much of Galicia in 1914, but were stopped by the Germans in East Prussia. German-led counterattacks in 1915 recaptured Galicia and took all of Russian Poland.*

KEY FIGURES

CZAR NICHOLAS II

Czar Nicholas II (1868–1918) succeeded his father, Alexander III, in 1895. While Alexander was strong-minded, his son was indecisive.

A year before he became emperor, Nicholas married Alexandra of Hesse-Darmstadt, a member of the royal family of a German state. Alexandra was a domineering personality, one who exerted considerable influence over her husband. Under her direction, Nicholas attempted to expand Russian influence in Asia in the 1890s, which led to a disastrous war with Japan (1904–1905). Russia's humiliating defeat and Nicholas's unwillingness to make political reforms sparked a short-lived revolution in 1905. Although the revolution was contained, Nicholas was forced to make some political concessions, chiefly the creation of a representative government (Duma). However, he continued to rule with absolute authority and rejected many of the Duma's proposals for moderate reforms.

At the outbreak of World War I, Czar Nicholas II continued his role as the embodiment of Russia and its people, even changing the name of his capital from the German-sounding St. Petersburg to the more Russian Petrograd. However, military disasters, the growing role of his wife in day-to-day government, and political unrest led to his abdication in 1917. Arrested and placed in internal exile by the revolutionaries, he and his family were killed in 1918.

when the heavy fall rains made the roads virtually impassable and slowed the German advance considerably.

The Russian armies had been badly mauled in 1915, suffering two million casualties, but they were still able to fight on in 1916. In total, Austria-Hungary and Germany reported around one million casualties in the same period. Germany, still facing a war on two fronts, was having its military resources stretched to the limit.

The Russian defeats in 1915 were destined to have profound political repercussions, however. The Russian commander in chief, Grand Duke Nicholas, was held responsible for the loss of Russian Poland and was sacked in September. On the 15th Czar Nicholas II took personal charge of future Russian operations on the eastern front. It would prove to be a bad decision. The czar had no military experience yet would not delegate responsibility to those advisers who had. Henceforth, he would be personally identified with the military operations of the Russian Army. His indecisiveness and the growing unrest at the front that was in part a product of his mismanagement were to contribute to the outbreak of violent revolution in 1917.

Turmoil in the Balkans

There had also been ferocious combat in the Balkans during 1915. Germany was eager to open up an overland supply route to Turkey, which had sided with the Central Powers on October 29, 1914, when two of its warships—the *Breslau* and *Goeben* (both vessels provided by Germany)—shelled three Russian ports on the Black Sea. To make this route feasible, Serbia would have to be defeated, as the main railroad to Turkey ran through the country. In support of this aim, German diplomats had been attempting to encourage neighboring Bulgaria to side with the Central Powers. Promised considerable territorial gains, the Bulgaria govern-

▲ *Bulgarian troops man a trench in southern Serbia following the rapid invasion of the country in October 1915. They are in position to oppose any advance by the British and French forces garrisoning the Greek province of Salonika to the south.*

Skopje. Marshal Radomir Putnik's Serbian forces, outnumbered by two to one, evaded the attempted encirclement but had to retreat to the southwest, fighting all the way. Attempts by French and British forces, stationed in the Greek province of Salonika to the south of Serbia, to lend assistance to the Serbians eventually came to nothing. By November the Serbians were in headlong retreat, heading for the coast of the Adriatic Sea through Montenegro, a Serbian ally, and Albania.

The withdrawal took place under dreadful winter conditions, and Serbian casualties were severe—some 100,000 killed or wounded and 160,000 troops made prisoner. Yet the remaining Serbian forces held together and were evacuated by Allied warships, reaching the Greek island of Corfu in early 1916. From there they would be moved to Salonika, where they joined the ever-growing force of British, French, and Russian troops in the region.

The buildup of troops in Salonika had begun in October 1915, chiefly in response to the mobilization of Bulgarian forces in September for the invasion of Serbia. Greece, of which Salonika was a part, was supposedly neutral, but the Greek prime minister, Eleuthérios Venizélos, had permitted

ment threw in its lot with Germany on September 6, 1915, and prepared its forces to invade Serbia

The new invasion of Serbia began on October 6. Two armies, one Austro-Hungarian and one German, invaded from the north, while two Bulgarian armies reinforced the attack by invading from the east five days later. The Bulgarian objectives were Nish and

▶ *Serbian artillery-men attempt to halt the invasion of their country by Austro-Hungarian, Bulgarian, and German troops, which began in the latter part of 1915.*

▶ *French colonial troops from Cochin China (now southern Vietnam), part of the growing—and often inactive— Allied garrison in the Greek province of Salonika.*

the Allies to land at the port of Salonika and move north to support Serbia. In fact, Venizélos had resigned shortly before the operation began, and his permission had also been revoked. Nevertheless, the movement of troops continued. France's General Maurice Sarrail and two divisions, one British and one French, arrived on October 5. More units would flow into Salonika over the following years—a total of 600,000 by 1917. However, many of these troops, often more than 80 percent, were incapable of service due to illnesses, and their commanders were often beset by jealousies and rivalries.

Russia's Brusilov Offensive

In 1916 Germany's war planners opted to focus their efforts on the western front, chiefly an all-out onslaught against the French fortress city of Verdun, which began on February 21. The attack was launched with such ferocity that the French called on their chief allies, Britain and Russia, to launch counterattacks to relieve some of the pressure by drawing off some of the German troops committed at Verdun. The Russian element in this strategy opened with the Battle of Lake Naroch on March 18. Despite being preceded by a two-day bombardment,

▼ *Captured Russian machine-gunners are moved to the rear under escort during the Brusilov Offensive, mid-1916.*

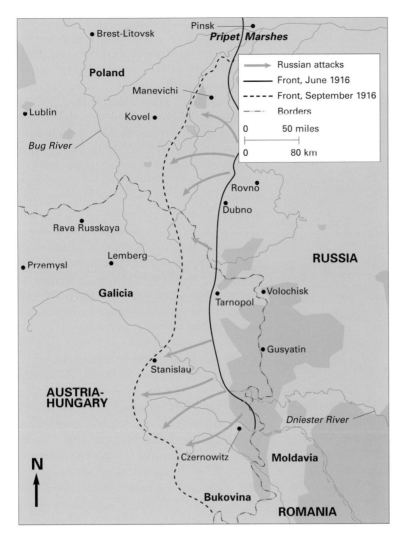

the Russian offensive, which was directed toward Vilna, quickly became bogged down in the spring thaw. Little progress was made, and a further 100,000 men were added to the growing Russian casualty list.

The Russians launched a much larger offensive during the summer. The Southwestern Army Group, four armies now under General Alexey Brusilov, attacked along a 300-mile (480 km) front. Brusilov, the most competent Russian commander of the war, had assembled his armies in great secrecy and did not forewarn the Austro-Hungarian and German forces arrayed against him by conducting a long preliminary artillery bombardment. When

▲ *The Brusilov Offensive in the summer of 1916. It was initially successful but was blunted by German-led counterattacks. Casualties among the ordinary Russian soldiers were heavy, and the survivors lost what little faith they still had in their senior commanders.*

the storm broke on June 4, the Russians achieved almost total surprise. Two Austro-Hungarian armies were totally destroyed and 70,000 prisoners taken; only the German units in the theater managed to blunt the offensive.

Brusilov continued to attack over the following months but was hampered by a lack of reinforcements and the steady arrival of fresh German forces from the western front. By the time the attacks ended on September 20, some of Brusilov's units had reached the Carpathian Mountains. It was the most spectacular Russian victory of the war, and it was to have enormous, if unforeseen, consequences. The Russian forces had suffered more than 500,000 casualties, and the soldiers were at the end of their tether after more than two years of fighting. Their morale was low, and they began to question both their officers and their allegiance to Nicholas II, who was in charge of the country's strategy.

As the Brusilov Offensive was entering its final stages, fighting again flared up in the Balkans. Romania, an ambitious regional power, had been persuaded to join the fight against the Central Powers. Its political and military leaders had been overly impressed by the early successes of the Brusilov Offensive, mistakenly believing that the Russian advance heralded the imminent collapse of Austria-Hungary. They had also been promised Austro-Hungarian territory if they threw in their lot with those fighting the Central Powers.

The Romanian government, headed by King Ferdinand, declared war on both Germany and Austria-Hungary on August 27. Russian troops to the north and British and French forces in Salonika had been earmarked to support any military operations. However, the Romanians were poorly prepared for war against the Central Powers.

For their part, the Central Powers also had military designs on Romania, chiefly because of its oil fields around Ploesti, its supplies of grain, which

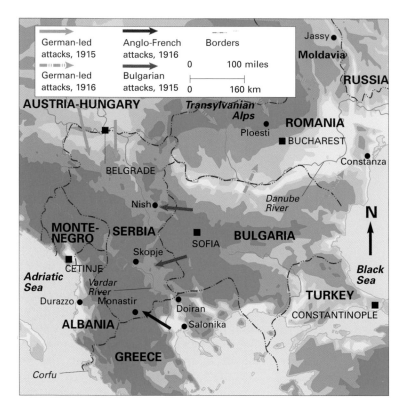

▲ The war in the Balkans, 1915–1916. Germany organized and led the invasions that succeeded in crushing Serbia and Romania, while the British, French, Russians, and Serbians all kept large forces in Salonika.

November 23, beating off a token counterattack by General Alexandru Averescu and then linking up with Falkenhayn's forces, which were advancing into Romania through the passes of the Transylvanian Alps.

The Romanians were decisively defeated during the Battle of the Arges River in early December, and Mackensen occupied the capital, Bucharest, on the 6th. The Romanians, who had suffered some 350,000 casualties during the brief campaign, many of them civilians, were left in possession of a small fragment of their territory in the northeast of their country. Their seat of government was moved to Jassy, the capital of the Romanian province of Moldavia. The invaders announced casualties totaling some 60,000 men.

A year of contrasting fortunes

The promised support to Romania offered by Britain, France, and Russia never really materialized. The Russians were still recovering from the Brusilov Offensive, and the French and British were deeply committed to the western front. The various forces in Salonika, which had been pushed back to the line of the Struma River by a joint German and Bulgarian offensive in the second half of August, did finally advance along the broad valley of the Vardar River in September. The troops committed to the offensive did have some success— Monastir in Serbia was captured on November 19—but the advance was too slow to have any impact.

Thus, by the end of 1916 the Central Powers seemingly held the upper hand both on the eastern front and in the Balkans. Romania had been occupied with very little difficulty; the Russians' Brusilov Offensive had been eventually contained; great swathes of Russian territory were still occupied; and a large enemy force remained bottled up in Salonika, which the Central Powers contemptuously referred to as their "biggest prisoner of war camp."

would alleviate shortages brought about by the British-led naval blockade of Germany, and its position to the north of the rail route between Germany and Turkey. The Central Powers reacted swiftly to Romania's war declaration and its slowly developing attacks into southeast Austria-Hungary.

Some Romanian forces advanced into the Austro-Hungarian province of Transylvania, where there was a large ethnic Romanian population, by moving through the passes of the Transylvanian Alps and the Carpathian Mountains. The advances quickly stalled, however, as the German Ninth Army, led by the former chief of the general staff, General Erich von Falkenhayn, struck back.

A second counterattack developed in the south of Romania, where General August von Mackensen led an invasion mounted by the Bulgarian Danube Army, which had been rapidly reinforced by German units. Mackensen's force crossed the Danube River on

▶ *Germany's General August von Mackensen (left) looks on as Austro-Hungarian troops celebrate their capture of Bucharest, Romania's capital. Mackensen was the driving force behind the swift victory of the Central Powers and was promoted to the rank of field marshal for his achievement.*

On the debit side it was clear that Austria-Hungary was in increasingly bad shape. The combat effectiveness of its armies grew even more limited, and the tensions among the various ethnic groups contained within their ranks were growing. Germany, increasingly overstretched, would have to continue to shoulder the greater part of the Central Powers' war efforts.

Similarly, deep-seated political problems were evident within the fragile Austro-Hungarian Empire itself, as the various groups it contained became increasingly vocal in their demands for independence and self-determination. Some of the last words uttered by the aged emperor of Austria-Hungary, Franz Joseph I, who died on November 21, 1916, after 68 years on the throne, reflected the parlous state of the nation: "I took over the throne under the most difficult conditions and I am leaving it under even worse ones." His successor, Charles I, was destined to be the last Austro-Hungarian emperor. However, Germany's fortunes in 1917 were seemingly destined to be revived by events in Russia, which was rent by revolutionary fervor. If Russia left the war, German armies there could be sent to the west.

The scandal of Rasputin

One of the events that typified the growing instability of Russia's ruling class in late 1916 was the murder of a monk, Rasputin, little known outside the empire but a close confidant of the royal family. Rasputin took to the religious life at an early age and became a well-known personality in Russia because of his pilgrimages to distant holy places. In two years he is believed to have traveled some 2,000 miles (3,200 km), visiting Greece and the Middle East. Back in Russia after his wanderings, he built up a loyal band of followers and gained a reputation for being able to cure the sick by prayer. At the time Russia was gripped by an interest in the occult and spiritualism, and one of the many people convinced of the efficacy of such beliefs was Grand Duchess Militsa, Czar Nicholas II's sister-in-law. Visiting a monastery in Kiev, she met Rasputin, probably in 1903.

Rasputin returned to St. Petersburg, the Russian capital, with the grand duchess, and his reputation grew. He met the czar and his czarina, Alexandra, in 1904. A year before, the czarina had given birth to an heir, Alexey. However, Alexey suffered from hemophilia, an inherited and life-threatening genetic disorder that prevents the blood from clotting after a minor injury.

In 1907 Alexey had a fall, which produced serious internal bruising. Both the czar and czarina, who were distraught, sought help. Rasputin was called in and apparently through the power of prayer the young heir was brought back to health. The czarina made Rasputin part of her inner circle, one of a small clique whose position and influence was increasingly resented and competed for by those who often craved an equally close relationship with the royal family.

Rumors, published in newspapers and also spread by word of mouth, began to circulate about Rasputin—that he was a drunkard and seducer of women. They were probably greatly exaggerated, but Rasputin also made enemies among Russia's political elite. Liberals, who craved greater freedoms, disliked him because they saw him as a reactionary. Some conservatives, individuals who opposed major reform, hated him equally because of his close association with the royal family, which they thought excluded them from decision making. In 1911, as stories of Rasputin's dissolute lifestyle threatened a major scandal, he was ordered by the Russian prime minister, Pyotr Stolypin, to leave St. Petersburg under pain of arrest.

Rasputin's exile did not last long. By the outbreak of World War I, he was back in favor with the royal family, having again helped the heir to the throne survive an illness. However, his luck began to run out. On June 27, 1914, the day that Austria-Hungary's Archduke Ferdinand was assassinated in Serbia, an event that precipitated World War I,

Rasputin was stabbed. He recovered from the attack, but the lurid rumors about him steadily mounted. It was falsely alleged that he was the czarina's lover and that both of them were German spies (Alexandra was, of course, of German origin).

In 1916, as the news from the eastern front worsened and Russian casualties rose alarmingly, Rasputin began to have premonitions of his own death. In December the monk wrote a note to the czarina: "I feel I shall leave life before January 1 [1917]." His message also declared that if he died at the hands of peasants, Czar Nicholas II would reign for many more years, but if he was killed by members of the aristocracy, then

▼ *Rasputin, a mystic and faith healer, developed a close attachment to the Russian royal family that many people resented.*

▲ *Rasputin pictured with a number of his followers. Women in particular were attracted by the mystical powers it was alleged he possessed.*

"none of your [the royal family's] children or relations will remain alive for more than two years."

On December 29 Rasputin was invited to the house of the dissolute Prince Yusupov, who had decided to kill him to "save" Russia. Despite friends trying to stop the monk from going, Rasputin attended the gathering. Yusupov poisoned Rasputin with cyanide, but a medical condition he had prevented the monk from absorbing the deadly poison. Next, Yusupov shot Rasputin several times in the back. Wounded, Rasputin staggered into the house's courtyard, where he was beaten with an iron bar, kicked about the face, and shot again. Rasputin was next tied up and taken by car to the Neva River, where his body was dumped into the freezing waters through a hole in the ice. The remains were recovered by the local police on January 1, 1917. The autopsy concluded that the monk had finally died from drowning.

Rasputin was assassinated because he was perceived as a manipulator of the czarina, who in turn was alleged to have undue political influence on her husband, Nicholas, an often weak and indecisive monarch. Those who murdered Rasputin hoped to weaken the czarina's supposedly malign influence on her husband. In fact, the connection was exaggerated, and Rasputin's role in political matters was limited. The outbreak of the Russian Revolution and the overthrow of the monarchy in 1917 was, by late 1916, virtually guaranteed. Rasputin was implicated in the weakness of Russia's ruling class, but the empire's problems ran much deeper. However, Rasputin did predict the end of the royal family. Within two years of his death its members had indeed been killed by revolutionaries.

Germany's war leaders

Although it was far less public, Germany was also undergoing political change at the highest level. As the war progressed, the military took an ever-tighter grip on German affairs. Power was mainly in the hands of two senior generals—Paul von Hindenburg and Erich Ludendorff. In 1914 the two men had forged an out-

167

standing military partnership, which would continue until the end of the war. That first year they inflicted major defeats on the Russians at Tannenberg during August and then again at the First Battle of the Masurian Lakes in September. Before the latter, Hindenburg had been made the commander of all German forces on the eastern front, with Ludendorff as his deputy. Further great victories were won in 1915. On November 1 Hindenburg was promoted to field marshal and made commander of all Austro-Hungarian and German forces on the eastern front.

In 1916 the chief of the general staff, General Erich von Falkenhayn—effectively Germany's most senior officer—was sacked for the failure of his offensive against the French at Verdun. Falkenhayn's replacement was Hindenburg, who appointed Ludendorff his deputy. The latter was named first quartermaster general. By the end of the year the two men dominated Germany's military affairs. Kaiser Wilhelm II, although the country's supreme war leader, allowed the two to formulate war strategies. Ludendorff, the younger, was much more than Hindenburg's deputy. Hindenburg, often willing to accede to his supposed deputy's decisions, became a figurehead, albeit one with power and public respect.

By early 1917 the military authority of both men was virtually unchallengeable. However, less sure were their respective positions within Germany's mainstream political life. Questions about Germany's war policy were to propel the two generals into the field of national politics. The leading figure in the country's government, Chancellor Theobold von Bethmann Hollweg, was

▼ Germany's wartime leaders, Field Marshal Paul von Hindenburg (left) and General Erich Ludendorff (right), discuss military strategy with their emperor, Wilhelm II.

opposed to a proposal by the German Navy that it should be allowed to recommence unrestricted submarine warfare, fearing that such a move would lead to war with the United States.

Hindenburg and Ludendorff backed the navy's demands and were able to engineer Bethmann Hollweg's resignation in July 1917. His replacement, Georg Michaelis, was chosen by the two commanders. He was a weak, pliable character and little suited to the role of chancellor. With Bethmann Hollweg's departure the last restraint on the generals' ambitions had been removed.

Wide-ranging powers

How far did the power of the two men stretch? In war terms they wholly dictated Germany's military efforts from late 1916, deciding where and when offensives were to be launched. Ironically, the decision by Ludendorff, an ardent believer in the pre-eminence of the military in all matters, to launch an all-out attack on the western front in the spring of 1918 to win the war outright ended in failure and destroyed the fighting spirit of the German Army.

One of their other major interventions was in the economy. The two generals, who had supporters among Germany's top industrialists, placed the running of the economy in the hands of the armed forces (chiefly with themselves at the head) and the same supportive industrialists.

In late August 1916, for example, Hindenburg ordered a doubling of the output of machine guns and a trebling in the production of artillery—all to be completed the following spring. In exchange, the industrialists were given a free hand in setting their own prices and profit margins. Industrial output certainly rose, but at a high cost. The industrialists' profits soared, paid for by the government and, ultimately, the ordinary citizen. Inflation rocketed, many nonmilitary products became scarce, and the illegal black market flourished. Labor relations rapidly worsened and outbreaks of political unrest grew in number.

The two men were destined to dominate Germany until the final weeks of the war. Ludendorff, his nerve wrecked by severe defeats on the western front in August 1918, was one minute demanding an immediate end to hostilities by the end of the next month and then arguing for the war's continuation. He was finally forced to resign on October 26 and fled to neutral Sweden in disguise. Hindenburg stayed in place, arguing that the country should sue for peace and also advising the emperor to abdicate on the eve of Germany's defeat in November 1918.

▼ *The leader of the German government, Theobold von Bethmann Hollweg, resigned in the middle of 1917, conceding political power in his country to a small group of generals.*

The War at Sea,
1914–1916

Although all of the combatant nations deployed warships at the outbreak of World War I, the two key navies were Britain's Home Fleet and Germany's High Seas Fleet. Britain had the largest force of warships in the world, but Germany was its nearest rival.

In the key areas of dreadnought battleships and battle-cruisers (ships with similar armaments to battleships but a higher speed gained at the cost of armored protection), the British could deploy 20 and 8 respectively and the Germans 13 and 5 in 1914. The British also had a greater building program. However, the British had to protect their far-flung colonies around the world and the sea-lanes that connected them to Britain.

Of the other major European naval powers from 1914 to 1916, France was primarily concerned with protecting the various Mediterranean sea-lanes to its colonies in North Africa, while Austria-Hungary and Italy were fighting for control of the Adriatic Sea and entry from there into the Mediterranean. Russia's navy had been badly mauled by the Japanese in the Russo-Japanese War (1904–1905), and its operations were mainly restricted to the Baltic and Black Seas. Farther afield in the Pacific, the greatest naval power was Japan, victor of the Russo-Japanese War.

In 1914 many expected a battle between the fleets. However, no one was willing to risk such a venture, and both sides settled down to impose blockades.

The naval war in 1914 had several elements. The Allies were intent on capturing Germany's colonies, principally those in the Pacific and China, and destroying the warships that protected them. Britain was also set on imposing a naval blockade of the Central Powers to halt the flow of the goods and raw materials that fueled their war efforts. The blockade was to be imposed by the major component of the Royal Navy, the Home Fleet, which was based primarily at Scapa Flow in the Orkneys to the far north of Scotland. Germany, with fewer warships, could not hope to protect all of its colonies. Its strategy was to strangle the flow of maritime trade to Britain using small forces of powerful, fast-moving cruisers or converted passenger liners, while its main fleet would remain in home waters as a counter to the Royal Navy's Home Fleet.

▲ The British fleet at anchor shortly before the outbreak of war. The largest naval force in the world, it was more than twice the combined size of the U.S. and German navies— its nearest rivals.

▶ German battleships pictured on maneuvers shortly before the war. Although smaller than the British fleet, the German naval forces were a potentially major threat to Britain's overseas trade.

War in the Far East

The first element of the Allied naval strategy, the elimination of Germany's Pacific colonies, was accomplished quickly. The Japanese, who declared war on Germany on August 23 and had colonial ambitions of their own, quickly took over the German-held Marshall, Caroline, Mariana, and Palau Islands in October. New Zealand forces captured the German portion of Samoa.

The largest Allied military operation involved the capture of the German base of Tsingtao, part of its Kiaochow colony on mainland China. Some 23,000 Japanese troops under General Mitsuomi Kamio, backed by more than 100 warships, landed in September, and began siege operations on October 31. They were later joined by a token British force of some 1,500 men under General Nathaniel Barnardiston. The Germans at Tsingtao finally surrendered on November 7 after having suffered 700 casualties out of 4,000 troops. The Japanese, who were to remain in control of Tsingtao until 1922, reported some 1,800 of their troops killed, wounded, or missing.

These early amphibious operations were wholly successful and achieved at relatively little cost. However, the elimination of the German warships that protected the colonies or acted as commerce raiders was far more protracted and costly. The key element was Admiral Maximilian von Spee's East Asiatic Squadron, consisting of two cruisers, *Gneisenau* and *Scharnhorst*, and four light cruisers—*Dresden*, *Emden*, *Leipzig*, and *Nürnberg*.

When Japan declared war, Spee recognized that his small squadron, based at Tsingtao, would be heavily outnumbered in the Pacific, and he therefore decided to abandon his plans to use his whole force to attack British merchant ships. He planned to detach the *Emden*, which was to commence attacks on enemy merchant ships, and return home with the remainder of his warships by sailing around Cape Horn at the tip of South America and then into the southern Atlantic.

Spee was at Valparaiso, Chile, when he received intelligence that a British light cruiser, *Glasgow*, was at Coronel, some 200 miles (320 km) to the south,

on October 31. The *Glasgow* was part of a squadron commanded by Rear Admiral Christopher Cradock, which was based at a British refueling station in the Falkland Islands in the southern Atlantic and had been alerted to Spee's intentions. He sailed to confront Spee on October 23. Cradock's role was to protect British trade routes from attack; he commanded an armored cruiser, *Good Hope* (his flagship), a cruiser, *Monmouth*, and an armed merchant cruiser, *Otranto*, as well as the *Glasgow*. A fifth warship, *Canopus*, an old battleship, had been sent to reinforce Cradock but arrived in the Falklands only after the admiral had left.

The two forces met some 50 miles (80 km) off Coronel shortly before 5 P.M. on November 1. Cradock was both outnumbered and outgunned but did not withdraw. Spee used his superior firepower to devastating affect. At long distance, with the British warships silhouetted against the setting sun, he pounded them to destruction. *Good Hope* sank after three hours, followed by *Monmouth*. *Glasgow* and *Otranto* escaped in the gathering gloom, but Cradock and 1,600 others had been killed. The German warships suffered no damage and not one casualty.

Action in the Falklands

Spee's victory was short-lived, however. The British reaction was swift. Vice-Admiral Frederick Sturdee was dispatched immediately from Britain to the South Atlantic to seek out Spee. He sailed on November 11, commanding a powerful force of five warships—two battlecruisers, *Invincible* and *Inflexible*, and three cruisers, *Cornwall*, *Kent*, and *Glasgow*. Sturdee headed for the Falklands, where he intended to refuel his ships and link up with the *Canopus*. Meanwhile, Spee had decided to destroy the naval facilities at Port Stanley in the Falklands and arrived there on December 8, only to find Sturdee waiting for him, having arrived the day before. Spee recognized the hopelessness of his situation and attempted to escape, but he was pursued to destruction by the faster, better-armed British warships.

▼ *The British battlecruiser* Invincible *steaming at full speed to engage the German fleet at the Battle of the Falklands in 1914. In this southern Atlantic action, Germany lost four warships and 2,100 sailors, the British just 10 men.*

The action began at 1 P.M. *Scharnhorst* was sunk some four hours later, followed by the *Gneisenau. Leipzig* was destroyed by *Glasgow* and *Kent,* and *Nürnberg* by the *Kent. Dresden* was able to escape but was pursued by *Kent* and *Glasgow* back into the Pacific and was scuttled in Chilean waters after a brief fight with the two British warships three months later. The East Asiatic Squadron had been destroyed. Spee and close to 2,000 of his men had been killed at a cost of virtually no British casualties.

While these battles were being fought, the lone raider *Emden,* under Captain Karl von Müller, was ranging far and wide in the Indian Ocean, Bay of Bengal, and the southwest Pacific, creating havoc. Between August and November, the light cruiser captured or sank 23 merchant ships, the Russian light cruiser *Zhemchug,* and the French destroyer *Mousquet,* and bombarded oil installations at Madras, India.

However, Allied warships were searching for the *Emden,* whose end came on November 11 while some of its crew was attempting to destroy communication facilities on Cocos Keeling Island. An Australian light cruiser, *Sydney,* surprised the *Emden* and destroyed it after a brief fight. Some of the *Emden*'s crew escaped in a schooner, before making

▲ *The German cruiser* Emden *was sunk in the Indian Ocean by the Australian light cruiser* Sydney *in November 1914, in the first wartime action fought by an Australian warship.*

an epic seven-month journey overland through what is now Saudi Arabia before they reached Constantinople, the Turkish capital.

There were two other German warships threatening maritime trade—the cruiser *Königsberg,* which was based in East Africa at the outbreak of war, and the *Karlsruhe,* which operated off the east coast of South America. On August 6 the *Königsberg* sank the British light

▶ *Thick, acrid smoke rises from oil storage tanks in Madras, India, after the surprise bombardment by the German light cruiser* Emden *on September 22, 1914.*

▼ **The wreck of the German cruiser Königsberg.** *Its big guns were saved by German troops for use on land.*

cruiser *Pegasus* off Mombasa, the principal port of the colony of British East Africa (now Kenya). However, the British set out to destroy the German warship, and it was forced to shelter in the estuary of the Rufiji River, which flowed through the colony of German East Africa (now Tanzania). The *Königsberg* was finally destroyed in July 1915 after its location had been confirmed by aerial reconnaissance, but its main armaments were removed and used by German land forces operating in East Africa. The *Karlsruhe* had a brief, if spectacular, career. Between August and early November 1914, the cruiser sank 14 British merchant ships but succumbed to a mysterious internal explosion on November 4.

The only other German surface raiders at large during this period were four converted high-speed liners fitted with some armaments. One, *Cap Trafalgar*, was sunk in the South Atlantic by the similar British armed merchant cruiser, *Carmania*, in September 1914. The month before, a second, *Kaiser Wilhelm der Grosse*, was sunk off North

Africa by the British cruiser *Highflyer*. The remaining two, *Kronprinz Wilhelm* and *Prinz Eitel Friedrich*, were interned in U.S. ports in the spring of 1915.

Back in European waters the two rival fleets avoided large-scale action. The bulk of the British Home Fleet commanded by Admiral John Jellicoe remained at anchor, mostly at Scapa Flow in the Orkney Islands and at Rosyth in Scotland, while his opposite number in the German High Seas Fleet, Admiral Friedrich von Ingenohl, maintained a similar posture at his bases at Kiel, Helgoland, and Wilhelmshaven.

Naval blockades

Neither side was willing to risk all on a single battle, as a major defeat would have had catastrophic consequences on the two countries' war efforts. Without a navy, Britain could not protect the sea routes along which vital supplies flowed, and Germany would be unable to prevent the British blockade of its territory from being tightened to an intolerable degree. Britain's First Lord of the Admiralty, Winston Churchill,

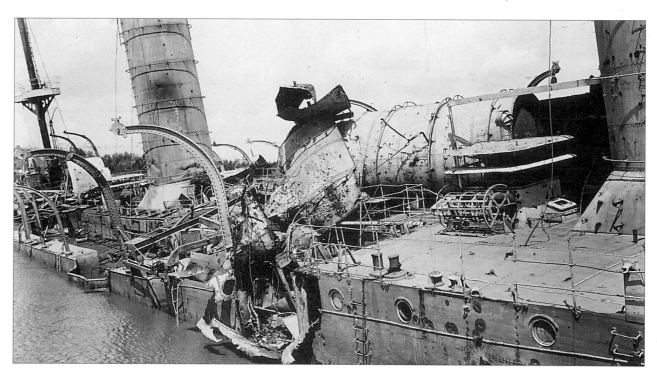

Blockading Germany

As soon as the war began, the British implemented a plan to bring Germany to its knees by imposing a blockade to starve it of vital supplies from overseas. On its own it would not end the war quickly, but as hopes evaporated of a swift victory on land, the blockade became a cornerstone of the overall Allied strategy.

A key strategy devised by Britain's war planners to defeat Germany was the idea of a naval blockade. It was felt that Germany was vulnerable to this policy—it had the largest maritime trade of all the continental European nations, and its merchant fleet was second in size only to Britain's. If Germany could be denied key materials, such as iron ore from Sweden—and, indeed, food—then its war machine might collapse or the morale of its ordinary civilians might disintegrate.

The fine details for any future blockade were initially drawn up in 1912 and then amended in 1914, shortly before the outbreak of war. The plan was simple—destroy Germany's merchant fleet and halt the flow of imports and exports between the country and its international trading partners.

The British plans took full advantage of the country's geographical position. In effect, it allowed Germany only two routes to the world's oceans. First there was the English Channel. This narrow stretch of water was to be blocked by mines and barrages, both covered by various warships known collectively as the Dover Patrol.

The second area, the 120 miles (192 km) of the North Sea between the Shetland Islands and Norway to the north of Scotland, was more problematic. Considerably more resources would be necessary to close off this sea route than were required to protect the 20-mile (32 km) wide Channel. The force committed to blockading the much larger North Sea area was known as the Northern Patrol.

The impact of the British blockade intensified gradually as the war progressed. For example, the Northern Patrol stopped

▶ *The crew aboard the British trawler* **Principal** *undergo gun drill in 1916. Shortages of ships forced the British to convert ordinary vessels to enforce the maritime blockade of German trade.*

▶ *The British propaganda poster "How the Hun Hates." The mining issue aroused strong passions on both sides. The Germans believed that many of the minelayers were little better than modern-day pirates, little more than criminals.*

HOW THE HUN HATES!

THE HUNS CAPTURED SOME OF OUR FISHERMEN IN THE NORTH SEA AND TOOK THEM TO SENNELAGER. THEY CHARGED THEM WITHOUT A SHRED OF EVIDENCE WITH BEING "MINE LAYERS." THEY ORDERED THEM TO BE PUNISHED WITHOUT A TRIAL.
THAT PUNISHMENT CONSISTED IN SHAVING ALL THE HAIR OFF ONE SIDE OF THE HEAD AND FACE.
THE HUNS THEN MARCHED THEIR VICTIMS THROUGH THE STREETS AND EXPOSED THEM TO THE JEERS OF THE GERMAN POPULACE.

BRITISH SAILORS! LOOK! READ! AND REMEMBER!

and searched 1,610 merchant ships between December 1914 and July 1915. A further 1,400 had been added by the end of the year. Cargoes thought to be bound for Germany were often confiscated. As for Germany's own merchant fleet, various armed British vessels were widely deployed to sink them.

By the spring of 1915, Germany's economy was beginning to feel the pinch—exports had virtually dried up and

imports were falling. Industry was increasingly short of vital raw materials. although goods originally intended for civilian production were diverted to military production. Certain foodstuffs were also increasingly in short supply. Early in 1916 things were made worse still when the British established the Ministry of Blockade to oversee

a more coordinated approach to tightening the continuing stranglehold on Germany.

The blockade was one of the less publicized strategies devised to defeat Germany. Nevertheless, it was an important part of the effort to defeat Germany and played a considerable role in bringing about the final Allied victory.

the political head of the navy, summed up the position: "He [Jellicoe] is the only man who could lose the war in an afternoon." The same could have been said of Ingenohl. The British were content to maintain what they termed a "distant blockade" of Germany.

Plans to impose an economic blockade of Germany were drawn up in 1912 and overhauled in 1914. The British knew that Germany had the greatest level of maritime trade of any of the continental European countries and a merchant fleet second in size only to that of Britain. Although the legality of Britain's plans were dubious in international law, the move toward a blockade began shortly before the war.

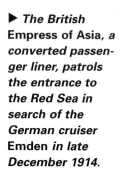

▶ *The British* **Empress of Asia**, *a converted passenger liner, patrols the entrance to the Red Sea in search of the German cruiser* **Emden** *in late December 1914.*

▼ *The German warship* **Frauenlob** *was damaged during the Battle of Helgoland Bight in August 1914.*

First Lord of the Admiralty Winston Churchill ordered the main fleet to its stations on July 29. From these locations it could block the German High Seas Fleet's only exits into the Atlantic and beyond—the Straits of Dover, which marked the easterly entrance of the English Channel, and the passages between Norway, Scotland, and Greenland. Minefields were laid in certain areas to lend additional support to the efforts of the Home Fleet's warships.

Civilian ships, often fast passenger liners or cargo vessels, were converted to warships just by adding armaments. These became known as armed merchant cruisers, and their role was to search for German surface raiders preying on Allied and neutral merchant ships. They also played a leading role in preventing maritime trade with Germany by stopping and searching the suspect vessels of any country, much to the annoyance of neutrals—not least the United States. One of the most successful of such units was the Northern Patrol, which operated in the North Sea and consisted of 24 vessels. Several thousand vessels were boarded and searched for contraband in the first year. Only the Baltic Sea was open to German merchant ships, which carried

vital Swedish iron ore to supply the country's armaments industries, but even here British submarines began to menace the trade.

Skirmishes in the North Sea

Although the two country's rival battleships did not meet in action in 1914, their lighter forces did, as each side probed the North Sea seeking an advantage. The British took the lead, making a diversionary attack against German warships active in the Helgoland Bight off the coast of northern Germany. Its aim was to distract German attention from the English Channel, where ships were moving the British Expeditionary Force (BEF) to France. The attack on August 28 was spearheaded by the 1st Light Cruiser Squadron under Commodore Reginald Tyrwhitt.

Initially, Tyrwhitt held the upper hand, but his forces began to suffer as more and larger German warships entered the fray. He was saved by the intervention of Vice-Admiral David Beatty's powerful 1st Battlecruiser Squadron. Three German light cruisers, *Ariadne*, *Köln*, and *Mainz*, were sunk and three others damaged. Several British warships were damaged, but none was sunk. Helgoland Bight was a great boost

FRANZ VON HIPPER

Hipper (1863–1932) was the ablest of Germany's admirals in World War I. For all but the final few weeks of the conflict, he led the High Seas Fleet's scouting forces—chiefly cruisers and battlecruisers—which could act either as the eyes of the main fleet or carry out independent actions, often hit-and-run raids on the east coast of England.

Before World War I Hipper served on torpedo boats and then progressed to larger ships, principally light and armored cruisers, between 1908 and 1912. After hostilities commenced, his first major engagement was at the Battle of the Dogger Bank in 1915, where one of his vessels, *Blücher*, was sunk and his flagship, *Seydlitz*, badly damaged. The following year he took part in the Battle of Jutland, where his actions enabled the bulk of the High Seas Fleet to escape destruction under the guns of the British Home Fleet.

In August 1918 Hipper replaced Admiral Reinhard Scheer as overall commander of the High Seas Fleet, but he had little opportunity for further action. He planned a last sortie against the British by his forces—one that had little chance of influencing the outcome of the war—but it only prompted an outbreak of mutiny in October and December. His last act of the war was to oversee the surrender to the British of the warships under his command as part of the armistice arrangements.

to British morale, but the euphoria masked shortcomings in naval planning and the coordination of large forces. The action confirmed to the Germans that they needed to avoid large-scale battles with the British Home Fleet.

The Germans did mount aggressive operations of their own using surface warships. These consisted of bombarding towns along the east coast of England. Such actions had several aims: to tie up the British Home Fleet or lure elements of it into an unequal struggle; to cause damage to port facilities; and to undermine the morale of British civilians. The first attack occurred on November 3, when Great Yarmouth and Goreleston were bombarded with little impact. A more serious raid occurred on December 16, when Admiral Franz von Hipper's 1st Scouting Division (the battlecruisers *Derfflinger*, *Moltke*, *Von der Tann*, and *Seydlitz* and the heavy cruiser *Blücher*), supported by light cruisers and destroyers, attacked West Hartlepool, Scarborough, and Whitby. There were civilian casualties—Scarborough was hit by 300 shells in thirty minutes, and 17 civilians died; West Hartlepool recorded 1,150 shells and 102 dead; and 50 shells struck Whitby, killing two.

The Germans had to break off their attacks after two hours as they were aware that strong elements of the Home Fleet, which had been forewarned of the German attack on the 15th by intelligence sources, were steaming to engage them. Due to a combination of luck, poor coordination between British vessels, and sea mist, Hipper escaped. In Britain the public response was one of outrage—apart from West Hartlepool none of the coastal targets had any major military significance. There was

KEY FIGURES

ADMIRAL DAVID BEATTY

Beatty (1871–1936) joined Britain's Royal Navy as a teenager and reached the highest level of command. He won a reputation for boldness in battle, calm leadership, and first-rate tactical skill. Beatty played a leading part in all of the major surface actions against Germany's High Seas Fleet in the North Sea during World War I.

As a young man Beatty saw considerable active service and was promoted to captain in 1900 and to rear admiral seven years later. Shortly before the outbreak of the war, he was given command of the British Home Fleet's battlecruiser squadron. As the squadron commander, he fought at Helgoland Bight (1914), the Dogger Bank (1915), and at Jutland (1916). Although his battlecruisers suffered two losses in the last battle, Beatty emerged with his reputation enhanced.

In December 1916 he replaced Admiral John Jellicoe as commander of the entire Home Fleet. Beatty's initial concern in his new position was to rectify deficiencies in the Home Fleet's warships, shells, and command and control systems that had been highlighted at the Battle of Jutland. In terms of strategy, Beatty continued the existing policy of maintaining a distant economic blockade of Germany—which bore fruit as the war continued.

also strong press criticism of the Home Fleet's seeming inability to prevent the German raiders' escape.

Hipper attempted to launch a second attack on Britain's east coast in late January 1915. The German battlecruisers sailed on the 23rd, unaware that British intelligence knew about the attack and had sent Admiral David Beatty with several battlecruisers to intercept Hipper. The two forces clashed off the Dogger Bank shoals on the 24th. Hipper was outnumbered and outgunned and turned for home at full speed. However, Beatty's warships were able to close on an older German vessel, *Blücher*, and sink it. Hipper's flagship, *Seydlitz*, was also damaged. By concentrating on the *Blücher*, Beatty had allowed the rest of Hipper's fleet to escape, although not before it damaged Beatty's flagship, the *Lion*.

Although the battle was a British victory, it highlighted several weaknesses in the Royal Navy. British signals were often garbled and ambiguous, and the level of gunnery was far from impressive. *Lion*, for example, had scored just

▲ Just after noon on January 24, 1915, during the Battle of Dogger Bank, the German cruiser *Blücher* **is filmed sinking. Some 800 Germans went down with the warship.**

◄ The war in the North Sea was relatively limited as both the British and Germans had no wish to suffer a decisive defeat. There were skirmishes, one major battle, and several bombardments of Britain's east coast but it was the British blockade that was to prove vital in Germany's ultimate defeat.

Germany's submarine blockade

As 1914 ended, the threat posed by German surface warships to Britain's maritime trade had been all but eradicated, and the rival fleets remained in their various anchorages around the North Sea, less than 24 hours of steaming apart. However, Britain's maritime security was to be much more severely tested in 1915 by a relatively new weapon—the submarine.

There had been warning signs in the first months of the war. On October 17, 1914, a German submarine (U-boat) had penetrated the defenses of the Home Fleet's main base at Scapa Flow and then launched two ineffective torpedo attacks before escaping. More successful attacks had occurred, however. On September 22, the submarine *U-9* under Captain Otto Weddigen sank three light cruisers, *Aboukir*, *Cressy*, and *Hogue*, in quick succession off the Dutch coast. More than 1,400 men were killed.

EYEWITNESS

CAPTAIN OTTO WEDDIGEN

Weddigen was the commander of the German submarine *U-9*, which sank three British cruisers off the coast of the Netherlands on September 22, 1914. Weddigen later recounted his exploits. Here, the story is taken up after he has already sunk two cruisers, *Aboukir* and *Hogue*, and is attacking the third, *Cressy*:

"When I got within suitable range I sent away my third attack. This time I sent a second torpedo after the first to make the strike doubly certain. My crew were aiming like sharpshooters and both torpedoes went to their bull's eye. My luck was with me again, for the enemy was made useless and at once began sinking by her head. Then she careened far over, but all the while her men stayed at the guns looking for their invisible foe. They were brave and true to their country's sea traditions. Then she eventually suffered a boiler explosion and completely turned turtle. With her keel uppermost she floated until the air got out from under her and then she sank with a loud sound, as if a creature in pain.

"The whole affair had taken less than one hour from the time of shooting off the first torpedo until the *Cressy* went to the bottom. Not one of the three had been able to use any of its big guns. I knew the wireless of the three cruisers had been calling for aid. I was still quite able to defend myself, but I knew that news of the disaster would call many English submarines and torpedo-boat destroyers, so, having done my work, I set course for home."

From *The First Submarine Blow Is Struck* by Captain Otto Weddigen.

---

four hits from 243 shells fired. On the plus side, the victory put a halt for some time to German raids on the east coast. Kaiser Wilhelm II, was alarmed by the loss of the *Blücher*, fearing that it confirmed Britain's naval supremacy in the North Sea. He ordered his secretary of the navy, Admiral Alfred von Tirpitz, and the commander of the High Seas Fleet, Admiral von Ingenohl, to act with extreme caution in the area.

▶ *A German submarine looks on as an enemy ship is consumed by fire. This image is from a wartime German postcard and was printed by the government to boost the morale on the home front.*

A final indicator of the submarine's potential came on October 27, when the British battleship *Audacious* was fatally holed by a submarine-laid mine off the southeast coast of Ireland.

Few on either side at the outbreak of World War I appreciated the military possibilities of the submarine. Many senior figures believed that it had neither the endurance nor the hitting power to provide a serious threat. Some also felt that to sink ships by torpedo without warning was too barbarous for anyone to contemplate. Indeed, at the onset of hostilities, Germany had no plans to use submarines to sink merchant vessels. However, at the close of 1914, Germany's naval high command began to press for their use, despite a reluctant emperor and German chancellor, Theobald von Bethmann Hollweg. In February 1915 the navy had its way. On the 2nd the announcement was made: "Germany hereby declares all of

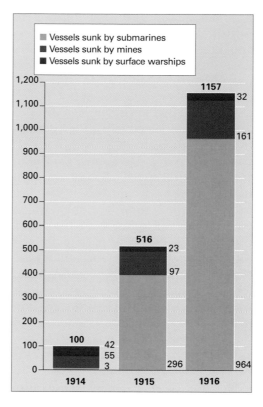

Vessels sunk by submarines
Vessels sunk by mines
Vessels sunk by surface warships

◄ *The growing importance of submarines in Germany's naval strategy is evident from this diagram of Allied ship losses during 1914, 1915, and 1916. It should also be borne in mind that many of the mines that accounted for sinkings were laid by submarines specially designed for the job.*

the waters surrounding Great Britain and Ireland, including the entire British Channel, an area of war, and will therein act against the shipping of the enemy. For this purpose, beginning February 18, 1915, she will endeavor to destroy every enemy merchant ship that is found in this area, even if it is not always possible to avert the peril which threatens persons and cargoes. Neutrals are therefore warned against further entrusting crews and passengers and wares to such ships."

Unrestricted warfare

Although Germany had just 20 U-boats available for the unrestricted submarine campaign (sinking any vessel without due warning), of which just four were immediately available, they had already shown their worth—some 12 merchant ships had been destroyed before the February 18 deadline—and U-boat successes were destined to soar throughout 1915 and beyond. In 1914 submarines sent to the bottom a little more than

1.25 percent of the total tonnage of British shipping sunk (surface raiders and mines accounted for the remainder). By the end of 1915 the figure had risen to 87.2 percent. In the same period, 20 U-boats had been lost, but 61 new models had been completed.

Submarines could use either gunfire or torpedoes to attack vessels but generally preferred surface actions where their superior speed allowed them to outrun most merchant vessels. Gunfire would be used to halt a ship, which could then be sunk by close-range shelling or a boarding party equipped with explosive charges. Torpedoes were expensive, and the early boats carried as few as six, and these were reserved for use against warships. However, the torpedo had to be fired underwater, where the submarine's speed was much slower, and it was inaccurate at distances beyond 800 yards (730 m).

That the submarines were successful was in part due to Britain's lack of preparedness to counter them. There was no way to track submarines beneath the surface, and although the most potent weapon available for use against them, the depth charge, was invented early in the war, it did not score any successes until March 1916. Nets or barrages stretching across routes in the English Channel, some fitted with mines, did deter U-boats, and an ad hoc force, the Auxiliary Patrol, comprising yachts, motor-boats, and trawlers, was formed but had little impact. The most likely way to succeed in destroying a submarine was to catch it on the surface and sink it with gunfire or ram it. Destroyers and speedy warships armed with torpedoes might have been used to attack U-boats, but these were needed to protect the battleships of the Home Fleet from Germany's own destroyers.

The British did attempt one tactic to defeat the U-boats that met with some initial success. Knowing that U-boat captains preferred to attack merchant vessels on the surface, decoy vessels known as Q-ships were developed. These had the outward appearance of an unarmed merchant ship or trawler, but instead they carried concealed weapons. It was intended to lure a U-boat to close range on the surface and then destroy it. They had their first success on July 24, 1915, when the Q-ship *Prince Charles* sank the *U-36*. Q-ships had some positive results, but their value declined as submarine captains become wary and attacked targets with torpedoes while submerged.

The successes of the submarines did have dangerous political consequences for Germany, chiefly due to attacks on neutral vessels. Although Germany did warn neutral countries not to allow their citizens to travel on enemy ships, diplomatic incidents did occur. In May 1915 a U-boat torpedoed the *Gulflight*, a U.S. oil tanker. Vigorous protests by the U.S. government led to a German offer of compensation. As the *Gulflight* sinking was still being discussed, a second, more serious incident occurred. On May 7, the *Lusitania* was sunk off the coast of Ireland by the *U-20*; 128 U.S. citizens died (see pages 238–239). President Woodrow Wilson issued increasingly stern warnings, but the Germans prevaricated. On August 19, a third ship, *Arabic*, was sunk by submarine, again with the loss of American lives. Wilson responded in the strongest terms, and Germany agreed to curtail its campaign of unrestricted submarine warfare—for the time being.

Attacks on Turkey

While the submarine campaign was being waged in 1915, the Allies, chiefly the British and French, launched the greatest amphibious operation of the war against Turkey. Discussions on its feasibility began in late 1914; it had several purposes. It was planned to relieve some of the pressure off Russia, which had suffered severe losses on the eastern front in 1914, was facing a major Turkish attack in the Caucasus, and was being starved of supplies due to the

Turkish blockade of the Dardanelles—which was the only route between the Black Sea and Mediterranean Sea. Turkey might be knocked out of the war if the assault was to prove successful; and any defeat of Turkey might induce more Balkan states to throw in their lot with the Allies.

Initially the plan envisaged a purely naval operation, using older battleships to conduct a three-stage operation: the destruction of the Turkish forts and batteries that lined both sides of the Dardanelles; the clearing of the minefields that lay in the narrow straits; and an advance through the Sea of Marmara to Constantinople, the capital of Turkey. Although the plan was enthusiastically adopted by some of Britain's war planners, chiefly First Lord of the Admiralty Winston Churchill, others were doubtful of its chances of success, not least the First Sea Lord, Admiral John Fisher, who believed that a naval operation would only be successful if it was supported by a ground attack.

Despite foreboding in some quarters, the first naval attack began on February 19, 1915, when the fleet, commanded by Admiral Sackville Carden, opened fire. Although the long-range bombardment of the Turkish forts had some impact, it was not sufficient to silence them entirely, and it was decided that closer-range fire would be needed. Following a period of bad weather, the second attack began on the 25th, and progress was better. The forts at the western entrance to the Dardanelles—at Seddülbahir and Kumkale—were subdued (although soon reoccupied by the Turks), and some minefields were successfully cleared. The ships were able to enter the narrows but were still confronted by forts and minefields.

Carden now faced a dilemma. The minefields prevented his warships from getting closer to the key forts at Kilidülbahir and Canakkale, and his minesweepers could not clear the fields without being brought under intense fire from the forts, which were positioned on either side of the narrowest point of the Dardanelles. Attempts to clear the mines, both at night and in daylight, failed. Carden became increasingly pessimistic about his chances but agreed to launch another assault on March 17. However, he became ill and was replaced by Vice-Admiral John de Robeck, his deputy, on the 15th. Three days later, de Robeck attacked with 18 battleships, 4 of which were French.

Eight miles (12 km) from Kilidülbahir and Canakkale, the warships opened fire, inflicting damage on the forts. By midday, de Robeck believed he had inflicted sufficient damage to allow his minesweepers to begin operating and he ordered some of his warships to withdraw. The French *Bouvet*, in the midst of executing a 180-degree turn, struck a

▼ *The British submarine* E11 *returns to base after a mission in the Sea of Marmara. Its captain, Lieutenant-Commander Martin Naismith, spent 96 days at sea during two operations and destroyed 101 enemy ships. However, 50 percent of the submarines in the area were sunk by the Turks or lost in accidents.*

mine in a field laid secretly by the Turks on March 8 and went down with virtually all hands. British battleships then struck Turkish mines; first the *Inflexible* and then the *Irresistable* were damaged, the latter mortally. A rescue ship sent to the scene, *Ocean*, was also sunk.

The attack was a disaster. The Turks had used up all of their large artillery shells and had little left to oppose any further naval attack; the British, however, did not make any further naval attack, believing that the risks were too severe. It was decided that ground troops had to forge a route to Constantinople—a decision that would lead to the operation against the Gallipoli Peninsula (see pages 193–196).

▼ The main areas where Germany's U-boats operated around the British Isles and the sites of several of their most significant sinkings.

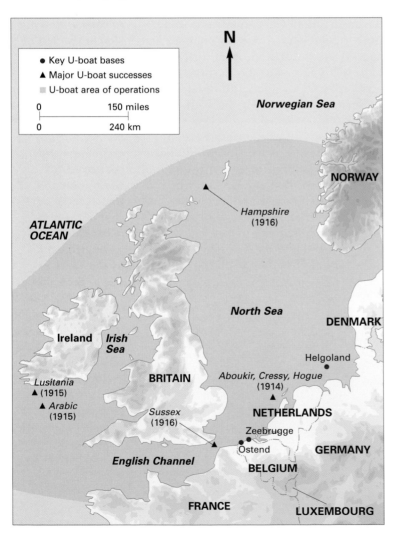

The British did have considerably more success with their submarine forces in the region during 1915. Several vessels were able to push through the Dardanelles and enter the Sea of Marmara, one even attacking shipping in Constantinople's harbor. The submariners faced several difficulties, not least the treacherous and fast-running currents in the Dardanelles, the limited space for maneuver, and minefields. Nevertheless, the first submarine to make the passage successfully, the Australian *AE2*, did so in April 1915. Other boats duly followed, and Turkish movement across the Sea of Marmara was soon halted. The operations ended in late 1915, by which time the strength of the Turkish merchant fleet had been halved, every Turkish battleship had been sunk, and virtually no surface vessels were willing to sail.

Germany relies on its U-boats

By early 1916 it was clear to some of Germany's leaders that if Britain was to be defeated, the submarine campaign had to be intensified, despite the dangers of antagonizing the United States. On February 21 it was announced that Allied merchant ships—but not passenger ships—sailing in the waters off the British Isles would be sunk without warning. However, on March 24, 1916, a German submarine sank the ferry *Sussex* in the English Channel, killing 50 passengers, including three U.S. citizens. President Woodrow Wilson issued warnings, and Germany again agreed to call off surprise attacks.

Despite these restrictions, the U-boats continued to be highly successful. Their torpedoes and deck guns—and mines laid by specially built submarines—exacted a fearful toll on Allied shipping. One of the successes of Germany's mine-laying submarines came on June 5, when the British cruiser *Hampshire* was sunk off the Orkneys. On board was Field Marshal Horatio Kitchener, a key member of the country's War Cabinet,

◀ **The British battlecruiser Indefatigable** *sinks beneath the waves of the North Sea during the Battle of Jutland, June 1, 1916. More than 1,000 men were drowned. The ship was destroyed when a shell fired by the German* **Von der Tann** *caused a magazine to explode.*

design. Three other light cruisers were also sunk. Scheer lost an old battleship, *Pommern*, and the battlecruiser *Lützow*, as well as four cruisers. However, the outcome of the battle was more complex than the losses might suggest.

Most important was the psychological impact Jutland had on Germany's senior commanders. It became clear that the High Seas Fleet was unlikely to inflict a decisive defeat on the British and that the blockade of Germany was still in place. If the High Seas Fleet was unlikely to inflict a crushing defeat on the British, then Germany's naval strategy would have to rely on its U-boats. This was a strategy that had the potential to achieve outstanding results—but it also held potentially disastrous risks.

who was heading a mission to discuss strategy with Russia's military chiefs. There were 12 survivors, but Kitchener was not among them.

Although its submarine fleet dominated Germany's maritime strategy in 1916, its surface forces also attempted to inflict a severe defeat on the British Home Fleet. The commander of the High Seas Fleet, Admiral Reinhard Scheer, devised a plan in which he would lure Britain's battlecruisers into an unequal action in the North Sea against the bulk of his own fleet, using his battlecruisers under Admiral Franz von Hipper as bait. The resultant Battle of Jutland was the only major action involving a large part of the rival fleets during the war. However, the British became aware of the German plan and sailed in full force to meet the threat.

German failure at Jutland

The action, which took place on May 31 and June 1, was not the decisive battle that both sides were looking for. In a sprawling series of encounters involving a total of more than 250 warships, Hipper's command was able to inflict greater losses on the British. Three British battlecruisers, *Indefatigable*, *Invincible*, and *Queen Mary*, were torn apart by internal explosions caused by accurate enemy fire and poor warship

---

EYEWITNESS

GEORGE CRACKNELL

Cracknell, a British sailor, served on the Royal Navy's light cruiser *Champion* during the Battle of Jutland. Here he describes the action:

"I was on the deck most of the time and saw mostly all of it—it was providence which saved us from being blown out of the water—shells, 12-inch [30-cm] etc., fairly rained round us. Saw the *Queen Mary* [a battlecruiser]—about 440 yards [400 m] from us go up in a puff of smoke and flame—afterwards there was nothing more to see only six or seven saved [actually nine]. It was a magnificent sight. Especially after our battlefleet engaged them. But the night was very thrilling. The sky was lit up with flame and intermittent actions were going on all round us. Saw two or three ships on fire and one Hun [derogatory name for German] dreadnought blown up by a torpedo [probably the battlecruiser *Seydlitz*, which survived]. We ran into some big German ships who turned their searchlights on us and blazed away but did not touch us, although bits of shell were picked up on deck. Next morning we had the devil's luck, a torpedo passed within a yard of the stern."

Extract from a personal letter written by Cracknell to his family on June 4, 1916.

The Wider War, 1914–1916

World War I spread beyond the borders of Western and Eastern Europe as other nations joined the conflict. Major campaigns were fought in the Middle East, the Caucasus, Africa, and northern Italy.

At the outbreak of the fighting in August 1914, Germany lost one ally but gained another. Italy, which in 1882 had been a signatory to the Triple Alliance with both Germany and Austria-Hungary, refused to honor its military obligations. On August 3 it declared that the alliance was essentially defensive in nature—one originally drawn up to counter any external threat to its signatories—and that it was Germany and Austria-Hungary who were the aggressors. The Italians stated that they had no obligation under the Triple Alliance to go to war.

However, there were other reasons why Italy shied away from a war declaration. Its government before the war had developed close and friendly ties with those countries opposing Germany and Austria-Hungary. Within Italy itself the alliance had never received widespread public support, as there was considerable animosity toward Austria-Hungary. At its root was the popular cause of irredentism, whose supporters aimed to incorporate external, foreign-controlled areas with large Italian-speaking populations into Italy proper. These were chiefly within the Trentino region to the north of Italy and around the port of Trieste to the northeast,

▼ *Turkey joined the Central Powers and declared war on the Allies in October 1914. Here, Turkish troops march to the front in Palestine.*

both controlled by Austria-Hungary. Equally, the two countries were regional rivals in the Balkans and along the Adriatic Sea. So in 1914 Italy adopted a position of neutrality, one designed not to offend either the Central Powers or those opposing them. However, both the British and French began strenuous diplomatic maneuverings to bring Italy into the war, chiefly by offering considerable territorial gains at the expense of the Austro-Hungarian Empire. The discussions would bear fruit on April 26, 1915, with the signing of the Pact of London. The following month the Italians announced their impending withdrawal from the Triple Alliance.

Ottoman Turkey goes to war

The loss of Italy as an ally was partially offset by Ottoman Turkey's decision to side with the Central Powers. Both Germany and, to a somewhat lesser extent, Austria–Hungary had successfully strengthened their ties with Turkey before 1914, sealing their relationship with a treaty just two days before the outbreak of war. Although the treaty did not pledge Turkey to support Germany militarily, events moved quickly. The following day the British authorities requisitioned two dreadnought battleships, originally destined for Turkey, that were nearing completion in British shipyards. The German response was to offer two of its own warships—the battlecruiser *Goeben* and the light cruiser *Breslau*—to the Turks. These reached Constantinople (now Istanbul) and were incorporated into the navy. The two warships tipped the balance. Turkey's leadership, eager to restore some of the country's prestige as the major power across the Middle East and in the Black Sea, joined the Central Powers. On October 29, the *Goeben* and

▼ *Evidence of Italy's commitment to the war against the Central Powers—civilians look on as troops head for the front to face the Austro-Hungarians in northern Italy, late spring 1915.*

Breslau and Goeben

At the outbreak of war Germany was eager to find further allies to support the cause of the Central Powers. The transfer of two German warships to the Turkish Navy in the first days of the war led to Turkey's siding with the Central Powers against the Allies. The inability of the Allies to prevent the transfer of the two warships proved to be a costly blunder.

At the outbreak of World War I, the British commandeered two dreadnought battleships, *Sultan Osman I* and *Reshadieh*, that were nearing completion in a British shipyard and destined for service in the Turkish Navy. As both warships had been paid for, the Turks took an unfavorable view of the British act. Germany looked to exploit the situation in the hope of bringing Ottoman Turkey into the war. The means to this end lay with two German warships in the Mediterranean—the battlecruiser *Goeben* and the light cruiser *Breslau*—under the command of Vice-Admiral Wilhelm Souchon.

The first act of the war for the *Breslau* and *Goeben* was to shell the French ports of Bône and Philippeville in Algeria on August 4 to disrupt convoys transferring troops from the colony to mainland Europe. Souchon then used, later on the same day, the speed of his two vessels to escape two British battlecruisers, *Indomitable* and *Indefatigable*, under Admiral Archibald Milne. The British continued to patrol the western Mediterranean, believing that the two German warships would continue to stalk troop convoys. However, Souchon now made for the eastern Mediterranean, heading for Constantinople, the Turkish capital, by way of the Dardanelles.

During the German warships' cruise through the eastern Mediterranean, a British force of four light cruisers under Rear Admiral Ernest Troubridge had a chance to close on the *Breslau* and *Goeben*, but Troubridge, acting on strict orders, believed they constituted a superior force and allowed them to progress eastward without seeking battle. On August 10, Souchon passed through the Dardanelles and reached the Turkish capital the following day. The warships were then nominally transferred to the Turkish Navy, although Souchon remained in charge of them (he later commanded the whole Turkish Navy until September 1917) and the crews were overwhelmingly German. The *Goeben* was renamed *Yavuz Sultan Selim*, while the *Breslau* became known as the *Midillu*.

▶ Goeben, *later named* Yavuz Sultan Selim, *did not put to sea between August and late October 1914, when it shelled Russian Black Sea ports.*

▲ Breslau, *a light cruiser formerly serving with the German fleet, was completed in 1912.*

The transfer brought the likelihood of a Turkish declaration of war for the Central Powers ever closer, and it was indeed the warships that later signaled Turkish intentions. On October 29–30, they and other Turkish vessels attacked a number of Russian ports on the Black Sea, including Odessa. Hostilities officially began on the 31st. For the price of two warships Germany had added a third member to the Central Powers.

The subsequent careers of the *Breslau* and *Goeben* were far from distinguished, however.

The *Breslau* was finally destroyed in January 1918 during a raid on Mudros. Initially holed by a mine, it was finally sunk by air attacks. The *Goeben* was more fortunate; it saw action against the Russian Black Sea Fleet and made a number of sorties into the Mediterranean. The warship also took part alongside *Breslau* in the sortie of January 1918, struck a mine, and ran aground. However, it survived a fierce air bombardment, during which 500 bombs were dropped on it, but only two hit. The *Goeben* was finally towed to safety. Later repaired and modernized, the warship continued to serve with the Turkish Navy until 1960.

◀ *Troops of the Indian Army and their British officers man defenses along the Suez Canal in Egypt. Although vital to the British cause, the Turks made only one unsuccessful attempt to capture it.*

▼ *British naval infantry undergo training in assault tactics prior to the amphibious assault on the Turkish-held Gallipoli Peninsula in April 1915.*

Breslau signaled Turkey's future intentions by bombarding three Russian ports on the Black Sea.

The Turkish war declaration presented the Allies with several strategic problems. Chief among these was the closure of the Dardanelles, which effectively blocked the major sea route between Britain and France on the one hand and Russia on the other. Equally, the British were concerned about the potential Turkish threat to the Suez Canal, which linked much of the British Empire with Britain itself.

Fighting for the Suez Canal

The Suez Canal cut through Egypt, which had a border with Palestine, a Turkish province, to the east. A Turkish advance from Palestine against the virtually undefended canal had potentially disastrous consequences. The British moved to protect their interests around the Mediterranean Sea and Egypt. On November 5 the island of Cyprus was annexed for possible use as a forward base for future operations against Asia Minor, and a protectorate was declared over Egypt on December 18. British

troops under the command of General John Maxwell were immediately sent to protect the Suez Canal.

By early 1915 Maxwell had organized his defenses along the canal but seemed unwilling to take the battle to the Turks in Palestine; indeed, the enemy made its own move against Egypt. On January 14 a force of 22,000 men under the Turkish minister of marine, Djemal Pasha, moved from its base at Beersheba in Palestine and crossed the Sinai Peninsula, heading for the canal. Thanks to the organizational skills of Djemal's chief of staff, German General Friedrich Kress von Kressenstein, the Turks had all they needed to make a successful crossing of the Sinai Desert (the provision of water would become a major problem for both sides during the war in the Middle East). However,

despite the best efforts of Djemal and Kressenstein, the Turkish attack on the Suez Canal on February 2 was easily rebuffed by the British. The Turks were forced to withdraw to Beersheba after having suffered some 2,000 casualties.

Invasion of Gallipoli

While the fighting in the Sinai Peninsula was dying down in early 1915, the Allies, primarily at the instigation of the British, were preparing to deliver what they believed would be a decisive blow against Turkey itself, considered to be one of the weaker of the Central Powers. The British plan was to break the deadlock of the war—typified by the stagnation on the western front—by mounting a direct naval attack on the Turkish capital, Constantinople (now Istanbul), by way of the Dardanelles and the Sea of Marmara. Success would force the Turkish authorities to sue for peace, and such a breakthrough would open the sea route to Russia by way of the Black Sea. The naval attack, which was delivered between February and March 1915, had been a failure (see pages 184–186), but the Allies opted to continue the campaign with a ground assault on the Gallipoli Peninsula.

The plans were rushed through in March and April, while the troops, equipment, and transports were gathered in the eastern Mediterranean and Egypt. A general, Ian Hamilton, was placed in overall command of some 78,000 troops—mostly British, but with a French division and significant numbers of men from Australia and New Zealand. The armada was supposed to have gathered in Mudros Bay on the island of Lemnos in mid-March, but the loading of the various vessels had been so haphazard in England that they moved to Alexandria, Egypt, to reorganize. A four-week delay ensued, allowing the Turks—forewarned of the impending assault—to improve their defenses in the threatened sector. Some 60,000 Turkish troops under German

---

KEY FIGURES

MUSTAFA KEMAL

Mustafa Kemal (1881–1938) remains a revered figure in Turkey and is regarded as the father of the modern Turkish state. Born Mustafa Rizi, he attended Harbiye Staff College in Istanbul, where he proved exceptional in mathematics and earned the name Kemal, meaning perfection.

After taking part in several campaigns against rebels within the Ottoman Empire, his first taste of full-scale warfare was in the Italo-Turkish War (1911–1912) and the First and Second Balkan Wars (1912 and 1913). In the months following Turkey's entry into World War I Kemal played a key role in defeating the Allied assault on the Gallipoli Peninsula (1915–1916), and then he fought against the Russians in the Caucasus, where he was promoted to general in April 1916.

By mid-1917 Kemal was active in Syria, where he wrote a report suggesting that Turkey should abandon many of its far-flung provinces to concentrate on the defense of the Turkish homeland. The suggestion was badly received, and Kemal was given indefinite sick leave in December. However, as the Turkish position in Palestine deteriorated, Kemal returned to active service. Facing superior enemy forces, there was little he could do but retreat into Turkey.

After 1918 Kemal became a key figure in driving out the Greek forces that had been allowed by the victorious Allies to occupy much of Turkey's Mediterranean coastline, and he became head of a new government. Resisting pressure from the Allies, who virtually wanted to end Turkish independence, and from Turkey's ruling elite, he was able to establish the Republic of Turkey in 1923. Kemal was able to transform Turkey into a modern state and was given the title Atatürk, meaning Father of the Turks.

General Liman von Sanders were available to defend the peninsula, but they were initially widely dispersed.

The Allied landings began on April 25. The two main assaults, by the British at Cape Hellas on the tip of the peninsula and the Australian and New Zealand Army Corps (ANZACs) at Ari Burna some 15 miles (24 km) further along, failed to gain their objectives. French troops landed at Kumkale on the other side of the straits with some success. At Ari Burna the ANZACs began well, moving inland to seize the lower slopes of Chunuk Bair Ridge. Further progress was blocked by the local Turkish commander, Mustafa

Kemal, who rushed troops to the threatened point of the line and pushed back the ANZACs almost to their landing beaches, where they dug in after suffering 5,000 casualties. Progress was little better at Cape Helles. The landings, which were poorly coordinated, ran into a wall of heavy Turkish fire, and the British 29th Division suffered severe losses. Some units managed to advance to their first objective, the commanding heights of Achi Baba, but lacking firm orders they did not secure the position, thereby allowing it to be occupied by the Turks. As the first day ended, the landings had failed, and the overland route to Constantinople had been

blocked by comparatively few Turks. Reinforcements were also en route to ensure that the Allies did not break out.

For the next three months the fighting was stalemated. The Allies sent various new units to Gallipoli, but each attempt to gain ground made little progress and resulted in severe losses. The Allied soldiers had to endure horrendous privations. Disease became rife in the insanitary conditions, the food was putrid, water was often in short supply, the heat was frequently unbearable, and no beachhead was entirely safe—all were overlooked by the Turks, for whom matters were little better.

Attempts to break the stalemate
In August Hamilton made a bold attempt to break the deadlock with a new amphibious assault in force. There was also to be a major effort by the ANZACs, who were tasked with attacking Chunuk Bair and other points on Sari Bair Ridge, and a subsidiary attack in the direction of the town of Krithia by the force at Cape Helles. A further diversionary attack was to involve three divisions, which were to launch an amphibious attack at Suvla Bay to the north of the ANZAC beachhead. The various attacks met with mixed fortune. The ANZAC assault, although fierce,

▼ *A shell from a Turkish gun bursts near one of the piers used by the British to unload supplies at Cape Hellas on the Gallipoli Peninsula. Virtually every sector of the beachhead was overlooked by Turkish positions.*

KEY FIGURES

C. ALLANSON

Allanson, a British major, took part in the fighting at Gallipoli during 1915. In August he and his men took part in a major attack on the Turkish forces. Allanson's troops, accompanied by a unit of Gurkhas (Nepalese soldiers fighting for the British), were to attack a position known as Hill Q:

"I never saw such artillery preparation; the trenches were being torn to pieces; the accuracy was marvellous, as we were just below. Then off we dashed. At the top we met the Turks: [Lieutenant] Le Marchand went down, a bayonet through the heart. I got one through the leg and then, for about 10 minutes, we fought hand to hand, we bit and fisted, and used rifles and pistols as clubs; blood was flying about like spray from a hair-wash bottle.

"As I looked round I saw we were not being supported, and thought I could best help by going after those [Turks] who had retreated in front of us. We dashed down, but had only got 300 feet [90 m] down when I saw a flash in the bay and suddenly our own navy put six 12-inch [30-cm] monitor shells into us, and all was terrible confusion; it was a deplorable disaster; we were obviously mistaken for Turks, and we had to get back. It was an appalling sight; the first hit a Gurkha in the face; the place was a mass of blood and limbs and screams, and we all flew back to the summit."

Extract from Allanson's personal diary, July–December 1915.

was blunted by strong Turkish resistance, while the attack at Cape Helles enjoyed only moderate success. It was Suvla Bay that briefly suggested victory. The landing, led by General Frederick Stopford, was made virtually unopposed. A general with drive and initiative could have moved inland rapidly, offering the possibility of cutting off the Turkish troops farther down the peninsula from Constantinople and forcing them to retreat in haste or surrender. Stopford was not the man for the job, however, and little progress had been made before Turkish reinforcements flooded into the area.

Again the fighting became a trench-bound stalemate. As summer gave way to fall, hopes of reaching Constantinople ended. Hamilton was sacked. His replacement, General Charles Monro, recommended a total withdrawal. Under the circumstances this was a tricky proposition, and losses were potentially high. Nevertheless the plan was approved on November 23. The two-stage evacuation began in mid-December 1915 and it continued into January 1916. Overseen by General William Birdwood, the withdrawal was a remarkable masterpiece of organization and planning—not a single Allied soldier became a casualty, and the Turks had little indication of what was taking place until it was too late. However, Allied casualties were severe enough—some 250,000 men. The Turks recorded similarly large losses.

The Mesopotamian campaign

With Turkey's entry into the war, the British faced an immediate threat to their interests—centered on the oil fields—in the Persian Gulf. A major force drawn from the British-led Indian Army was already protecting Bahrain, which had major oil-refining facilities, and it was detailed to launch an attack into Turkish-controlled Mesopotamia. The amphibious landings began on October 23. The small Turkish garrisons were forced to retreat, and Basra was captured on November 23.

Although the initial British attacks into Mesopotamia were small scale and limited in scope, by early 1915 more

▼ *Indian troops board local craft at Basra, the recently captured Turkish port at the head of the Persian Gulf, in 1915. Their initial objective was to protect British oil installations in the Gulf, but their mission was soon enlarged to include the capture of Baghdad. The decision had disastrous consequences.*

ambitious plans were being laid to capture Baghdad. If it were captured, the British would be able to use it as a springboard for an advance into the heart of Turkey itself or perhaps to support operations in Palestine. To this end reinforcements were sent from India, and overall command was placed in the hands of General John Nixon.

While the British built up their forces, the Turks launched probing attacks toward Basra. From April 12 to 14 a Turkish attack on a British outpost at Qurna, north of Basra, was repulsed; a similar attack on Ahwaz, some 50 miles (80 km) north of Basra, was blocked on the 24th. Sensing that the Turks had few resources to protect Baghdad, Nixon ordered General Charles Townshend to scout along the Tigris River toward Baghdad to discover the Turkish dispositions and strengths.

Townshend began well. On May 31 his troops took a Turkish outpost near Qurna and moved forward to occupy Amara on June 3. He was supported by General George Gorringe, whose force advanced along the Euphrates River in

The various war theaters in the Middle East between 1914 and 1916. The fighting centered on three areas—Mesopotamia, the Caucasus, and Egypt and Palestine.

a move to protect Townshend's left flank. The principal objective was the Turkish garrison at Nasiriya, which was compelled to withdraw after a month-long campaign that ended with the fall of the town on July 24. With his flank secure Townshend now led his enlarged force northward toward Baghdad, but every mile he advanced took him farther and farther away from the main supply base at Basra.

Townshend's first objective was Kut-el-Amara, and by September 16 he was at Sannaiyet, just a little way from his goal. The local Turkish commander, Nur-ud-Din Pasha, had entrenched his 10,000 men, and they were supported by 38 artillery pieces. Townshend had fewer

guns—28—and just 1,000 more troops. Despite his clear lack of superiority, Townshend attacked and won a considerable victory. The Turks were forced to retreat toward Ctesiphon, halfway between Kut-el-Amara and Baghdad, after having suffered 5,300 casualties. The British lost a total of 1,230 men. Baghdad seemed within range, but the British advance halted, chiefly due to a lack of transport.

Senior British military figures, seeing that Baghdad was nearly within their grasp, ordered Nixon and Townshend to move on the city as soon as it was practical. They brushed aside concerns that the British force was too overstretched to undertake such a major operation and that the Turks would undoubtedly oppose it with as much strength as they could muster. Despite these worries, Townshend resumed his advance toward Baghdad by way of Ctesiphon on November 11, unaware that Nur-ud-Din now commanded some 18,000 strongly entrenched troops backed by 45 artillery pieces. Having been forced to detach several units to protect his lines of communication, Townshend had around 11,000 troops and 30 artillery pieces.

Townshend began his attempt to crush the Turkish forces on November 22. Initially he was successful, breaking through their first line of defenses and holding onto their gains in the face of several counterattacks. However, more Turkish reinforcements then arrived, and Townshend, increasingly outnumbered, was forced to order a retreat back to Kut-el-Amara on the 26th. British losses totaled 4,600 men, while those of the Turks reached some 6,200.

Arriving at Kut-el-Amara, Townshend ordered the town to be fortified. He had two months of supplies to hand and expected to be able to survive any Turkish siege until a relief column could arrive. The Turks arrived outside the British-held town on December 2.

Any British relief efforts directed toward Kut-el-Amara were delayed by the need to bring troops from overseas, chiefly from India; as a consequence relief operations did not begin until January 1916. The first attempt to breach the Turkish siege lines around Kut-el-Amara was led by General Fenton Aylmer; it failed. In March a second, led by Aylmer's replacement, General George Gorringe, also broke down in front of the Turkish defenders, who were being organized by German General Kolmar von der Goltz. Inside Kut-el-Amara, the situation was fast reaching crisis point. Casualties were mounting steadily and food was desperately short, despite attempts to air-drop supplies. On April 29 Townshend was forced to accept the inevitable and surrender with his 8,000 troops.

The defeat of Townshend and the forces sent to break the siege of Kut-el-Amara provoked something of a crisis within the British leadership, and the military activity in Mesopotamia came

▲ The British garrison besieged by the Turks at Kut-el-Amara from late December 1915 quickly ran short of supplies. Attempts at air-dropping rations by small aircraft proved wholly inadequate. Here, a British ground-crew prepares one such aircraft for a supply drop.

◄ British forces near Ctesiphon, south of Baghdad. It was the high-water mark of the first attempt to capture Mesopotamia in 1915 but was soon followed by a headlong retreat.

▼ Following the British defeat at Kut-el-Amara, reinforcements were rushed to Mesopotamia, including many drawn from the Indian Army. Here, Sikh troops are being transported up the Euphrates River to a forward base, 1916.

operation was ambitious and was argued against by Germany's senior military adviser in Turkey, General Otto Liman von Sanders. Despite his protests and concerns, the attack went ahead.

At its head was the Turkish minister of war, Enver Pasha. He had little military experience yet decided to advance from his base at Erzerum in the depths of winter and through mountainous and inhospitable terrain. Enver's objective was the city of Kars, a little way over the Russo-Turkish border. The advance soon stalled, though, as the Russians moved into Turkey to block the Turks.

At the Battle of Sarikamish the Turks suffered a defeat. The Russian commander, General Vorontsov, launched a counterattack at the end of December. Although the fighting continued into the new year, the Turks were soundly beaten, incurring heavy losses. As many as 30,000 became casualties during the five-day battle and many more died during the 14-day retreat back to Erzerum—fewer than 18,000 troops actually survived the ordeal. Enver Pasha temporarily surrendered his command and returned to Constantinople. Abdul Kerim was named his successor.

Although Enver Pasha's ambitious offensive into the Caucasus was defeated, Vorontsov did not act decisively. Because of his lack of drive he was replaced by General Nikolai Yudenich,

almost to a halt for most of what remained of 1916. Only in August did matters change, with the appointment of General Frederick Maude as the local commander. Initially, however, he was forced to remain on the defensive until reinforcements arrived. On December 13, Maude resumed his advance on Baghdad at the head of some 165,000 men. The fate of the ancient city would not, however, be decided until 1917.

War in the Caucasus

The Turks made their first move against Russia in November 1914—an advance from the northeastern corner of Turkey into the Russian-held Caucasus. The

PEOPLE AND WAR

ARMENIAN GENOCIDE

Turkey's entry into World War I gave its leadership the opportunity to undertake in Asia Minor a deliberate policy of what today would be called ethnic cleansing. The policy, directed by Interior Minister Mehmed Talaat Pasha and Minister of War Enver Pasha, focused on two ethnic groups.

One of these groups, the Greeks, lived along the Mediterranean coast of Turkey, and the other, the Armenians, lived in northeast Turkey along the borders with Russia and Persia (now Iran). The Armenians, a Christian minority in a Muslim country, bore the brunt of the campaign, particularly as they were suspected of supporting and being armed by Russia during the conflict.

Actions against the Armenians began in February 1915. Some were massacred outright, particularly the 100,000 serving in the armed forces and the leaders of local communities, while others were transported to inhospitable parts of the Ottoman Turkish Empire, principally Syria and Mesopotamia. Many never reached their final destination due to outright murder or the effects of disease, illness, and the lack of food.

Although the scale and degree of official backing for the campaign against the Armenians has been questioned by some, there is little doubt that it was prosecuted with considerable force. Estimates vary, but it has been suggested that between 750,000 and 1.5 million Armenians—out of a population of two million or so—died in massacres, by starvation, or during the forced resettlement. In the second half of 1915 alone some 500,000 were massacred.

who launched an attack into northeastern Turkey in the spring of 1915. The Russian advance was supported by an uprising of the Christian Armenian minority that lived in Muslim Turkey. The Turks had recently launched a murderous campaign against the Armenians. Men, women, and children were massacred, and their towns and villages razed to the ground in a government-directed genocide intended to rid Turkey of what it feared was a dangerous, pro-Russian "enemy within."

Despite the Turkish campaign the Armenians' uprising had some success. They seized the fortress city of Van on April 20, which they held until the arrival of some of Yudenich's troops on May 19. However, the Turks under Abdul Kerim counterattacked toward Van, inflicting two defeats on part of Yudenich's command in quick succession at the Battles of Malazgirt and Karakose. Yudenich, one of the more talented Russian commanders of the war, did not panic and laid his own plans for a counteroffensive. He sent 22,000 men under General N. N. Baratov to fall on the left flank of the advancing Turks. Kerim was taken by surprise and forced into making a retreat after suffering major losses.

The fighting in Armenia continued to ebb and flow over the following weeks until the Turks eventually gained the upper hand. The Russians were forced to abandon Van, which the Turks occupied on August 5. In part in response to the loss of Van, the Russian command structure was reorganized. Although Yudenich kept his local command, he was given a superior to answer to—Grand Duke Nicholas, the uncle of Czar Nicholas II. For the grand duke, the appointment was a demotion. He had recently overseen a headlong retreat of the Russian Army on the eastern front and, as the commander in chief, had been blamed for the catastrophe. The czar effectively sacked him and assumed his position as supreme commander. Despite the setback, the grand duke was an experienced commander and began to lay plans for an offensive in the Caucasus. Shortages of troops and equipment, however, would delay the offensive until the beginning of 1916.

Italy joins the Allies

Following their abandonment of the Triple Alliance with Austria-Hungary and Germany on May 3, 1915, the Italians moved swiftly. A declaration of war on Austria-Hungary was announced on May 24 and on Bulgaria on October 20 (Germany did not follow until August 28, 1916). Italy's military leadership, under its commander in chief, General Luigi Cadorna, implemented its military plans rapidly. In the north holding forces were detailed to defend those parts of northern Italy that ran around the salient of the Austro-Hungarian Trentino region. The main thrust of the Italian Army was in the northeast, directed against the line of the Isonzo River, chiefly in the direction of the town of Gorizia. Although Gorizia was the initial target, the Italians hoped to crash through the Austro-Hungarian defenses to take Trieste and then advance on Vienna, the Austro-Hungarian capital. As events proved, such plans were too ambitious.

Between the outbreak of war in 1914 and Italy's declaration of war in May 1915, the Austro-Hungarians had heavily fortified their border with Italy along the Isonzo. Troop reinforcements had been sent there and defensive lines built. The area's natural terrain—steep-sided mountains with narrow river valleys—also greatly aided the defenders. Within weeks of the May declaration the local Austro-Hungarian commander, General Svetozan Borojevic von Bojna, had some 100,000 troops available to meet the expected Italian onslaught along the Isonzo. Many had recent experience of combat in the Balkans and on the eastern front. The Italian Army, although numerically stronger with some 875,000 men in total, was far from ready for a full-scale war and had had little time to prepare for action since war had been announced. It was also acutely short of basic supplies and equipment and was particularly deficient in artillery and machine guns.

Two Italian armies—the Second Army under General Pietro Frugoni and the Third Army commanded by the Duke of Aosta—were committed to the attack, which became known as the First Battle of the Isonzo. A total of 200,000

▲ Austro-Hungarian troops on the Italian front man an isolated mountain outpost along the Isonzo River during the summer of 1915.

troops and 200 artillery pieces were available for the enterprise, which began on June 23. The Italians hammered away at the Austro-Hungarians until July 7 but made little progress.

The Second Battle of the Isonzo took place between July 18 and August 3. Despite Cadorna's having increased the provision of artillery in the sector, the Italians failed to make any breakthrough and suffered 60,000 casualties. Austro-Hungarian casualties totaled close to 45,000 men. The Third Battle of the Isonzo began on October 18, with the Italians deploying some 1,200 artillery pieces. By November 4, however, they were no nearer to capturing their initial objective of Gorizia, let alone advancing to Trieste and beyond. A fourth battle followed in quick succession. Fought between November 20 and December 2, it took the same pattern as the others. Total Italian casualties in the final two attacks along the Isonzo reached 117,000 men. Austria-Hungary announced a figure of more than 70,000 troops.

Russian successes against the Turks
Back in the Caucasus, by early 1916 the senior Russian commander, Grand Duke Nicholas, had finally overcome

his shortages of troops and equipment and was ready to launch a broad-front offensive against the Turks. Leading the advance, which began in January, was General Yudenich, who moved forces from Kars toward Erzerum on the 11th. Yudenich inflicted a key defeat at the Battle of Köprukoy on the 18th, forcing the Turks under Abdul Kerim, who were almost surrounded, to retreat back to Erzerum. Turkish losses of 25,000 were severe, many of them having succumbed to the severe cold. Yudenich continued his advance toward Erzerum over the following weeks and succeeded in smashing through the city's ring of forts in a three-day battle in mid-February. A Russian naval force acting in support of Yudenich moved along the coast of the Black Sea to the north. Against minimal Turkish opposition, it captured the port of Trebizond.

The surrender of Erzerum and Trebizond was a serious blow to Turkish morale, but their local commander, Enver Pasha, laid plans to recapture the lost territory. He opted for a broad-fronted advance against the Russians, involving two of his armies. The Third Army, under Vehip Pasha, was tasked with striking out along the coast of the Black Sea, while the Second Army, under Ahmet Izzim Pasha, was to drive on the town of Bitlis in an attempt to move around the Russian left flank.

General Nikolai Yudenich acted promptly to deal with the twin threat, which developed in late June. On July 2, Yudenich attacked the Third Army at Erzinjan. By the 25th the Turks had been shattered, suffering 34,000 casualties. Yudenich now turned his attention to the Second Army. The Turks scored a number of local and temporary victories, notably the capture of Mus and Bitlis by one of the Second Army's corps commanders, Mustafa Kemal, the hero of the recent Turkish victory at Gallipoli. Kemal's successes were short-lived, though, and the Russians recaptured both Mus and Bitlis in the second half of August. Exhausted by the recent battles, both sides went into their winter quarters to recuperate and reequip. There would be no more major fighting in the theater until 1917.

The Trentino counteroffensive

In the spring of 1916 Italy's commander in chief, General Luigi Cadorna, resumed his attempts to break through the Austro-Hungarian defenses along

▼ *Turkish troops with a supply train of pack animals in the Caucasus. The men wear heavy coats to protect them from the bitter weather.*

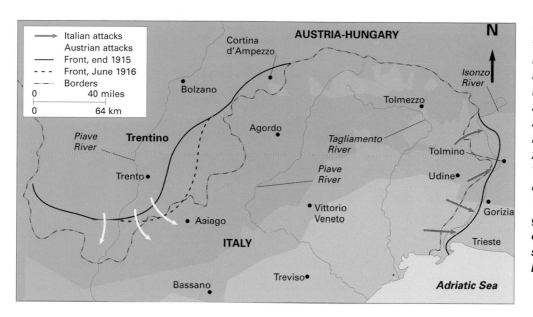

Legend:
→ Italian attacks
→ Austrian attacks
— Front, end 1915
--- Front, June 1916
-·-· Borders

0   40 miles
0   64 km

◀ *The fighting in the southern Alps in 1915 raged to and fro, with Italy making little over-all headway against the Austro-Hungarians. The Austro-Hungarian Trentino counter-offensive in spring 1916 did gain some ground but was ended by supply shortages and Italian attacks.*

the Isonzo River. It was part of an agreement made with the British, French, and Russians at the Chantilly conference north of Paris in December 1915 that roughly simultaneous offensives would be launched on the western, eastern, and Italian fronts. It was believed that Germany and Austria-Hungary would be overstretched and unable to offer an effective counter to Allied offensives delivered on all fronts. However, the fifth battle along the Italian Isonzo sector, which was fought between March 11 and 29, ended in the same way as the preceding four. Italian gains were extremely limited.

Austria-Hungary's senior commander in the theater, Archduke Eugene, was planning his own counterattack. The ground he chose was not along the Isonzo but in the Trentino. The long-planned attack began on May 15. Two Austro-Hungarian armies were earmarked for the advance—the Eleventh Army and the Third Army. Opposing them was General Roberto Brusati's First Army. Brusati's defenses were over-run in the initial stages of the advance and the Austro-Hungarians made some progress, but, as with the Italians along the Isonzo, the mountainous terrain prevented any rapid exploitation of the

initial breakthrough, and the troops began to outpace their heavy artillery and its equipment. Italian reinforcements were able to block the Austro-Hungarian advance by June 10.

The Russian Brusilov Offensive on the eastern front, which had begun on the 4th and was directed against Austro-Hungarian forces there (see pages 162–163), forced Count Franz Conrad von Hötzendorf, Austria-Hungary's commander in chief, to withdraw some of Archduke Eugene's troops from the Trentino and send them to reinforce his crumbling front line in the east. Eugene had to abandon some of his gains in the face of an Italian counter-attack, and the fighting had died down by July 17. The Italians had suffered greatly—their casualties reached some 147,000 men, including 40,000 taken prisoner; they had also had 300 artillery pieces destroyed, captured, or abandoned. Austro-Hungarian losses were around 80,000 men.

The action on the Italian front now switched back to the Isonzo. Cadorna rapidly moved troops from the Trentino, hoping to catch the Austro-Hungarians off balance, and attacked in the direction of Gorizia, believing that the withdrawal of Austro-Hungarian troops to the eastern front might at last make possible a breakthrough of some kind. Cadorna had 22 divisions for the assault, while the Austro-Hungarians had just 9. This sixth battle began on August 6, and the Italians crossed the Isonzo and finally captured Gorizia three days later, but then their advance faltered. When the battle was concluded on the 17th, the Italian casualties were more than 50,000 men, while the Austro-Hungarians had 40,000 killed, wounded, or captured. Despite the losses, the morale of the Italians rose due to the capture of Gorizia.

There were three further Italian attacks along the Isonzo before the end of 1916, in September, October, and November. Each assault was designed to exploit the capture of Gorizia. However, the illusion of total victory engendered by the Sixth Battle of the Isonzo quickly evaporated. Few gains were made, and a further 75,000 Italians became casualties, some 10,000 more than those suffered by the Austro-Hungarians.

War in colonial Africa

Although the fighting in Italy and across the Middle East dominated the thoughts of the leadership both of the Allies and of the Central Powers from 1914 through 1916, there were a number of other commitments around the globe. These were chiefly in Africa, which mostly consisted of colonies run by the warring nations.

Germany was at a distinct disadvantage in the war in Africa. It had just four colonies—Togoland, Kamerun (modern Cameroon), German Southwest Africa (Namibia), and German East Africa (Tanzania)—and each was surrounded by colonies belonging to one or another of the Allies. The forces available to defend them—small numbers of German troops backed by local forces (*askaris*)—were far from adequate, and they could expect little additional support from Germany, whose resources were already overstretched. The Allies, though, could call on considerable reserves of men if needed.

The difficulties of Germany's African colonies were soon exposed. Togoland fell quickly to an Anglo-French attack. The colony's vital radio station at Kamia was first attacked on August 22, 1914, and as larger Allied forces converged on it, the local German commander surrendered to them four days later.

German Southwest Africa was the next colony to fall. At the beginning of the war the German authorities, who had some 9,000 troops available, abandoned the coast and concentrated on defending the capital, Windhoek. The attacking force put together by the Allies consisted of some 50,000 men and was composed of forces from neighboring South Africa, a semi-autonomous member of the British Empire. The South Africans launched their invasion in April 1915, using two

▼ *South African mounted troops near Upington on the Orange River. This was the frontier between the Union of South Africa and German Southwest Africa.*

columns, one of them under the leadership of General Jan Smuts and the other under General Louis Botha. Botha took Windhoek on May 20. The Germans still had forces in the north and offered to partition the colony, but Botha continued his advance. The last German forces surrendered on July 9.

Kamerun proved to be a much tougher proposition. Initial Allied attacks were repulsed, and a larger Anglo-French expeditionary force was raised by General Charles Dobell. On September 25, 1914, this landed near the German coastal radio station at Duala, which surrendered the next day. However, the bulk of the German forces escaped to the central region, where they received some reinforcements. The Allies resumed their advance toward Yaunde, the main German base. Progress was slow, but Yaunde was finally captured on January 1, 1916. The remains of the German force retreated into neighboring Spanish Guinea, a neutral territory where they were interned. German resistance was finally extinguished in February.

The fourth German colony, German East Africa, proved more difficult still to capture, chiefly because of its excellent local commander, Colonel Paul von Lettow-Vorbeck. Lettow-Vorbeck commanded a force of some 10,000 troops at the outbreak of the war and decided to take the fight to the British in neighboring Uganda and British East Africa (now Kenya), where the British could field fewer than 5,000 troops. Lettow-Vorbeck cut the colony's chief railroad, which linked Uganda with Mombasa on the coast. The British rushed reinforcements to the theater in response, but an amphibious assault on Tanga was repulsed in November 1914.

While the British paused for further troops, Lettow-Vorbeck waged a guerrilla campaign against British East Africa, launching numerous hit-and-run raids on isolated outposts. Finally a new Allied commander was appointed,

South Africa's General Jan Smuts, and extra forces poured into the region.

Smuts devised a strategy that involved large forces invading German East Africa from several directions. The attacks developed over the spring and summer of 1916. British and South African troops drove south from British East Africa, Belgian units struck eastward from the Belgian Congo, while other British contingents attacked northward from neighboring British-controlled Northern Rhodesia (now part of Zimbabwe). Amphibious landings also occurred at several points along the coast of the German colony.

Lettow-Vorbeck proved an elusive foe. He avoided major battles against the superior enemy forces and continued his guerrilla strategy, tying down huge numbers of Allied troops that might have been more profitably employed elsewhere. Allied casualties soared throughout 1916—chiefly because of disease—while the elusive Lettow-Vorbeck remained at large.

▼ *British colonial troops board a train in East Africa during the campaign to hunt down the small German force operating in the region.*

The Western Front, 1916

The year 1916 was to see intensive activity by the Central Powers and the Allies, each convinced that victory might be won. As early as December 1915 General Joseph Joffre, the French commander in chief, had headed a major war conference at Chantilly, a town a north of Paris, to discuss strategy against the European Central Powers in 1916. The delegates—British, French, Italian, and Russian—eventually agreed to conduct offensives, probably in July when

The western front in 1916 saw a year of constant combat. The Germans, British, and French launched attacks or counterattacks. Yet by December the combatants had gained little.

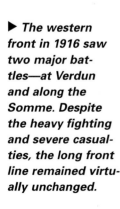

▶ The western front in 1916 saw two major battles—at Verdun and along the Somme. Despite the heavy fighting and severe casualties, the long front line remained virtually unchanged.

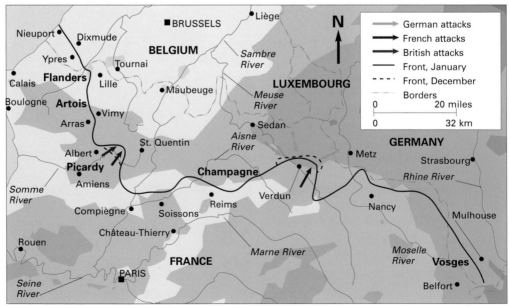

◀ *A German heavy howitzer opens fire on Verdun from its camouflaged emplacement.*

The focus of this activity would be the French forces defending the border fortress of Verdun, some 120 miles (192 km) east of Paris. Falkenhayn believed that manpower shortages were severely weakening France (the country had suffered more than 1.25 million casualties

STRATEGY AND TACTICS

FALKENHAYN AND VERDUN

General Erich von Falkenhayn opted for an offensive against the French at Verdun in early 1916. He could draw on 26 new divisions, which he had formed by scouring troop depots for men, to launch his major attack. Here, he summarized his strategic views for the year:

"As I have already insisted, the strain on France has almost reached breaking point—though it is borne with the most remarkable devotion. If we succeed in opening the eyes of her people to the fact that in a military sense they have nothing more to hope for, that breaking point would be reached and England's best sword [the French Army] knocked out of her hand. To achieve that objective, the uncertain method of a mass breakthrough, in any case beyond our means, is unnecessary. We can probably do enough for our purposes with limited resources. Within our reach behind the French sector of the western front, there are objectives for the retention of which the French would be compelled to throw in every man they have. If they do so, the forces of France will bleed to death—as there can be no question of a withdrawal—whether we reach our goal or not. If they do not do so and we reach our objectives, the effect on France will be enormous.

"For an operation limited to a narrow front, Germany will not be compelled to spend herself so completely that all other fronts are practically drained. She can face with confidence the relief attacks [by the Allies] to be expected on these fronts and indeed to hope to have sufficient troops to reply to them for counterattacks. For she [Germany] is perfectly free to accelerate or draw out her offensive, to intensify it or break it off from time to time, as suits her purpose."

Extract from Falkenhayn's summary of his vision for the Verdun attack presented to Kaiser Wilhelm II, late 1915.

the Russians would be ready to take part. The Russians were desperately short of artillery, rifles (some 160,000 frontline soldiers had none at all), and machine guns by the end of 1915 and were reorganizing their inefficient and often corrupt supply services. The country was also accepting substantial volumes of equipment from the other Allies.

The European Central Powers, their policies chiefly driven by Germany's chief of the general staff, General Erich von Falkenhayn, opted for a complete reversal of the strategy they had pursued in 1915. In 1916 they decided to adopt a defensive posture on the eastern front and concentrate their efforts on the western front.

on the western front in 1915) and that its forces—and the will of the French population as a whole to carry on the war—would collapse if they continued to suffer losses on a similar scale. French troops were, therefore, to be killed in large numbers through a deliberately attritional battle around Verdun.

Falkenhayn was not concerned with breaking through the French trenches at Verdun and then advancing on Paris to the west; he was intent on killing as many French soldiers as possible. The code name for Falkenhayn's offensive was Operation *Gericht*, meaning the sentence of a court or punishment.

Verdun, lying on the Meuse River, was at the center of a large salient projecting into the German lines and had been an anchor of the French defenses since 1914. It was partly surrounded and could be fired on from strong German-held positions to the east, north, and south. Its defenses comprised a series of huge forts, which circled the town at a distance of 5 miles (8 km). Each fort consisted of earth-covered concrete

positions linked by underground passageways and ringed by deep dry ditches strewn with dense masses of barbed wire, which could be swept by machine-gun fire. Large-caliber artillery pieces were fitted to retractable steel cupolas, which could be raised to fire on targets and then lowered for protection while being reloaded. The forts' garrisons lived and worked underground, protected by great thicknesses of reinforced concrete and hard-packed earth. Three miles (5 km) or so beyond the various forts lay the actual front lines, where the extensive French and German trenches stood in opposition.

Verdun's defenses had been seriously weakened in the months preceding the German offensive—many of the garrison's heavy artillery pieces had been removed for service elsewhere on the western front, where the French were desperately short of such weapons. At the opening of Operation *Gericht*, there were just 270 artillery pieces to protect Verdun. The French also had fewer railroads or serviceable roads leading into

▼ *A German shell explodes yards from a French frontline trench at the opening of the Battle of Verdun, February 21, 1916.*

Verdun, along which supplies and reinforcements could be moved, than the Germans. For their part the Germans had built several railroads leading to their positions around Verdun; the railroad center of Metz was less than 20 miles (32 km) from the front, and not far away was the iron-and-steel works of Briey-Thionville, which provided vast quantities of shells. The principal force committed to the attack, Crown Prince Wilhelm's Fifth Army, had ample supplies of artillery, some 1,200 pieces, and huge stockpiles of shells by early 1916.

Falkenhayn's offensive commenced on February 21 and was heralded by the largest bombardment seen in warfare to date. In 21 hours more than one million shells fell on the positions occupied by the French defenders, a large proportion on the two divisions along an 8-mile (13 km) sector of the front on the east bank of the Meuse. The French fell back in confusion once the ground assault began late in the afternoon, surrendering two of their three lines of trenches. In this sector the keys to the

third line were two forts—Douaumont and Vaux. Douaumont was inadequately garrisoned by a mere 57 artillerymen and was captured by the Germans at little cost on the 25th—none of the garrison was killed and the wounded consisted of only a single German soldier. After a few days of intense fighting at Verdu the Germans had advanced up to a maximum depth of 3 miles (5 km).

Joffre acted swiftly to stem the tide, recognizing the severity of the threat posed by the German onslaught. He issued explicit orders that there would be no further retreats, that every piece of land around Verdun was to be fought over to the bitter end, and that a new commander, General Henri Philippe Pétain, was to take charge of the embattled Second Army at Verdun. Pétain took over on the 26th, by which time the Germans had scaled down their attacks on the French lines.

Verdun became much more than a battle to the French. It came to symbolize a nation under immense threat but one willing to endure any sacrifice to ensure its survival. Prime Minister Aristide Briand caught the national mood when he berated Joffre and his generals: "If you surrender Verdun, you will be cowards, cowards! And you needn't wait till then to hand in your resignation. If you abandon Verdun, I will sack you on the spot." Verdun, then, was to be held at all costs—and it was.

By the end of the battle in December nealy three-quarters of all of France's troops had served at Verdun at one time or another. The German high command began to lose its tight grip on the battle and the initial objective of destroying the French Army. More and more German units were thrown into the fighting, despite the cost in lives. French casualties were horrendous, but those of Germany were on an almost equal scale. Verdun was no longer the one-sided attritional battle that had been envisaged by Falkenhayn.

◄ *The scene in a frontline French trench at Verdun. By 1916 France had dispensed with its original bright uniforms and adopted a more subdued color known as horizon blue. Steel helmets had also been introduced to reduce head wounds.*

KEY FIGURES

MARSHAL HENRI PHILIPPE PÉTAIN

Pétain (1856–1951) was a career soldier who rose to be one of France's national heroes through his actions in World War I. He was commissioned in 1876 and rose slowly in seniority until the outbreak of World War I in 1914, which began his meteoric rise to the highest command.

In August 1914 Pétain was in charge of a regiment, but within the same month he had been made a brigade commander. His calm leadership in the First Battle of the Marne (September) led to the command of a division, and the following October he was placed in charge of a corps. In May 1915 his corps came close to crashing through the formidable German defenses placed on Vimy Ridge.

In February 1916 Pétain was given the task of holding Verdun, which he proceeded to accomplish. However, he was considered too defensively minded, and in early May he was replaced by the more offensive-spirited General Robert Nivelle. Pétain was given command of Army Group Center, of which Nivelle's forces were part. In 1917 Nivelle, by this stage France's commander in chief, launched a disastrous attack along the Chemin des Dames in Champagne and was sacked. His replacement was Pétain, who was successful in quelling a large-scale mutiny that had broken out after the Nivelle-led attack. Pétain played a leading role in the final Allied battles of 1918 and was promoted to the rank of marshal in November. He was considered a national hero by the French.

As winter gave way to spring, the intensity of the fighting around Verdun was maintained. The French position improved somewhat, in large part due to Pétain's efforts. He ordered more French units forward to defend Verdun and rotated them from the front line for furlough on a regular basis. Previously, units had stayed in their trenches until virtually annihilated, an intolerable situation that was having a profoundly adverse impact on the morale of the ordinary French soldiers. Pétain also greatly strengthened the French artillery support in the sector.

Both of these efforts were monumental undertakings. Verdun was poorly provided with railroads—just one at the outbreak of the battle, which was soon smashed by German artillery fire. All that remained was a single narrow road running into Verdun some 38 miles (60 km) from the village of Bar-le-Duc to the southwest. Pétain organized large bodies of engineers to improve and

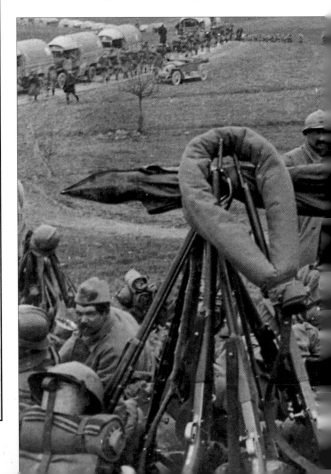

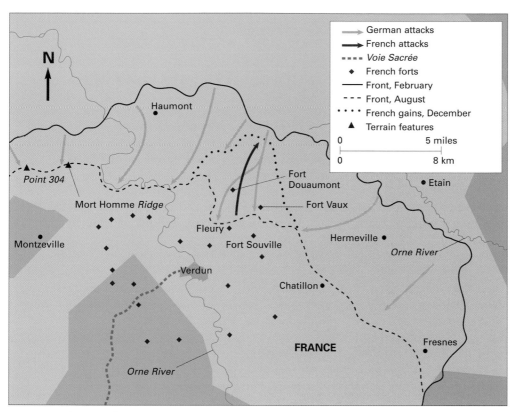

◄ *The ebb and flow of the Battle of Verdun. During the action, which lasted from February to November, the German attacks were concentrated on the east and north of the city.*

◄ *French troops and vital supplies flow into Verdun along the* **Voie Sacrée** *(Sacred Way), the only viable route into the city once the German offensive against it had begun.*

repair this vital artery and ordered his transport officers to gather trucks from all over France to move men and equipment into Verdun. This fragile lifeline was central to the defense of the city and became known as the *Voie Sacrée* (Sacred Way). At the height of the fighting, which was to last for 10 months, a truck carrying supplies was passing any point on the road every 14 seconds.

Renewed pressure at Verdun

The Germans, who had halted their opening attacks to the northeast and east of Verdun shortly after capturing Fort Douaumont on February 24, switched their attentions in early March to the northwest of Verdun. In this sector the French were using artillery positions on two pieces of high ground to bombard the attackers, with considerable effectiveness. The Germans recommenced their onslaught against Verdun on March 6 with the objective of capturing the elevated sites.

EYEWITNESS

MAJOR SYLVAIN-EUGÈNE RAYNAL

An officer in the French Army, Raynal was the commander of Fort Vaux during the Battle of Verdun. For several days (June 2–6) he held off repeated German attempts to capture his position. The fighting mostly took place underground in narrow darkened corridors lit by flickering kerosene lamps. Water was in short supply for the French garrison—Raynal and his men licked condensation off the walls. The garrison also had to face gas, grenade, and flamethrower attacks. Here, Raynal records the conditions he experienced and witnessed on the night of June 5–6:

"The short but violent fights of the morning had necessitated the employment of the whole garrison, and our men's strength had been drained away. I saw them gasping in the dust and smoke. Yesterday I had already noted that they had scarcely touched their rations because of the lack of water. The preserved meat was salted and could scarcely be forced down our dry throats. For my own part, I had eaten nothing yesterday, and today I felt little hunger, only thirst.

"I could see my men broken with fatigue, silent and gloomy. If I had to call on them for still another effort, they would be incapable of carrying it out. So I decided to serve out the last drops of the corpse-smelling water that remained in the cistern. It represented scarcely a quart [1.1 liters] per man; it was nauseous, it was muddy, and yet we drank this horrible liquid with avidity. But there was too little and our thirst continued."

Extract from Raynal's memoirs of the fight for Fort Vaux.

The fighting that occurred around one French position—Point 295—produced horrendous losses on both sides, and this key patch of territory became known as Mort Homme (Dead Man) Ridge. For the next three months this shell-blasted and crater-strewn high ground would be the focus of intense and bloody combat. The German assault troops slowly advanced toward its summit with the French contesting every inch of ground. It was finally captured at the end of May. While the battle for the Mort Homme area still raged, the Germans broadened their offensive in the sector to tackle another piece of high ground a little to the west of the ridge—Point 304. Again the fight was fierce and prolonged, with the Germans reaching Point 304's lower slopes by early April. By August their assault troops held half of it, but the French clung on to the other half.

While the Germans continued to batter away against Verdun, there were changes in the French command. Pétain, who had led Verdun's initial defense against the German attacks and had become a national hero, was promoted to command several armies in April and was replaced by the relatively inexperienced General Robert Nivelle, one of his deputies at Verdun.

Pétain had been content to block the attacks on Verdun to preserve his forces as much as possible and minimize their casualties. Nivelle was much more ambitious—he had convinced his superiors that he had a formula to recapture the lost ground. Pétain was left in overall charge, but Nivelle would be responsible for any major counterattacks around Verdun. Echoing his predecessor's dogged courage, Nivelle issued a message of defiance against the Germans to his troops: "Ils ne passeront pas!"—They shall not pass! For the moment the defense of Verdun was paramount. It would be several months before the French had the means at hand to launch a major counterattack.

While the battles continued to the north of Verdun around Mort Homme and Point 304, the Germans recommenced attacks southeastward from Fort Douaumont, beginning on April 9. Little ground was won or lost over the following weeks, thus forcing the Germans to switch the focus of their offensive in June toward Fort Vaux, which lay little more than 5 miles (8 km) from the center of Verdun itself.

The Germans found Vaux a tougher nut to crack than Douaumont. Vaux was defended by 600 men (350 more than it was designed to take) led by Major Sylvain-Eugène Raynal. The fort's garrison lacked artillery, and drinking water was scarce, yet for four days (June 2–6) Raynal and his men fought for every inch of the darkened corridors, dealing with repeated gas and flamethrower attacks. On the morning of the 7th the French raised the white flag, having had 20 men killed and 80 wounded inside Vaux and others killed in attempted

breakouts. The Germans lost more than 2,700 men killed, wounded, or missing.

The German attacks in May and June increased the pressure on the French. Pétain feared the worst, particularly when the Germans attempted to capture Souville and Tavennes forts, both uncomfortably close to Verdun. He asked his commander in chief, General Joseph Joffre, for permission to surrender some ground. Joffre refused the request, knowing that four Russian armies under General Alexey Brusilov were to attack on the eastern front in the first week of June (see pages 162–163) and that the British were to launch an offensive along the Somme River later in the month. Either or both of these operations were likely to force the Germans to withdraw troops from Verdun. Joffre was correct—the Brusilov Offensive led to the transfer of 15 divisions. The Germans halted their attacks against Souville and Tavennes on July 11, and the fighting subsided for the next three months.

Offensive on the Somme

The Somme attack had originally been planned to begin earlier in the year and was intended to be a joint Anglo-French operation. However, the German attack at Verdun disrupted the timetable, and

▼ *The reality of the Verdun battlefield after months of prolonged artillery bombardments—a moonscape of craters and shell-torn tree stumps. This is the area around Mort Homme (Dead Man) Ridge to the northwest of the fortress town.*

Life in the Trenches

Life on the western front for the ordinary soldier was punctuated only rarely by large-scale violent action, chiefly during the major offensives. For the rest of the time the average day developed its own routine.

▲ *French troops occupy a trench on Vimy Ridge. Cold, damp, and insanitary conditions led to many noncombat casualties.*

▲ *A German shelters in a front-line bunker with a few home comforts—his pipe, a family photograph, and a flask of liquor.*

On all sides a daily routine developed, one varying in its detail, depending on the nationality of the soldier or the local circumstances, but essentially the same. Shortly before dawn the frontline soldiers "stood to," manning their positions with weapons ready to repel any attack—dawn was a popular time to launch offensives as it was believed the enemy might be asleep. If nothing untoward happened most soldiers were "stood down," while sentries remained watching the enemy lines, and attended to other matters. Some

tried to snatch more sleep; others dealt with personal matters such as writing letters home, reading mail, books, and periodicals, or repairing and maintaining uniforms and equipment.

At the same time individuals could wash, shave, and eat breakfast, often consisting of cold food from tins, supplemented sometimes by much-valued food parcels sent from home or bought locally from

behind the lines. Hot food was at a premium and much coveted, particularly in winter when cold and damp were prevalent.

At dusk there was a similar "stand to," and if nothing developed, the soldiers could enjoy a hot meal before nightfall. However, their day's work was often far from over. Darkness gave the men a measure of protection from enemy fire that allowed them to undertake routine tasks above ground that were otherwise impossible in the full glare of daylight.

Some would be detailed to repair and strengthen the trenches, often venturing into no man's land to construct or renovate barbed-wire entanglements. Others might be sent to the rear

▶ *Australian troops stand ready to repel any German attacks. A soldier (right) scans no man's land with a periscope, while another (center) holds a U.S.-developed Lewis machine gun.*

to bring up rations or vital equipment. More aggressively, small patrols might venture into no man's land to listen to the activity in the enemy's trenches. Sometimes full-scale raids might be launched. These had several aims—to gather more concrete intelligence, to disrupt the enemy's established routine, and to gain some control over the local sector of the front.

Death was an ever-present danger during even the quietest day on the western front. It was common to unleash artillery bombardments in the hope of inflicting casualties on the unwary, and random machine-gun fire or sniping could add to the toll of dead and wounded.

Equally, soldiers could succumb to various debilitating ill-nesses and diseases associated with living in unhygienic and insanitary conditions. Although estimates vary enormously, it has been suggested that a unit of 1,000 men in the front line suffered an average of 60 casualties per month, even in the quietest periods of the war. Roughly 50 percent of this total was caused by enemy action.

Aside from the dull routine, the constant danger, and the fear of death, the soldiers had to endure the almost continuous noise of enemy fire and the loss of close companions. Both mentally and physically trench life was a nightmare that most hoped to endure and survive at best. Many frontline veterans of the conflict described their time in the trenches as a mixture of weeks of boredom interspersed by hours or days of great fear.

▼ *British troops wait to be served hot food from a field kitchen.*

French forces were drawn off to bolster the defenses of the town. Consequently, the offensive was to be a predominantly British affair with some French support.

The new commander of the British Expeditionary Force, General Douglas Haig, was confident of success. He was in command of the largest British force ever seen in warfare, and it was seemingly well provided with artillery and shells. It was believed that a prolonged bombardment of great intensity would smash the enemy trenches and cut swathes through its barbed wire. Some 1.5 million shells had been stockpiled. Many of the German defenders would be killed or wounded or left so disoriented that they would not be able to put up a fight. When the infantry units went "over the top," it would simply be a matter of occupying ground methodically, step by step. One British officer of a regiment in the 32nd Division shared Haig's optimism, telling his men: "You will be able to go over the top with a walking stick, you will not need rifles. When you get to Thiepval [a village to be captured on the first day] you will find the Germans all dead, not even a rat will have survived."

The main British attack by General Henry Rawlinson's Fourth Army was along an 18-mile (29 km) front between Gommecourt in the north and Maricourt to the south. This was to be supported by a limited advance a little farther north by the Third Army under General Edmund Allenby. South of Rawlinson, across the Somme River, was General Marie Emile Fayolle's French Sixth Army occupying a 10-mile (16 km) front opposite German-held Péronne. Fayolle's troops were to support the main British advance.

When the British attack began on July 1, 14 divisions would be committed and a further 8 (5 of cavalry) were in reserve to exploit any breakthrough. Only 4 of the divisions in the opening attack had seen action before. The remainder were made up of volunteers who had joined

▶ *An indication of the immense effort needed to support a major offensive. Here, troops load, unload, and then redistribute ammunition and grenades for the front shortly after the opening of the Battle of the Somme.*

up since 1914. Opposing the British and French on the Somme was General Fritz von Below's German Second Army.

The preparation for the attack began eight days earlier. On June 23 British artillery began to pound the well-protected German positions around the clock. Some 200,000 shells were unleashed on the defenses every day, and the constant rumble of the barrage was so loud that it could be heard as far away as southern England. Morale in the British camp was high, from the most senior general to the ordinary soldier in the frontline trenches.

The advance commences

On July 1 the bombardment ceased. A few minutes before the infantry advanced, several large mines, which had been dug under the German front line, were detonated, obliterating trenches and German soldiers. Then

▶ *A British 6-inch (15 cm) artillery piece pictured during the weeklong bombardment of the German trenches that heralded the Somme attack. Although impressive numbers of such weapons were used, their actual impact on the German defenses was much less decisive than had been predicted.*

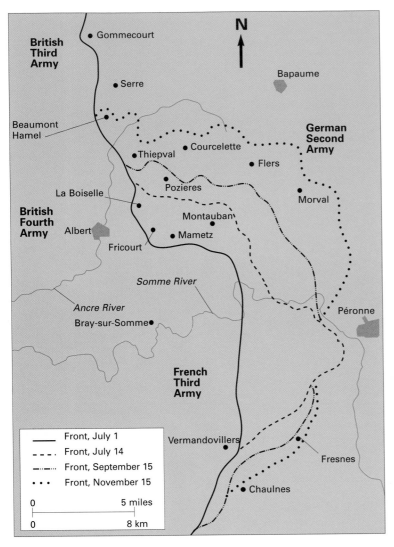

N

British
Third
Army

Gommecourt

Bapaume

Serre

Beaumont
Hamel

German
Second
Army

Courcelette

Thiepval

Flers

Pozieres

La Boiselle

Morval

British
Fourth
Army

Albert

Montauban

Mametz

Fricourt

Somme River

Ancre River

Bray-sur-Somme

Péronne

French
Third
Army

Vermandovillers

Fresnes

Chaulnes

Front, July 1
Front, July 14
Front, September 15
Front, November 15

0   5 miles
0   8 km

▲ The British-led
Battle of the
Somme in 1916
was planned to
rupture the
German front line
and allow a deci-
sive breakthrough
to end the war.
After the first few
hours of the bat-
tle, it became
obvious that
thoughts of crash-
ing through the
German lines were
wildly optimistic.

There were some territorial gains, chiefly in the south, where the two villages of Mametz and Montauban were captured—by the French—but the attack was largely a disaster. By the end of the day some 57,000 British troops had been killed or wounded, constituting around 60 percent of the officers and 40 percent of the ordinary infantrymen. German casualties on the day are estimated at just 8,000. July 1 remains the most sanguine day in the history of the British Army. Why had the battle gone so disastrously wrong?

The British high command had greatly overestimated the impact of the preliminary bombardment. Although the British had some 1,400 artillery pieces, many were too light to be of use in cutting barbed wire or smashing hardened defenses. Heavy guns firing large high-explosive shells were essential for this work, and the British were short of such weapons. To make matters much worse, as many as 30 percent of all the shells fired were duds that did

whistles blew all along the line to signal the advance. It was 7:30 A.M. on what was to be a very hot day.

The first wave, some 120,000 men, clambered out of the trenches and advanced into no man's land, making its way forward slowly. Most of the troops were burdened with extra equipment—ammunition, rations, signaling flags, etc. No man's land varied in width between some 300 and 600 yards (275–550 m), and many of the assault troops had barely got out of their trenches before being hit by machine-gun fire. Some of the units persevered throughout the hot day, but hopes of a breakthrough evaporated.

not explode at all. Consequently, much of the German barbed wire was left intact, sections of trenches were also relatively untouched, and many German soldiers sheltered in dugouts and emerged unscathed. When the artillery fire ceased shortly before the attack, the Germans had a few minutes to prepare.

▲ Lines of British infantrymen move forward at a steady pace as the Somme offensive opens. Most are heavily laden with extra equipment. The slow advance allowed the Germans to man their trenches and pour heavy fire into the attackers.

◄ Moments before the infantry attack on the Somme began, the British detonated a series of huge mines under the German trenches. Here, smoke, dust, and debris rise from the mine detonated at Beaumont Hamel.

▲ *British guards escort German prisoners and wounded to the rear on July 3 during the Battle of Albert, two days after the opening of the offensive on the Somme.*

They left their dugouts and manned their trenches. When the British soldiers advanced, they approached an alert enemy. German machine-gun and artillery fire did the rest.

The balance of losses reflected this situation. Advancing on the village of Thiepval, the British 8th Division suffered 5,121 men killed, wounded, or missing on July 1; the German 180th Regiment defending it recorded 280 casualties. Among the greatest losses of the day were those suffered by the 1st Newfoundland Regiment; it advanced with 752 men and suffered 684 casualties in an hour. The British divisions present on July 1 lost at least 25 percent of their total strength.

A battle of attrition

Haig continued to hammer away along the Somme River over the following weeks and months. Initially, he still hoped for a breakthrough, but the battle steadily became one of attrition, and Haig seemed willing to accept this. It was considered a victory if proportionately more casualties were inflicted on the defenders than were sustained by the attackers. The British renewed their stalled attack of July 1 on the night of the 13th–14th. Four of Rawlinson's divisions struck in the south against the small village of Bazentin and the surrounding high ground in a surprise advance. The Germans were forced to cede ground before some reinforcements could be rushed forward to plug the gap in the line. The British success worried the Germans so they moved more reinforcements from Verdun, where the fighting had temporarily died down, to the Somme and also reorganized their command structure. The threatened sector was split between General Fritz von Below to the north and General Max von Gallwitz, the overall sector commander, who took charge of the south.

On the 23rd Rawlinson tried a second assault, this time against the village of Pozières to the west of Bazentin. The village eventually fell to two Australian divisions, but the progress elsewhere was minimal. The fighting on the Somme died down during August, although casualties on all sides continued to mount. For example, the British were averaging two to four thousand casualties per day even in the "quiet" periods. Haig returned to the offensive in mid-September. On this occasion his objectives were the two smashed villages of Flers and Courcelette. On the 15th of the month, twelve divisions attacked on a 12-mile (19 km) front.

For the first time in war, tanks were committed to battle. The British, who had developed these tracked armored fighting vehicles in great secret, had 36 on hand. They had some impact at Flers, where a number of German troops fled their positions on seeing them, but many suffered mechanical

---

EYEWITNESS

FRIEDRICH STEINBRECHER

Steinbrecher, a former student who was to be killed in action on the western front during 1917, served with the German Army during the Battle of the Somme. In early August 1916 he and his unit were transferred to the sector of the battlefield to the southwest of the town of Péronne, which was being attacked by the French Sixth Army commanded by General Marie Emile Fayolle. On August 12 Steinbrecher and his comrades received urgent orders to stem a possibly major French breakthrough in the vicinity of two villages close to the front line:

"At noon the gunfire became even more intense, and then came the order: 'The French have broken through. Counter-attack!' We advanced through the shattered wood in a hail of shells. I don't know how I found the right way. Then across an expanse of shell craters, on and on. Falling down and getting up again. Machine guns were firing. I had to cut across our own barrage and the enemy's. I am untouched. At last we reached the front line. Frenchmen are forcing their way in. The tide of battle ebbs and flows. Then things get quiet. We have not fallen back a foot. Now one's eyes begin to see terrible things. I want to keep running on—to stand still and look is horrible. 'A wall of dead and wounded!' How often have I read that phrase. Now I know what it means.

"I have witnessed scenes of heroism and weakness. Men who can endure every privation. Being brave is not only a matter of will, it also requires strong nerves, though the will can do a great deal. A divisional commander dubbed us the 'Iron Brigade' and said he had never seen anything like it. I wish it had all been only a dream, a bad dream. And yet it was a joy to see such heroes stand and fall. The bloody work cost us 177 men. We shall never forget [the villages of] Chaulmes and Vermandovillers."

Letter written to his family, published in *German Students' War Letters*, 1929.

failure or became bogged down in the shell-cratered terrain. Nevertheless, the British were able to advance an average of one and a half miles (2.5 km) in the sector, but bad weather and the appearance of German reinforcements ended the advance after a week.

Haig persisted with another attack in September. Between the 25th and 27th small gains were made at Morval and around Thiepval. Similar offensives were made as the weather worsened— around the Transloy ridges for most of October and, lastly, at Beaumont Hamel in November, after Haig had been urged on by Joffre. The well-fortified village, originally an objective to be taken on July 1, finally fell on November 13.

The Battle of the Somme finally ended on November 19 after five months of action in which the British and French had recaptured a mere 125 square miles (310 sq km) of territory. The average advance was just 6 miles (9.5 km). The list of casualties was staggering—420,000 British troops killed, wounded, missing, or taken prisoner (70,000 of whose remains have never been found or were impossible to identify at the time); some 194,000 French; and 450,000 German.

French counterattacks at Verdun

While Haig was hammering away along the Somme, the Battle of Verdun continued. The Germans scaled down their increasingly fruitless efforts around the citadel and adopted a more pragmatic defensive posture. The French, however, had been reinforcing their troops in the sector during the summer in preparation for a major counterattack.

Organized and managed by General Charles Mangin, Nivelle's deputy, the counterattack began on October 24. The French immediately recaptured what little remained of Fort Douaumont, which had been lost the previous February, and followed this by carrying Fort Vaux on November 2. A month-long pause followed, but Mangin struck again on December 15, pushing the shaken Germans back in some areas by the 18th almost to the lines they had

▼ *British troops and one of the first tanks take shelter behind an embankment after the fighting around the Somme village of Flers, September 15. The attack had marked the first appearance of the tank in battle.*

held at the beginning of their offensive. These French successes ended the fighting at Verdun, the longest battle of World War I. French losses totaled some 542,000 men, while the German forces recorded around 430,000 casualties.

The fighting of 1916 on the western front had profound repercussions for Britain, France, and Germany. Britain's General Douglas Haig, architect of the Somme offensive, was promoted to the rank of field marshal and would lead the British forces in France until the end of the war. However, the luster of his command had been badly tarnished, and his political masters increasingly viewed his military plans and requests with deep skepticism.

The British political leadership was also transformed by the traumatic events of 1916. Herbert Asquith, who had led the British government into war in 1914 and had been subjected to vilification in the press for much of 1916, resigned in early December to be replaced by the irascible but dynamic Secretary of War David Lloyd George on the 7th.

The British Army had been decimated along the Somme. The enthusiastic volunteers of the early summer had been transformed into cynical veterans who had little faith in their superiors but would continue stoically to "do their duty" and fight on. However, the British could no longer rely on recruits like those volunteers who had fought in the Battle of the Somme. Conscription had been introduced in January 1916 with the first of two Military Service Acts (the second was enacted in April). These made it compulsory for all unmarried men aged between 18 and 41 to enlist. Between February 1916 and the end of the war some 2.3 million men would be conscripted, and they would constitute the bulk of the British Army until the armistice.

For their part the French—not least the frontline soldiers— found it hard to come to terms with the slaughter at Verdun. Many began to believe that after more than two years of severe losses their lives counted for little to either politicians or generals. Pétain, ever sympathetic to the plight of the

▲ *A machine-gun position manned by French troops at one of the forts near Verdun. The rapid rate of such automatic gunfire contributed greatly to the scale of infantry losses during the course of the war.*

▲ *A posed image of French troops gives some idea of the grim conditions endured by the men in the trenches.*

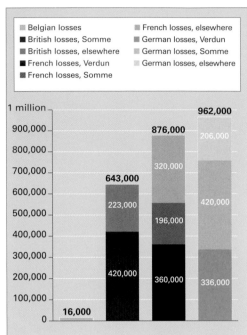

Belgian losses	French losses, elsewhere
British losses, Somme	German losses, Verdun
British losses, elsewhere	German losses, Somme
French losses, Verdun	German losses, elsewhere
French losses, Somme	

1 million

962,000

876,000

643,000

206,000

320,000

223,000

196,000

420,000

360,000

420,000

336,000

16,000

▼ *The bitter reality of the war on the western front in 1916, which produced huge casualties for little gain. Here, German dead lie outside their destroyed bunker.*

▲ *The casualties suffered by the various combatants on the western front in 1916. The chart includes killed, wounded, prisoners, and missing.*

men under his command, remarked on the impact that Verdun had on them: "In their unsteady look one sensed visions of horror, while their step and bearing revealed utter despondency. They were crushed by horrifying memories." Equally, France's politicians were filled with disquiet over their own military leadership. The commander in chief, General Joseph Joffre, was dismissed in December, although promoted to the rank of marshal a few days later. His replacement was to be one of the heroes of Verdun, General Robert Nivelle, a political sophisticate who was adept at soothing the politicians' fears by promising victories at little cost.

Germany had emerged from 12 months of almost constant bloodletting on the western front still able to carry on the war, but the German Army had been transformed for the worse. Verdun and the Somme had cost it dear,

not least in its corps of experienced officers of all ranks. These men had been the backbone of the prewar German Army and had led it into many battles since 1914 with great skill. They would be greatly missed, particularly in 1918.

There were changes in Germany's military leadership during 1916. The chief of the general staff, General Erich von Falkenhayn, had been dismissed on August 29, chiefly due to the failure of his Verdun plan. He was replaced by Field Marshal Paul von Hindenburg and his able deputy, General Erich Ludendorff. Shocked by the losses on the western front, the pair would adopt a defensive strategy in the west in 1917 and focus their attentions on the eastern front. To this end they opted to surrender territory on the western front to shorten their front line, thereby freeing units for service elsewhere.

This strategic withdrawal was sudden but planned well in advance. Some 20 miles (32 km) behind the line stretching between Arras and Soissons, the Germans were already constructing a broad zone of defenses—the Siegfried Line. Known to the Allies as the Hindenburg Line, it was a formidable barrier that marked a new concept of trench warfare—defense in depth.

POLITICAL WORLD

GERMANY'S PEACE OFFER

The German chancellor, Theobald von Bethmann Hollweg, believed that it might be possible to seek a negotiated settlement to the war in late 1916 from a position of some strength, as Germany's forces had held Allied attacks on the western front and overrun Romania.

Bethmann Hollweg also recognized that the German people were tiring of the struggle and that food shortages were damaging their morale. He thought that his peace offer would finally convince the German people that their leaders were not prolonging the war deliberately. If it was rejected by the Allies, as was likely, then the government could claim that they, not Germany, were blocking peace.

A further reason for the offer was that Bethmann Hollweg had considerable reservations about Germany's future war strategy. He was aware that several senior figures in the military were intent on resuming unrestricted submarine warfare. Such a tough naval strategy would inevitably lead to the sinking of neutral ships. The chancellor saw that the United States would declare war on Germany if its shipping were sunk. However, if Bethmann Hollweg's peace proposals were rebuffed, he could claim to U.S. President Woodrow Wilson that the resumption of unrestricted submarine warfare was forced on a desperate Germany by the Allied rejection of his offer.

The German peace call was made on December 12. Bethmann Hollweg requested that the United States and other neutrals communicate his offer of negotiations to the Allies. His proposal suggested talks but did not outline any specific topics. The note was immediately rejected by the Allies, who were intent on making Germany pay for the war that they believed its leadership had started.

The Allies formally rejected the proposal on the 30th, saying that it was "empty and insincere." British war leader David Lloyd George used words once spoken by U.S. President Abraham Lincoln to justify the rejection: "We accepted this war for an object, a worthy object, and the war will end when that object [the defeat of the Central Powers] is attained. Under God I hope it will never end until that time." On January 10, 1917, Kaiser Wilhelm II announced that unrestricted submarine warfare would recommence on February 1, thereby bringing the likelihood of U.S. entry into the war ever closer.

America and the Growing Conflict, 1914–1916

The United States reacted to the war by declaring its neutrality, but as the fighting continued it was forced ever closer to taking part in the conflict.

At the outbreak of war in August 1914 the United States immediately proclaimed its neutrality and offered to mediate between the powers embroiled in the conflict. However, there was considerable sympathy toward those fighting the Central Powers, which were seen as the aggressors by many Americans. Nevertheless, most U.S. politicians and citizens had key concerns closer to home. U.S. foreign policy centered on Latin America, particularly the Caribbean and Central America, where the United States was attempting to preserve its interests. Between 1914 and 1916 U.S. troops intervened in Mexico (1914 and 1916), Haiti (1914 and 1915), Nicaragua (1914 and 1915), Santo Domingo (1916), and the Dominican Republic (1916).

To many Americans, however, domestic issues were of much greater import. President Woodrow Wilson, a Democrat who had come to power in 1912, was a moderate political progressive. Backed

▶ *U.S. armed guards stand watch outside the Mexican Naval Academy at Vera-cruz, damaged by shelling in 1914 from the USS warship* Chester *during a brief intervention in Mexico.*

by Democratic majorities in both the House of Representatives and the Senate, he was able to introduce acceptable domestic reforms designed to curb some of the unbridled powers of those individuals and companies that dominated the nation's economic life. These measures antagonized many conservative politicians, who opposed any federal interference in the country's economic and social affairs.

Equally, liberal politicians argued that Wilson's reforms did not go far enough and did not reflect the aspirations of a considerable number of ordinary Americans. However, the majority of politicians of whatever persuasion agreed on one thing—the United States must remain wholly neutral. Wilson summed up his own view in a speech to the Senate on August 19, 1914, stating that the United States had to be "neutral in fact as well as in name during these days that are to try men's souls."

Apostles of neutrality

Wilson's inner cabinet consisted of figures who, on the whole, reflected the

▼ *The United States saw the Americas as its sphere of influence, and intervened often before and during World War I.*

▲ *Woodrow Wilson (1856–1924), the 28th U.S. president, was head of the U.S. government throughout the war in Europe.*

UNITED STATES

• New Orleans

N

Continental U.S.A.
U.S. protectorates
Borders

0   900 miles
0   1450 km

Gulf of Mexico

HAVANA   HAITI
1914, 1915

Veracruz
(1914)   CUBA   PUERTO
                                            RICO
MEXICO CITY
                    BRITISH
                    HONDURAS

MEXICO   DOMINICAN
(1916–1917)   HONDURAS   REPUBLIC
                              Caribbean Sea   (1916)

GUATEMALA   NICARAGUA   *Panama Canal Zone*
                  (1914, 1915)

EL SALVADOR   CARACAS
        COSTA RICA   VENEZUELA
        PANAMA   COLOMBIA

POLITICAL WORLD

PROCLAIMING U.S. NEUTRALITY

In August 1914 President Woodrow Wilson made clear his commitment to neutrality and called on all Americans of whatever origin or political persuasion to support the United States as a neutral power:

"The people of the United States are drawn from many nations, and chiefly from the nations now at war. It is natural and inevitable that there should be the utmost variety of sympathy and desire among them with regard to the issues and circumstances of the conflict. Some will wish one nation, others another, to succeed in the momentous struggle. It will be easy to excite passion and difficult to allay it. Those responsible for exciting it will assume a heavy responsibility, responsibility for no less a thing than that the people of the United States, whose love of their country and whose loyalty to its government should unite them as Americans all, bound in honor and affection to think first of her and her interests, may be divided in camps of hostile opinion, hot against each other, involved in the war itself in impulse and opinion if not in action.

"Such divisions amongst us would be fatal to our peace of mind and might seriously stand in the way of the proper performance of our duty as the one great nation at peace, the one people holding itself ready to play a part of impartial mediation and speak the counsels of peace and accommodation, not as a partisan, but as a friend."

Extract from Wilson's speech to the U.S. Congress, August 19, 1914.

▼ *William Jennings Bryan, Woodrow Wilson's secretary of state during his two terms of office.*

majority view regarding the war. One of the key members of the team was Secretary of State William Jennings Bryan, who was responsible for the conduct of U.S. foreign policy and was pacifist in outlook. At the outbreak of the conflict he suggested that Wilson should act as a negotiator between the warring countries and keep the United States strictly neutral. Wilson also relied on two other advisers. First, there was Counsellor of the State Department Robert Lansing, who also deputized for Bryan. Lansing was less pacific than the secretary of state, believing that it was his duty to defend the interests of the United States forcefully by absolute observance of international law but also to promote and maintain U.S. business interests worldwide. Wilson's other key adviser was Colonel Edward House.

▲ *General Leonard Wood at Plattsburg, New York, where a camp trained volunteers in the event of war.*

sympathetic to the Allied cause, an attitude reflected in their dispatches about the German conduct of the war. The British had a stranglehold on news transmission across the Atlantic, controlling the underwater cables along which information passed, and they painted their cause in terms acceptable to the United States. By July 1916 the British War Propaganda Bureau boasted that it had "swept the German news out of the American papers." The Germans did have two radio stations in the United States that could broadcast news favorable to the Central Powers, but their influence was small.

War and the U.S. people

From August 1914 onward some Americans were willing to offer their wholehearted support to the Allied cause and made calls for the United States to expand its armed forces. Chief among these was the Republican ex-president, Theodore Roosevelt. Backed by a former chief of staff of the U.S. Army, General Leonard Wood, Roosevelt believed that his country should take a more leading role in international matters. As a prelude to so doing, they wanted to establish a draft system for basic military training.

Roosevelt and Wood were supported by groups, such as the National Security League and the Military Camps Training Association, which promulgated their message under the umbrella title of the Preparedness Movement. Financial backing came from bankers, financiers, and the heads of large corporations, such as Cornelius Vanderbilt and Simon Guggenheim. Further support came from labor leaders. Chief among these was the president of the American Federation of Labor, Samuel Gompers. Both groups were benefiting from the expansion of the U.S. economy brought about by the growth in overseas trade engendered by the war. Order books were full and employees were enjoying high wages.

Although he had no official position, House was a trusted confidant of Wilson and his eyes and ears in Europe.

Although all these senior politicians were generally neutralist in outlook, most leaned toward support of the Allies, especially Britain. The same was true of some ordinary citizens. They viewed the German invasion of Belgium in August 1914 as a gross violation of that country's sovereignty by an illiberal and militaristic power and also took the view that Germany had engineered the crisis in the preceding July that had led to the outbreak of war. There were several reasons for this view. Many U.S. diplomats in Europe were broadly

Although a great many U.S. citizens were broadly sympathetic to the Allied cause, some ordinary Americans were less so—chiefly the German-Americans who constituted some 8.6 percent of the population. Most were recent immigrants who maintained strong ties with their former homeland and lived in close-knit communities within the United States. Some two million of them were believed to be members of the National German-American Central Alliance, a body established at the turn of the century to protect the German immigrant community, chiefly against organizations such as the Anti-Saloon League, which strongly supported the prohibition of alcohol. The alliance's original financial backers were U.S.-based brewers and alcohol dealers.

Some German-Americans took steps to combat the wealth of pro-Allied wartime propaganda being disseminated. In New York, for example, the German-American Literary Defense Committee distributed 60,000 pro-German pamphlets between August and December 1914. German-American journalist George Sylvester Viereck established a pro-German weekly newspaper, *The Fatherland*, on August 10, which by October had reached a circulation of some 100,000. Other activities by German-Americans included fundraising events, such as one held in St. Louis, Missouri, during October 1914, which raised $20,000 for war relief, and a rally at Madison Square Garden attended by some 70,000 in June 1915. Pressure was put on the U.S. administration to prevent the sale of equipment to the Allies, though with little success.

The second group that was less favorably disposed toward the Allied cause consisted of Irish-Americans, who made up a little over 5 percent of the country's population. Most had little sympathy for Germany, but the majority were decidedly anti-British. They believed that Britain had treated the Irish badly over the centuries and was continuing

PEOPLE AND WAR

U.S. ANTIMILITARISM

On November 4, 1915, President Woodrow Wilson announced plans to strengthen the U.S. forces, a move that provoked outrage among some. Less than two weeks later, progressives and reformers met to form the Anti-Militarist Committee, later renamed the American Union Against Militarism. Among its leading lights were several women, including Jane Addams and Florence Kelley.

The movement believed that many influential industrialists and financiers were using the Preparedness Movement as a cover to boost their profits and block political reform in the United States. One member, Frederic C. Howe, summarized this view, stating that war "is usually identified with a reaction at home. It checks social legislation." The Union stated that it intended to "throw a monkey wrench into the machinery of Preparedness."

The movement did not gain mass appeal, and as the war continued some of its leading members began to modify their opinions, not least because they began to believe that Wilson had exhausted all avenues to bring about peace. By 1917 some were arguing that war might be a driving force for social and political reform. One Union stalwart, Paul Kellogg, commenting on Wilson's highly moral stance on U.S. involvement in the conflict, wrote that the president had "lifted the plane of our entrance into the war from that of neutral rights to an all-impressing fight for democracy." Others strongly disagreed with this analysis, and the movement gradually split into opposing factions once the United States had gone to war.

to do so. Britain, many argued, would not voluntarily surrender its control of Ireland and that only force would make it grant the country independence. Why should the Irish fight for a country that many saw as their oppressor?

Both the German- and Irish-American lobbies, who had some formal links established before the war, argued that Germany was waging an essentially defensive war and that large sections of the U.S. press were biased against the country—although some press barons, most notably William Randolph Hearst, were anti-British. Neither group suggested that the United States should actively side with Germany (although some of their members probably felt so), but they did argue that strict neutrality ought to be observed and that the United States should not go to war in support of the Allies.

A few German-Americans, either acting alone or as German agents, did take direct action. In February 1914 Werner Horne was arrested after failing to blow up a railroad bridge at Vanceboro, Maine. Also, on June 2, 1915, a bomb planted by a German Cornell University tutor destroyed a room in the Senate, and the tutor also shot and wounded the pro-British banker William Pierpont Morgan. Direct evidence of German meddling in U.S. affairs came on July 24, 1915, when secret service agents found a briefcase on the New York subway. Later published in the *New York World*, documents found within the briefcase revealed that the Germans had paid Dr. Heinrich Albert, a U.S.-based German, some $28 million to wage a campaign of sabotage against U.S. industry. In January 1916 it was revealed that the German military attaché in the United States, Franz von Papen, had made payments to German agents. Diplomatic protests were issued, and Papen was forced to return home.

Other groups in the United States were committedly pacifist—opposed to any form of militarism both in the United States and elsewhere. On August 29, 1914, for example, 1,500 women led by Fanny Garrison Villard marched in New York under a banner depicting the dove and olive branch of peace. A few months later Villard formed the Women's Peace Party with suffragette Carrie Chapman Catt, president of the National American Woman Suffrage Association, and reformer Jane Addams. Several other groups followed, including the League to Enforce Peace and the American League to Limit Armaments. Though these groups directed part of their efforts against militarism, they also demanded social reform within the United States itself.

Unlike the Preparedness Movement, the various pacifist groups lacked major financial backing, and their campaign struggled to broadcast its message to the wider U.S. public. Some support was provided by industrialist Henry Ford, who organized a "peace ship," *Oscar II*, under the slogan, "Get the boys out of the trenches and back to their homes by Christmas." With a number of pacifists and journalists on board, the *Oscar II* sailed for Europe on November 4, 1915, although Ford's efforts to bring about an end to the war failed and were lampooned in the press.

▼ *The Henry Ford–sponsored "peace ship"* Oscar II *in New York harbor, prior to its departure for Europe in 1915.*

AMERICAN RELIEF CLEARING HOUSE
(COMITÉ CENTRAL des SECOURS AMÉRICAINS)

▲ Cars laden with goods outside the offices of the American Relief Clearing House in Paris, 1915.

Some Americans made much more personal decisions regarding the war. Often acting individually or in small groups, they decided to take some role in the war itself. Many working in war-ravaged Europe would write letters to friends or family or have articles published in national and local newspapers and magazines that would bring home the horrors and realities of modern warfare. Among these were people who were deeply shocked by the impact the war was having on European civilians and attempted to aid those affected by the fighting. Women were particularly prominent in these movements. For example, New York–born author Edith Wharton helped to establish the American Hostels for Refugees in Paris during November 1914. They were reception centers for civilians who had been forced to flee Belgium and northeast France because of the fighting. Some 4,000 refugees found permanent

shelter in buildings run by Wharton's organization, and many others fleeing the fighting received urgent care when they finally reached the French capital.

Nearer the front, other Americans, very often students from Ivy League universities, volunteered to attend to the needs of those who had been wounded in action. As early as September 7, 1914, the American Ambulance of Paris began operating on the western front, and it was followed by the American Volunteer Motor Ambulance Corps, organized by Richard Norton, and A. Piatt Andrew's American Ambulance Field Service. Some Americans played an even more direct role in the war, siding with the Allies. About 200 U.S. pilots, including Eugene Bullard, the only African-American pilot of the war, volunteered to serve in units of the French Air Service. Some formed the *Escadrille Americaine* (American Squadron) in April 1916. Others served in the British Army or the French Foreign Legion, including the poet Alan Seegar, who was killed in 1916.

The key question confronting U.S. politicians in August 1914 was how to maintain U.S. neutrality when the economy relied on overseas trade with the warring nations, which were all trying to strangle their opponents' trade. The cornerstone of their public policy was an international trade agreement, the Declaration of London, signed in 1909. In time of war the agreement identified three types of goods. First, there was absolute contraband, chiefly ammunition and weapons, that any belligerent could seize on the high seas if the cargo was bound for an enemy. Second, there

---

PEOPLE AND WAR

ESCADRILLE AMERICAINE

Among those individual U.S. citizens to volunteer to fight in World War I before U.S. entry into the war in April 1917 were the pilots of the *Escadrille Americaine* (American Squadron), which was part of the French Air Service. The squadron, raised on the initiative of U.S. aviators at the close of 1915, was commanded by a French officer and entered frontline service on April 20, 1916. Its opening mission took place on May 13, and its first air victory was achieved five days later by Kiffin Rockwell, who shot down a reconnaissance aircraft. The first U.S. volunteer casualty in air combat was Victor Chapman, who was killed on June 23.

As the squadron achieved public acclaim in France, Germany protested to the U.S. government that the use of the term "American" in its title was not in keeping with the country's neutral status. Promptings by the U.S. authorities led to the French renaming the unit the *Escadrille Lafayette*, after the French officer who had fought against Britain during the American War of Independence.

In February 1918 most of the squadron's pilots were placed under U.S. command. By this stage the U.S. volunteers had served in most sectors of the western front, downing 57 enemy aircraft. Nine of the squadron's pilots had been killed. Many of those who had served in its ranks became renowned wartime figures. Among these was the third highest scoring U.S. ace of the war, Raoul Lufbery. One of those associated with the volunteer pilots was William Wellman. A member of the French-American Lafayette Aviation Corps, a body that placed U.S. volunteers with French units, Wellman won the first best-picture Academy Award for his movie *Wings*, whose plot centered on air combat in World War I.

was conditional contraband, such as food, which could also be seized if bound for any enemy port, although not if it was destined for a neutral country, even if it was destined for end use by an enemy power. Third, there were several free goods, including cotton, ores, rubber, and animal hides, that were free from seizure, whatever the destination of the vessel carrying them.

U.S. Counsellor of the State Department Lansing requested on August 6, 1914, that the various European belligerents abide by the declaration's provisions. The Central Powers agreed, believing that they were favorable to their cause, but with the proviso that the Allies back the declaration. Britain, which had not ratified the declaration, responded on the 20th, stating that conditional contraband destined for a neutral port would be seized if its ultimate destination was to a Central Power. Subsequently, free goods were also deemed targets by the British.

Britain's decision to strengthen its naval blockade had a considerable impact on U.S. trade with Europe. Between December 1914 and January 1915, U.S. exports to Germany fell by 90 percent compared with the corresponding period the year before. U.S. exports to neutral countries, such as Denmark, the Netherlands, Norway, and Sweden, rose by 250 percent in the same period and helped compensate to some extent for the loss of trade with Germany. Nevertheless, various U.S. business interests complained bitterly about Britain's actions. Wilson attempted to secure agreement with Britain to modify its blockade, but it stood firm, although it released some detained American cargoes and agreed to buy shipments of U.S. copper it had seized.

Despite the friction over Britain's wartime trade policy, the U.S. administration remained broadly sympathetic to the Allied cause. Despite German protets, Counsellor Robert Lansing agreed to allow merchant ships armed

for defense to use U.S. ports, a policy that would clearly benefit the Allies because they had the bulk of transatlantic trade. The administration also did not make any objections to Britain's declaration of the North Sea as a military zone in November 1914, despite the fact that it might damage U.S. trade with Scandinavia. Lansing was under considerable domestic pressure from vested interests to maintain U.S. trade overseas. He stated that U.S. industry should be allowed to sell anything it wanted to any of the belligerents. In effect this policy benefited the Allies, whose blockade of Germany had put an end to any U.S. trade with the Central Powers. If U.S. businesses were going to trade in bulk in Europe, it would be with Britain and France, not Germany.

A number of U.S. financial institutions had been approached by the Allies to supply loans through which they

▲ *Robert Lansing (1864–1928), the U.S. secretary of state from 1915, was more hostile to Germany than his predecessor William Jennings Bryan.*

▶ *German U-boats rendezvous on the surface. They were responsible for a number of sinkings in the Atlantic and elsewhere in which U.S. citizens had been killed. Gradually the attacks on shipping were to erode U.S. neutrality.*

could finance their war efforts. These loans would be used to buy U.S. goods and were of obvious benefit both to U.S. industry and to the country's financial institutions. Initially Lansing warned such financial heavyweights as John Pierpont Morgan, financier, railroad-owner, and steel magnate, that such loans were not consistent with a neutral stance. However, Morgan and his fellow industrialists argued that if the Allies did not receive such loans, they would divert their trade away from the United States to other markets and damage the economy. Lansing repeated these concerns to Wilson, and the latter agreed to an unofficial relaxation of the laws governing finance. On November 26, 1915, for example, it was announced that some $50 million was to be extended to a number of London banks.

While Wilson and his advisers were grappling with the preservation of U.S. neutrality, they were also trying to bring about an end to the war. They believed that the United States had a moral duty to arbitrate a peace settlement. Wilson, though, had to tread a tightrope. While he did not want Germany to be humiliated, he believed that it was the aggressor and should shoulder a greater share of the blame for the outbreak of war. His view was shared by Lansing, who in a memo stated, "Germany must not be allowed to win this war or to break

KEY FIGURES

COLONEL EDWARD HOUSE

Texas-born Colonel Edward House (1858–1938) was a leading light among the advisers who had the confidence of President Woodrow Wilson both before and during the involvement of the United States in World War I.

A Democrat, House had helped secure Woodrow Wilson's election in 1912, and on the eve of the outbreak of war in 1914 he was entrusted with being Wilson's "eyes and ears" in Europe. In spring 1914 House was on a mission in Europe as the continent slid toward war. His report summarized the tension, beginning with the words "The situation is extraordinary. It is militarism run stark mad."

House, whose own personal view gradually favored intervention on the side of the Allies, traveled to Europe in 1915 and 1916 at the president's behest. The aim of the diplomatic trips was to bring the war to a conclusion, with the United States acting as a mediator. However, none of the warring parties, neither the Allies nor the Central Powers, were willing to compromise, and House failed.

Following the U.S. declaration of war in 1917, House coordinated Allied policy on finance, supplies, and shipping. He also aided the president in drafting his 14-point peace proposal. In 1919 House was a member of the delegation to the Paris Peace Conference. However, Wilson and House became distant over the terms of the settlement with Germany, and the two men never met again after the signing of the Treaty of Versailles in June.

even." The Allied nations likewise believed that Germany was wholly responsible for the war and would not accept any settlement that appeared to let Germany off the hook and make them shoulder some of the blame.

Wilson's tentative peace efforts in 1914 came to little, but in early 1915 hopes rose after German Secretary of State for Foreign Affairs Arthur Zimmermann gave some encouragement to U.S. mediation. The president's special adviser, Colonel Edward House, sailed for Europe on the passenger liner *Lusitania* on January 30. Once in

(see pages 238–239).

▲ *President Woodrow Wilson stands to take the cheers of an enthusiastic crowd as he passes through the streets of San Francisco in 1915. Many still believed that he would be able to keep the United States out of the war.*

Europe, House quickly discovered that neither the Central Powers nor the Allies were willing to contemplate a peace settlement. Germany, for example, was still confident of victory and stated that it would have to be allowed to annex Belgium and Poland. Britain and France were equally unwilling to contemplate peace without victory.

U.S. neutrality under threat

U.S. attitudes toward Germany began to harden in 1915, chiefly due to the latter's growing use of its submarines to impose a naval blockade around Britain. This strategy was intensified in February, when Germany declared all waters around Britain a war zone where any vessel, neutral or not, would be open to sudden attack. Under international law vessels could not be sunk without warning, and their crews and passengers had to be allowed to leave

without hindrance before any sinking could take place. Wilson responded to the German declaration by announcing the doctrine of strict accountability—if any U.S. lives were lost to submarine attacks, Germany would be held responsible no matter what the circumstances. Events soon tested Wilson's resolve.

On March 28 the merchant ship *Falaba*, bound for Liverpool, England, from West Africa, was sunk. Among the dead was Leon Thrasher, a mining engineer and the first U.S. citizen to be killed during the war. Similar events followed. On May 1 the U.S. tanker *Gulflight* was sunk and two of its crew killed. Six days later the British liner *Lusitania* was mortally wounded by a lone German submarine sailing off the south coast of Ireland. The striken vessel went down rapidly, taking with it 1,198 passengers and crew, including 128 Americans (see pages 238–239).

The U.S. response to the *Lusitania* sinking was one of widespread outrage, but would the loss of 128 American lives push the United States from neutrality into war? Wilson's confidant, Colonel Edward House, was in little doubt. In one of a series of cables to the president from Europe, he argued, "We can no longer remain neutral spectators. Our action in this crisis will determine the part we will play when peace is made." Wilson was more circumspect, however. He was still unwilling to countenance U.S. entry into the war, believing the United States could maintain its honor through vigorous protest.

Wilson could not be sure that the American people would back an overseas war, which many, despite their outrage over the loss of the *Lusitania*, still saw as having little to do with their country. Nor did he wish to alienate further the German-American and Irish-American immigrant groups, both of which were being pilloried for their presumed support for Germany by certain section of the press. Movies reflected the growing anti-German feeling. For example, on August 7, 1915, *The Battle Cry of Peace* opened—it showed an "enemy" in German-style spiked helmets taking over New York.

Not all politicians shared Wilson's viewpoint. The ex-president Theodore Roosevelt, who was strongly pro-Allied, was much more belligerent, particularly toward those he believed were attempting to prevent the United States from going to war to protect its international honor. These people he categorized as "the hyphenated Americans, the solid flub dub and pacifist vote, every soft creature, every coward, every weakling, every man whose god is money, or pleasure or ease, and every man who has not got in him both the sterner virtues and the power of seeking after an ideal." Although Roosevelt's words reflected his own views rather than majority public opinion, Wilson took the opportunity of the *Lusitania*'s sinking to remind the various U.S. immigrant communities of their responsibilities to their adopted country: "A man who thinks of himself as belonging to a particular national group in America has not yet become an American, and a man who goes among you to trade upon your nationality is no worthy son to live under the Star and Stripes."

Wilson moved to counter the fallout of the *Lusitania* sinking by issuing increasingly stern warnings to Germany. He began mildly on May 13 by asking

◀ *Theodore Roosevelt was outspoken and belligerent in his support of the Allied cause and was equally critical of those Americans whom he believed were not supporting their country in its time of need.*

The *Lusitania*

In 1915, with the Allied blockade beginning to bite, Germany announced that the waters off Britain and Ireland were an area of war and all shipping there was in peril. It was a strategy with major political risks.

On May 7, 1915, the British passenger liner *Lusitania,* with 2,000 people on board, was sailing off the south coast of Ireland on the final leg of its journey from New York to Liverpool. Despite Germany having publicly warned the United States that British ships in the area would be attacked by submarines without warning and that U.S. citizens should not embark on such vessels, the *Lusitania* took no special

precautions to avoid attack. The British Admiralty had warned of U-boat activity in the waters off Ireland; it had also recommended adoption of a zigzag course. The *Lusitania* crew felt no need of it.

Shortly after 2 P.M. the liner was struck by one of (possibly) two torpedoes fired by *U-20* commanded by Lieutenant Commander Walther Schwieger. The great liner sank within 20 minutes, taking with it 1,198 passengers and crew, including 128 U.S. citizens.

The loss of the *Lusitania* was greeted with outrage in the United States, despite the German warning published prominently in the U.S. press and subsequent claims that the liner was armed and carrying ammunition supplies to Britain (later proved true). Some Americans and many leading newspapers decried the sinking as an act of a barbarous nation and turned on the country's

◄ *Captain William Turner of the* Lusitania, *who survived the German submarine sinking.*

◀ *The liner* Lusitania *belonged to the British Cunard company and was one of its fastest ships.*

seen as grudging and unconvincing by many. For example, Schwieger was hailed as a hero for the attack and celebrated in the German press on his return home. One editor wrote: "The sinking of the *Lusitania* is a success to our submarines which must be placed beside the greatest achievements of this war."

A privately struck medal commemorating the attack—although not countenanced by the German government, which attempted to remove them from circulation—was seen as further evidence that the public regrets of the authorities were far from sincere. Finally, a German offer of compensation ($1,000 per U.S. citizen killed) was seen as ill judged and insulting.

German-American immigrant community. Slurs were cast on its loyalty, and U.S. papers were filled with speculation about subversives who might attack from within in the event that the United States went to war with Germany. Some leading figures called for a war declaration.

However, President Woodrow Wilson was determined that the recent event should not lead to war and an ending of U.S. neutrality. He issued a series of increasingly severe diplomatic notes to Germany over the following months that forced the German government to curtail its attacks on passenger vessels.

Nevertheless, the sinking of the *Lusitania* did serve to harden popular opinion in the United States against Germany, in part because Germany handled the crisis badly. Its apology for the destruction of the *Lusitania* was

▶ *The medal struck to commemorate the sinking of the vessel. Germany's government felt the need to placate U.S. opinion, but the German public and press were supportive of the sinking.*

Germany to apologize and confirm that the sinking was an isolated tragedy, one not related to ongoing military policy. The German response was to argue that the *Lusitania* was a legitimate target, as it was armed and carrying ammunition, and that Germany would continue with its unrestricted submarine warfare. Wilson's second note on June 9 was more forceful and called on Germany to cease unrestricted submarine warfare, adding that there could be no compromise. Secretary of State Bryan believed the second note effectively ensured that the United States would go to war with Germany at some stage. Germany was unlikely to end unrestricted submarine warfare permanently, thereby probably forcing a declaration of war by the United States in the future. Unable to reconcile Wilson's stand with his own views, he resigned and was replaced by Lansing. A third note followed on July 21.

While the United States and Germany continued their diplomatic wrangling, the unrestricted submarine campaign continued. Again U.S. lives were lost. On August 19 a passenger liner, *Arabic,* was torpedoed off the south coast of Ireland. Among the dead were three U.S. citizens. On this occasion the president's response was blunt—if Germany maintained its unrestricted submarine campaign, the United States would respond. On the 28th the German authorities announced that they would avoid attacks on passenger ships and withdraw from the waters off southern Ireland, southwest England, and the English Channel. For the moment, at least, the chances of U.S. entry into the war had been greatly reduced.

Despite the sinking of the *Arabic,* Wilson still tried to broker a peace settlement. In late December his trusted adviser House was again sent to Europe. He visited London, Berlin, and Paris in January and February 1916. Again, as in his 1915 mission, he had little success. It was agreed that Wilson would issue a

▲ A U.S. cartoon accusing Theodore Roosevelt of bidding for the White House on the strength of his enthusiasm for U.S. involvement in the war and trying to lead public opinion in that direction.

call for a peace conference on receipt of a note to that effect from Britain and France and that if Germany ignored the call or made unacceptable demands, then the United States would probably enter the war on the Allied side. However, there was no mention of timing and the wording was vague. In fact, both Wilson and House failed to appreciate the depth of the animosity between Britain and France on the one hand and Germany on the other. All sides still harbored hopes of outright victory. None was willing to contemplate a negotiated end to the war at the beginning of 1916.

Strengthening the U.S. armed forces

Although Wilson seemed committed to policies of neutrality and a U.S.-led search for peace, by late 1915 the advocates of the Preparedness Movement were having some impact on his thinking. Several of the movement's leading lights, including Theodore Roosevelt,

▶ A U.S. War Department poster promoting the military training camp at Plattsburg opened in summer 1915.

began an initiative to establish military training camps for ordinary citizens. The first, formed by General Leonard Wood at Plattsburg, New York, opened on August 10. Some 1,200 volunteers arrived for training. All paid for their own travel expenses, food, and uniforms. President Wilson was initially reluctant to endorse the scheme, but he eventually relented to pressure on November 4, although Secretary of State Bryan had actively campaigned against establishing any further "Plattsburg" camps. By summer 1916 some 16,000 U.S. citizens were actively training in such camps, and in June the president led a Preparedness Movement parade in Washington.

Wilson also began to strengthen the U.S. military in late 1915, despite considerable opposition from groups such as the American Union Against Militarism. In December the National Defense Act ordered that the strength of the U.S. Army be more than doubled to 288,000 men and authorized greater manpower increases in the National Guard, which was to be paid for by the federal government rather than individual states. Although seemingly impressive, the bolstering of the armed forces was to occur over five years. However, the act also allowed the president to call out the National Guard for an indefinite period in a national emergency and stated that all men could be drafted under such unusual circumstances.

Weaknesses in the U.S. Army were soon highlighted by the expedition to Mexico, a country racked by political unrest. Mexico was economically tied to its neighbor—80 percent of its trade was with the United States—and U.S. leaders had long been willing to intervene in the country's affairs. On April 21, 1914, for example, U.S. Marines landed at Veracruz to release U.S. sailors arrested by the Mexicans.

A far lengthier incursion began in March 1916, following a raid on Columbus, New Mexico, by guerrillas led by

Mexican bandit and revolutionary Francisco "Pancho" Villa in which 14 U.S. soldiers and 10 civilians were killed (see pages 244–245). The subsequent punitive expedition into Mexico ordered by the American government was to highlight many of the U.S. Army's shortcomings. The military intervention eventually involved a large proportion of the country's frontline strength. However, when the president mobilized National Guard units, many men refused to serve, while others were poorly trained or lacked motivation. Those who returned home felt that the U.S. Army was inefficient, poorly equipped, and badly led.

If the Army was woefully small and its troops ill prepared for combat compared with the millions of men fighting in the armies of the European powers,

◀ Growing evidence of the might of the U.S. Navy—several battleships steam in line astern.

attacks off southwest England and in the English Channel, although the ban on attacks on passenger ships remained in force. On March 24 a passenger ferry, the *Sussex*, was sunk without warning in the English Channel by a German submarine. Fifty passengers were killed, including three Americans on board. President Wilson responded by stating that unless the U-boats were reined in immediately the United States would sever diplomatic ties with Germany—

the navy was more able to protect U.S. interests. The U.S. Navy was already the third largest in the world in 1914, after those of Britain and Germany, but pro-navy lobbyists were convinced that it would have to be further expanded if it was to guard U.S. overseas interests effectively. The Naval Appropriations Act of 1916 called for a large-scale building program, which was to include 16 battleships and battlecruisers.

Although Germany had pledged to halt submarine attacks on passenger ships in August 1915, the promise was soon broken. Hawks in the German military argued strongly that a relaxation of the prohibition would allow the U-boat fleet to bring Britain to its knees by strangling its overseas trade. They had their way. In March 1916 U-boat captains were given permission to resume

---

POLITICAL WORLD

THE *SUSSEX* SINKING

The loss of several U.S. lives during the sinking of the *Sussex*, struck without warning in the English Channel by a German submarine on March 24, 1916, prompted a stern response from President Woodrow Wilson that forced the German authorities to apologize for the attack:

"I have deemed it my duty, therefore, to say to the Imperial German Government, that if it is still its purpose to prosecute relentless and indiscriminate warfare against vessels of commerce by use of submarines, notwithstanding the now demonstrated impossibility of conducting that warfare in accordance with what the Government of the United States must consider the sacred and indisputable rules of international law and the universally recognized dictates of humanity, the government of the United States is at last forced to the conclusion that there is but one course it can pursue; and that unless the Imperial German Government should now immediately declare and effect an abandonment of its present methods of warfare against passenger- and freight-carrying vessels this government can have no choice but to sever diplomatic relations with the government of the German Empire altogether.

"We owe it to a due regard to our own rights as a nation, to our sense of duty as a representative of the rights of neutrals the world over, and to a just conception of the rights of mankind to take this stand now with the utmost solemnity and firmness."

From President Wilson's address to the U.S. Congress, April 19, 1916.

The Mexican Expedition

The United States had a long-standing involvement in neighboring Mexico's affairs; in February 1913 it intensified when the Mexican president, Francisco Madero, was assassinated on the orders of General Victoriano Huerta and chaos ensued that threatened U.S. economic interests in its neighbor.

It was difficult for President Woodrow Wilson to remain aloof from Mexican affairs: the United States had major financial interests in the country, and some 40,000 U.S. citizens resided in the country.

Woodrow Wilson's administration did not accept Huerta's authority and backed a rival, Venustiano Carranza. Huerta was finally forced to resign on July 14, 1914, but only after the U.S. Marines had been in occupation of Veracruz since the previous April. Following the brief presidency of Francisco Carbajal and a period of political chaos, Carranza emerged as the country's new leader. In October 1915 he was recognized by the United States as Mexico's president.

However, Carranza's position was far from secure. The head of Mexico's northern administration, Francisco "Pancho" Villa, a former ally of Carranza, refused to accept his authority and several clashes between the two

rivals' forces ensued. Villa, a blend of revolutionary and bandit, developed a great hatred of the United States for its support of Carranza. Some of Villa's supporters stopped a train at Santa Isobel carrying a party of U.S. mining engineers bound for Chihuahua and killed several of them in cold blood, provoking outrage in the United States.

On March 9, 1916, a larger and more provocative incident took place when Villa crossed the Mexico-U.S. border and attacked the town of Columbus, New

▶ *General Pershing pursuing Villa in Mexico, 1916. In 1917 Pershing was made head of the American Expeditionary Force in Europe.*

Mexico, which was garrisoned by part of the U.S. 13th Cavalry. After a firefight, Villa retreated, having lost at least 100 casualties. U.S. losses totaled 14 soldiers and 10 civilians.

President Woodrow Wilson responded by using the National Guard to strengthen the U.S. garrisons along the border, and on March 15 he ordered a punitive expedition into Mexico.

The expedition consisted of a force of some 10,000 regular troops under Brigadier General John J. Pershing. It remained

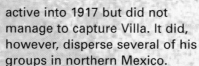

FRANCISCO (PANCHO) VILLA

active into 1917 but did not manage to capture Villa. It did, however, disperse several of his groups in northern Mexico.

The direct U.S. involvement was seen by President Carranza as an affront to Mexican sovereignty, and there were several clashes between his and Pershing's troops. The most severe of these was the battle fought between troopers of the African American 10th Cavalry and Mexican government forces at Carrizal on June 21. Although the U.S. forces had to retreat, the Mexicans suffered severe losses during the firefight.

The clash at Carrizal prompted some in the United States to argue that full-scale war should be declared. Wilson, however, was more circumspect. He recognized that the country's slender military resources were already overstretched by the

▲ *A U.S. reward notice for the apprehension of Pancho Villa.*

punitive expedition and border defense. Equally, he saw that the United States might need to preserve its military strength for any commitment to World War I. Still, Pershing remained in Mexico until February 1917, when he was ordered home by his government despite Villa's remaining at large.

In April 1917, following the introduction of a new Mexican constitution, Wilson accepted Carranza's presidency. Although it had become clear that German agents were agitating for Mexico to take some part against the United States in World War I, Wilson steadfastly refused both domestic and international demands that he take any further military action against the country's southern neighbor.

one step away from declaring war. A few days after Wilson's demand, on April 24, Germany reinstated orders for its U-boats not to attack any neutral vessels without adequate warning.

Despite the actions of the German submarines, Wilson remained publicly committed to keeping the United States neutral, and in 1916 he campaigned for reelection under the slogan, He Kept Us Out of the War. Supporters of the incumbent president could point to the recent German about-turn on its submarine campaign following the *Sussex* sinking as proof that Wilson was still firmly committed to maintaining U.S. neutrality in the conflict.

There was, some politicians argued, no pressing need to go to war with Germany to safeguard the country's economic and political interests. One delegate at the Democratic Party convention stated that U.S. rights and honor had been upheld following the loss of the *Sussex* "without orphaning a single American child, without widowing a single American mother."

Neutrality in the balance

Wilson's opponent in the presidential race was Republican Charles Evans Hughes, a former Supreme Court justice backed by some of those less enamored of Wilson's commitment to neutrality, including Theodore Roosevelt. In effect the electorate faced a single question: neutrality or possible war? Although Wilson's message was more powerful, the election on November 7 was close and probably hinged on the desire to avoid plunging the country into war. The incumbent president gained 277 votes from the electoral college, while Hughes received 254. The Democrats lost in the Senate, where their majority was cut to nine seats, and in the House of Representatives, where 216 Democrats were opposed by 210 Republicans (including the first woman to enter the U.S. Congress, Jeanette Rankin) and six Independents.

Wilson saw his victory, however narrow, as confirmation of his policies of keeping the United States neutral while attempting to broker a peace settlement. On December 18 he asked the various warring nations to state the terms upon which they would be willing to make peace and also secretly contacted both Britain and Germany to offer peace discussions under his leadership. His "peace note" proposals were not well received, either by Britain and France or by Germany. Wilson had already begun to admit—at least in private—that U.S. neutrality could not be preserved indefinitely. Speaking to the Cincinnati Chamber of Commerce on

▼ *Uncle Sam looms at Wilson's shoulder as the president gravely reads Germany's response to his requests for observance of international law and accepted norms of behavior.*

GERMANY'S REPLY.

PRESIDENT'S DESK

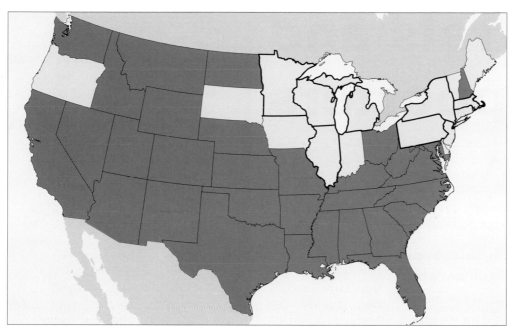

◀ *The voting patterns in the presidential election of 1916 reveal support for Wilson's defeated rival, Charles Evans Hughes, in the northeastern states (shown in yellow), which contained large German minorities.*

▼ *A German satirical cartoon depicts Wilson as Neptune, the god of the sea, muzzling the U-boats.*

October 26, President Wilson stated: "I believe that the business of neutrality is over. The nature of modern war leaves no state untouched."

Wilson may not have fully realized that for all his attempts to keep the United States neutral and to broker an end to the hostilities, the future course of the country did not rest entirely in his hands. The actions of Germany's military planners would help determine whether the United States remained neutral or went to war.

In late 1916—after 12 months of devastating casualties on the western front and with the likelihood of victory fast evaporating—these planners were arguing with their political masters that only a resumption of unrestricted submarine warfare offered a chance to win the war. Five months of unrestricted submarine warfare, they argued, would finish off Britain. If the campaign resulted in a U.S. war declaration, they believed it was unlikely that the United States would be able to intervene to any significant degree before the fighting in Europe was effectively over. It was an enormous gamble—if it failed Germany could not hope to win the war.

Neutrals and Supporters

World War I was a catastrophe on a global scale as countries and their peoples were drawn inexorably into the conflict. Colonies, supposedly independent nations, and neutrals alike had to face the fallout of a wide-ranging war. Britain, with its empire, seemed to have the greatest human assets of all the warring countries.

At the outbreak of war, Britain immediately called on the military and economic resources of its vast empire for assistance. Although there were some dissenting voices, the great majority of subject peoples responded with enthusiasm. In military terms the empire provided a major boost to Britain's strength. The greatest support came from Australia, New Zealand, Canada, South Africa, and India. Australia provided a total of some 332,000 soldiers out of a population of just 4.5 million; Canada, 595,000 out of 7.2 million; India, 1.3 million out of 315 million; New Zealand, 124,000 out of one million; and South Africa, 231,000 out of six million. Even the smallest colonies provided troops—Jamaica raised 10,280 men, while the tiny Leeward Islands, also in the Caribbean, sent 229 islanders to fight. In all cases, the majority of troops that served overseas in the war were volunteers.

These various contingents served in every major war theater, usually alongside British-raised forces. However, some played a more independent role. New Zealander troops quickly captured Germany's Samoan island colonies in the Pacific in the first weeks of the war; the Australian cruiser *Sydney* sank the

▲ *Indian troops take cover during the fighting in Belgium during late 1914. The subcontinent would provide the greatest number of colonial soldiers raised by the British Empire.*

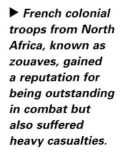

▶ *French colonial troops from North Africa, known as zouaves, gained a reputation for being outstanding in combat but also suffered heavy casualties.*

German raider *Emden* in November 1914; and the South African forces completed their capture of German Southwest Africa (now Namibia) in July 1915. A high price was paid by the empire for its demonstration of loyalty to the mother country. For example, Australia recorded a staggering 60,000 men killed and 212,000 wounded, a casualty rate of more than 80 percent—the highest of the war. Canada and New Zealand recorded similar figures: 48 and a little over 50 percent, respectively.

Supporting the empire's military commitment was its economic output—mainly foodstuffs, vital raw materials, and war equipment. This was often on quite an immense scale. For example, some 97 percent of Australia's meat production went to Britain, while some 35 percent of the latter's demand for copper was satisfied by Australian mines. Equally, Canada manufactured huge quantities of artillery shells and around 50 percent of Britain's total shrapnel (antipersonnel) shells. Many nonmilitary personnel from the empire served in noncombatant roles as laborers, merchant sailors, and teamsters.

In fact, so short were the Allies of such manpower that they had to cast their net beyond the borders of their respective empires. For example, local workers were hired from the Chinese authorities to serve overseas, chiefly on the western front and in Africa. By 1918 there were more than 200,000 Chinese nationals serving in Western Europe and a further 175,000 with the British forces operating in Africa.

France, too, could call on a large colonial empire, chiefly in northern Africa and Indochina (now Cambodia, Laos, and Vietnam). Its three possessions in North Africa—Algeria, Morocco, and Tunisia—provided substantial numbers of troops, the majority of whom served on the western front. Other colonial forces were deployed within Africa itself, chiefly in the campaigns to take over the continent's German colonies. Similarly Belgium deployed its colonial

The Easter Rising

At Easter 1916 Irish nationalists staged a rebellion against the British. The uprising centered on the Irish capital, Dublin. The British rushed troops to the country and defeated the nationalists. Many of their leaders were quickly tried and executed.

Before 1914 the British had been moving gradually toward granting a degree of political independence to Ireland through what was known as the Home Rule Bill. However, the process was suspended at the outbreak of World War I, and the intent was that it would not be enacted until the end of hostilities. The bill was not particularly popular with several sections of the Irish population. First, there were the island's Protestants. Mainly concentrated in the northeast of the country, they were determined to maintain absolute British rule. Second, there were various radical Catholic nationalist groups that wanted total independence. Among these were the Irish Republican Brotherhood, which enjoyed financial support from many Irish-Americans, and the Irish Citizen Army. Plans for an insurrection were first discussed in August 1914.

The nationalists had access to weapons, some of them provided by Germany. However, they were short of numbers to put their plan into effect. To make matters worse, a shipment of weapons due to be delivered by German submarine shortly before the rising was intercepted. The organizer of the arms smuggling, Roger Casement, was captured near Tralee in the southwest of Ireland and later executed. In the end, little more than 1,000

▼ *The destruction along Sackville Street in central Dublin in the wake of the Easter Rising by Irish Republicans in 1916.*

nationalists were available to take part in the rising, which began on April 24, 1916.

Events in Dublin went well initially for the rebels. Small units took key positions within Dublin, including the General Post Office, which became the rebels' headquarters. The British were caught by surprise, but quickly ordered troops and armed police based in various military camps outside Dublin to move on the city. Further reinforcements were later to arrive from Britain. The British began to counterattack with growing ferocity from the 26th onward, using artillery fire and even a gunboat to pound the rebels. Many buildings were consumed by fire, and civilian casualties were high. The last remaining nationalist surrendered on April 29. The British had suffered around 500 casualties in the fighting. Some

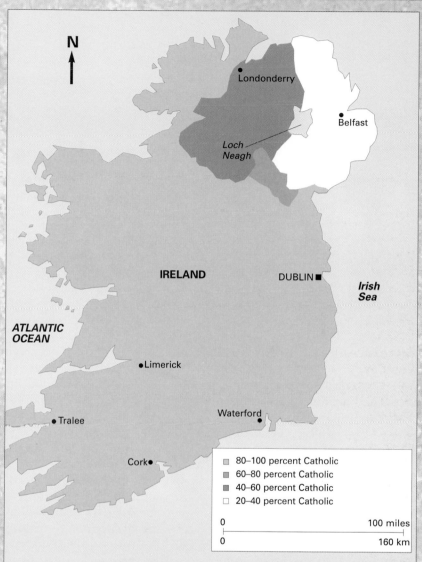

1,000 Republican rebels and Dublin civilians had also been killed or wounded.

The surviving nationalist leaders were punished swiftly. Tried by secret court, many were found guilty and executed immediately. Among these were James Connolly, head of the Irish Citizen Army, and Patrick Pearse, military leader of the Irish Volunteers group. The manner of their end—the news of their executions was not disclosed to the public until they

▲ Ireland's Catholic and Protestant communities were in 1916 geographically segregated.

were dead—caused much revulsion. The British, fearing further unrest, soon released many of the 3,000 nationalists they had imprisoned after the uprising. Many returned to Ireland, where they began organizing a stronger movement, one that they thought would have the support of the majority of the Catholic population.

Map legend:
- 80–100 percent Catholic
- 60–80 percent Catholic
- 40–60 percent Catholic
- 20–40 percent Catholic

◄ Captured Boer rebels in South Africa are led into confinement. About 10,000 Afrikaners participated, but they were opposed by far more troops and the uprising soon collapsed.

forces in Africa to protect the Belgian Congo. A 10,000-strong army was raised, which later participated in the campaign against the German forces operating in East Africa.

Unrest in the empires

Britain's empire was not immune from unrest from 1914 through 1916, however. A number of active nationalist movements opposed to colonial rule saw the conflict as a chance to press for independence. Most were purely local movements, but some received a measure of support from one or another of the Central Powers. Potentially the most serious of various nationalist incidents was an uprising in Ireland that occurred (with some German support) during Easter 1916. It ended in failure but signaled a blow to Britain's authority over the country. Elsewhere, in India, Germany attempted to back the Muslim independence group in Bengal, led by Har Dayal, with offers of weapons. The movement was suppressed by the authorities, but its leadership did prompt one of the few mutinies of the war. Har Dayal, who was based in Germany, was in part responsible for

the event, which occurred in Singapore. The mutiny took place on February 15, 1915, and broke out among a unit of the Indian Army that had been sent to defend what was a key British base in the Far East. The revolt was quickly suppressed, and 47 of the Indian ringleaders were duly executed.

South Africa also faced political problems at the beginning of the war. In August 1914 British-sponsored plans for the occupation of neighboring German Southwest Africa led to splits in the country's leadership. Some South Africans were loath to attack their neighbor because Germany had supported their rebellion against the British at the turn of the century (the Second Anglo-Boer War, 1899–1902). The rebels laid plans to march on Pretoria, the South African capital, and depose the pro-British government of General Louis Botha and his defense minister, General Jan Christiaan Smuts. However, the rebel uprising was badly planned from the outset and had little popular support. By mid-December, the majority of the rebels had been dispersed, and one of their key leaders, Christian Beyers, had drowned while

▼ Senussi desert tribesmen taken prisoner in Libyan North Africa in the wake of their jihad uprising in 1915.

fleeing the government's troops. Some 5,700 rebels were soon captured or surrendered—most of them were treated leniently—and the detailed planning for the invasion of German Southwest Africa proceeded unhindered.

Attempts at subversion by the Central Powers were not wholly confined to the British Empire. Both French and Italian colonies and possessions in North Africa saw German-led attempts to support local uprisings. France had controlled Morocco since 1912, much to the resentment of the local peoples, who were already resisting their new master as war was declared. Assisted by German money and equipment, several tribes opposed French rule, although many others sent men to fight for France. The fighting continued intermittently until 1926, but France's grip on Morocco was never seriously threatened by the rebels.

It was Italy, however, that faced the most serious threat to its prestige in North Africa, when its colony of Tripolitania (now chiefly Libya) was threatened. Several tribes, collectively known as the Senussi, after the family to which they owed their allegiance, were encouraged to rise by German and Turkish agents, who were hoping to use the colony as a springboard for an attack on neighboring Egypt, dominated by the British and the key to con-

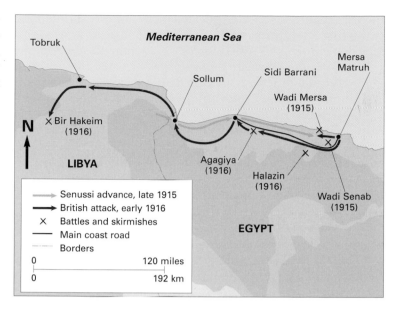

trol of the Suez Canal. The Senussi did rise in late 1915 and were defeated only with considerable difficulty in February 1916, although they continued sporadic raiding into 1917. Nevertheless, the Senussi revolt tied up some 35,000 British, 15,000 French, and 60,000 Italian troops that could have been used elsewhere in the war.

Allied-sponsored revolts
There was limited scope for those opposed to the Central Powers to sponsor local colonial rebellions. The Central Powers, chiefly Germany, had fewer colonies, and the majority of

▲ *The Senussi revolt in North Africa from 1915 to 1917 was in part created by German and Turkish agents who wished to undermine Italian and British authority in Libya and Egypt and tie up large numbers of their troops.*

those they did have were quickly taken in the first few months of the war by various detachments of Allied forces.

The Ottoman Turkish Empire, however, was quite different, and the British did attempt to foment uprisings within it, particularly in Arabia (now mainly Saudi Arabia). Turkish control of Arabia was patchy, mainly along the peninsula's coastal fringe with the Red Sea. The most important area was the Hejaz, the mountainous coastal region bordering the Red Sea. Here, the Turks held Mecca and Medina, as well as a number of key ports. All were linked by the Hejaz railroad, which ran from Damascus, Syria, to Medina. It unified the domains of the empire in this part of the Middle East, and along it Turkish troops and equipment flowed to keep the local peoples under control.

At the outbreak of war the Turks made attempts to force the local Muslims to declare a *jihad* (holy war) on the British, who held some territory in Arabia and controlled neighboring Egypt. One local leader, Husein Ibn Ali, the *sherif* (governor) of Mecca, refused, and in mid-1915 he asked for support from the British to rise against the Turks, in part to create an independent Arab state in Arabia. The support—weapons and equipment, as well as British and French military advisers (including British officer T. E. Lawrence) and forces—only trickled into

▲ *British-officered Indian troops keep guard on India's border with neighbor Afghanistan—the scene of much Central Power intrigue during the war.*

KEY FIGURES

KING FEISAL I

Feisal (1885–1933) was a son of Sherif Husein of Mecca and a key figure in the attempt by the Arabs of what is now Saudi Arabia to free their lands from Turkish rule.

The Arabs under Sherif Husein rebelled in June 1916, and Feisal was given command of the forces operating along the Red Sea, an area known as the Hejaz. Aided by British adviser T. E. Lawrence, the first success was the capture of Aqaba. Feisal's forces next pushed north, launching raids against the Hejaz railroad, a Turkish lifeline.

By late 1918, Feisal was nearing Damascus, Syria. It fell on October 1, and he was made king of Syria. After the war he attended the Paris Peace Conference, aiming to maintain Arab rights but the British and French made a deal, the Sykes-Picot agreement, that allowed France to take over Syria. Feisal was deposed in 1920.

road, was led by Husein's third son Feisal, who was aided by Lawrence; the Southern Army was under Husein's first son, Ali; and the Eastern Army was led by Abdullah, Husein's second son. In 1917 and 1918 these forces, particularly Feisal's, would conduct guerrilla attacks on the Turks in Arabia and beyond.

Subversion and subterfuge

Aside from their colonial possessions, the warring nations also exerted or attempted to exert influence over states that they considered to be within their zones of influence. These nominally independent countries often had a key strategic location, sometimes bordering the lands of two of the powers, or contained valuable raw materials, very often oil. Chief among these states were Afghanistan and Persia (now Iran). Afghanistan, on the borders of British India and Russia, had long been coveted by both powers, with each trying to control and use the local leadership to its own ends. The outbreak of World War I added another dimension—the Central Powers. In mid-1915 Germany and Turkey dispatched a supposedly secret mission under Oscar Niedermayer to Kabul, Afghanistan.

The Afghan ruler, Amir Habibulla Khan, kept the British informed of Niedermayer's activities, despite some domestic pressure for him to side with the Central Powers. Habibulla played the mission along, agreeing to a draft treaty in January 1916, but he demanded such huge recompense that Niedermayer concluded, as was intended, that Afghanistan would never side with the Central Powers. Niedermayer departed in May, and Habibulla was able to keep Afghan supporters of the Central Powers in check for the remainder of the war.

Similar issues arose in oil-rich Persia, which had, in effect, been divided between Britain and Russia since 1907. At the beginning of World War I, Germany sent a military mission and

▼ *British and Russian officers pictured in Persia during 1916. Their chief role in the war was to prevent subversion by German and Turkish agents.*

the region, and it was not until 1916 that the uprising began. Arab forces were able to crush the Turkish garrisons in Mecca and Jedda. In October 1916 Husein was proclaimed *sultan* (sovereign) of the Arabs, and the Arab Army was reorganized into three distinctive commands. The Northern Army, which was tasked with crippling the Hejaz rail-

▲ *Czech leader Tomás Masaryk fled to Switzerland soon after the outbreak of war and began organizing a government in exile. Its chief role was to win support from the Allies for a postwar independent Czech state, one free from the shackles of the Austro-Hungarian Empire of which it was a part.*

campaign that would take him across the country. He eliminated lawlessness and wholly undermined German influence in the country.

Unlike the other major powers Austria-Hungary and Russia did not have any overseas colonies. Their prestige rested on the sheer size of their homelands and the millions of people their monarchs ruled, but these empires were far from united. Like the colonial powers that faced challenges from nationalists in their overseas territories, the central authorities of both Austria-Hungary and Russia faced threats to their authority from internal nationalists who saw the war as an opportunity to press for greater freedoms and self-determination.

Austria-Hungary contained many ethnic groups, most of whom were concentrated in specific regions of the empire. One of the greatest areas of concern comprised the Czech- and Slovak-populated provinces of Bohemia, Moravia, Slovakia, and Ruthenia. Most of the inhabitants resented performing military service and paying taxes to the empire, but their aspirations for some degree of autonomy had been thwarted repeatedly. With the outbreak of World

agents to Persia. There were three main aims: to undermine Anglo-Russian influence, to take over Persian banks, and to raise local forces that could be used against British India. Their efforts failed in northern Persia due to the presence of Russian troops, but they had more success in the south, where Britain's control shrank to various ports on the coast. Turkish forces were also able to evict the Russians from the western region of Persia. Despite these successes the gains of the Central Powers were far from secure. The Germans proved little more popular than the British and Russians, and the British raised a local force led by General Percy Sykes in March 1916 to combat the German efforts. Sykes embarked on a

War I, demands for greater autonomy grew, chiefly inspired by exiled Czech and Slovak leaders, among them Tomás Masaryk and Edvard Benes. They hoped that support could be won from Britain, France, and Russia for an independent homeland. Although Britain and France warmed to the idea, Russia made the unacceptable offer to incorporate the provinces into its empire in the event of an Allied victory. Many Czechs took matters further. Some units, nominally part of the Austro-Hungarian Army, deserted wholesale, forming an initially small unit in the Russian Army in December 1915; it

would grow considerably over the next two years. Others fought alongside the French and Italians, but their aspirations would not be satisfied until the end of the war.

Russia had similar, possibly greater problems. Chief among these was Poland. Polish nationalists craved independence, but their country was to be a key battlefield on the eastern front during World War I. As such it was of vital importance not only to Russia and to Austria-Hungary, which contained a sizable Polish population in its province of Galicia, but also, to a somewhat lesser extent, to Germany.

▼ *Czechs serving with the Austro-Hungarian Army. As the war continued, their already weak commitment to the empire would evaporate in the face of the nationalist cause.*

▼ *Polish troops serving with the Austro-Hungarian Army. Some Poles briefly believed that Germany and Austria-Hungary would allow them to establish an independent Polish state once their homeland had been freed from Russian control.*

At the outbreak of war Russia moved first, asking for Polish support in return for a free and democratic Poland but under Russian supervision. However, Russian military setbacks in 1914 and 1915 suggested to some Polish leaders that greater freedom might be gained by siding with Austria-Hungary and Germany against Russia.

Chief among these figures was Józef Pilsudski, a leading light in the Polish Legions of the Austro-Hungarian Army. The legions had mustered 18,000 men by mid-1916. Germany and Austria-Hungary also made concessions to win Polish support in late 1916, a time when they controlled all of Poland. On November 5, it was announced that a semi-independent Polish state had been established under their protection. Its head was to be Pilsudski. However, both he and the majority of Poles doubted that the new state would be anything more than a puppet of Germany and Austria-Hungary. As with the Czechs and Slovaks, the Poles' desires for independence would not be satisfied until after the war.

Worldwide neutrals and war

There was also a further category of countries worldwide that felt the impact of World War I. These states were the neutrals, those that announced in the first weeks of the war that they would not become directly involved in the conflict. Some 24 countries remained wholly neutral throughout. Although

---

JAPAN'S 21 DEMANDS

Japan was an ambitious Pacific power and had plans to expand its control over China, which was internally weak and politically divided and lacked any effective armed forces. Following the Japanese-led capture of the German-run port of Tsingtao in November 1914, Japan demanded that China submit to its authority.

On January 18, 1915, the Japanese issued what became known as the 21 Demands. Drawn up by Japan's foreign minister, Takaaki Kato, and directed at the Chinese leadership, they were intended to give the Japanese virtual control of China's economic and political affairs. The main points would have allowed Japan to exercise effective control over large swathes of Chinese territory, granting it controlling interests in China's railroads and certain key industries. China was opposed to the demands, but with large Japanese forces based threateningly nearby, its government could do little.

Britain and France, Japan's allies, were alarmed at the demands (about which they had not been consulted) but could do little as they were overwhelmingly concerned with the war in Europe. However, President Woodrow Wilson of the neutral United States was able to exert some influence, and the Japanese dropped a few of their demands, fearing direct U.S. military intervention. Nevertheless, China had agreed to most of them by June. Japan had made major gains at the expense of Chinese independence, but its standing in the world had suffered by its highhandedness.

they were dotted across the globe, the greatest concentration of them was in the Americas. Much closer to the fighting on the western front, however, were several European countries, including the Netherlands, Norway, Switzerland, and Spain. Between 1914 and 1916 they continued to address their own affairs and deal with questions of their political relationships with neighbors and rivals, while attempting to avoid antagonizing any of the warring sides by seemingly siding with another. Many had negligible armed forces and so could not use military power to protect their interests as neutrals.

Globally, China was another case in point. During the period it was militarily weak, beset by great internal unrest, and was also a pawn in the struggle between the Allies and Central Powers. In 1914 Germany tried to encourage the Chinese leadership to declare war on Japan, one of the Allies. However, the Japanese quickly captured the only German military base in the country—Tsingtao—in November 1914 and immediately demanded the same favorable trading rights that Germany had enjoyed by issuing what became known as the 21 Demands. War between the two was only averted when the Chinese capitulated to the demands, which were wholly weighted in Japan's favor. The agreement greatly worried the United States, which saw Japan as an ambitious expansionist power in the Pacific, an area where there were considerable U.S. economic and strategic interests.

The war was to impinge on other neutrals in several ways. Many had sizable and powerful European minorities, often ones with considerable power over the local economy, that would endeavor to offer some assistance to their land of origin. Equally, many of these countries relied on overseas trade with Europe, often in one key product—crop, foodstuff, or raw material. For example, in Central America Guatemala's economy was dominated

▼ *Chinese troops prepare to police the streets during student protests against the Japanese. China was incapable of defending itself militarily against the ambitions of Japan, which was the main expansionist power in the Pacific.*

by coffee production and export, of which more than 50 percent was in German hands. The warring European nations were keen to exert as much diplomatic pressure as possible on this trade with the aim of halting the flow to a military rival.

The world's oceans and seas were turned into battlegrounds, and the merchant ships of neutral countries—or their produce—were likely to be caught up in the fighting. The importance of this international trade can be illustrated by Brazil. Although trade with the United States (both imports and exports) dominated the country's economy at the outbreak of war, Germany was the second greatest importer of Brazilian goods, while Britain was the second greatest exporter of goods to Brazil. Clearly, both countries had much to lose if their economic and trading links with Brazil were restricted or indeed severed.

As neutrals, Brazil and other nations in the Americas suffered as the war went on. Ships were sunk, territorial waters were violated, and trade revenue was threatened. Increasingly these threats were dominated by Germany's attempts to strangle Britain's maritime trade. Germany relied on its submarine fleet to halt this flow of vital supplies by resorting to unrestricted submarine warfare. Inevitably, this led to the neutrals' suffering ship losses and casualties, events that gradually moved various states toward favoring those opposed to the Central Powers.

Overriding all of this turmoil from 1914 to 1916 was one key issue—the role of the United States, the dominant political and economic power in the Americas. The United States gradually moved toward war against Germany in the period. When it declared war in 1917, many other neutral countries in the Americas followed suit. Their greatest contribution was not in troops but in vast quantities of foodstuffs and minerals that fueled the Allied war effort.

The United States Moves to War

Although events during 1916 had pushed the United States ever closer to a direct role in the conflict, in early 1917 few citizens expected to become involved in a distant European war that appeared to have little or no direct bearing on their own lives.

At the outbreak of the conflict in August 1914, the country had not entered into any overseas political alliances and President Woodrow Wilson declared a policy of strict neutrality. In the first two years of the conflict Wilson, a high-minded man of liberal leanings, endeavored to preserve

On April 6, 1917, Congress voted to back President Woodrow Wilson's call for a declaration of war on Germany, yet only a few months before, it seemed that the United States might avoid becoming embroiled in World War I.

his country's neutrality, while his support for free trade and an abhorrence of war encouraged him to seek peace.

However, by mid-1916 the United States was cautiously aligning with the Allies, and in April 1917 Wilson led his country into war. The reasons for this fundamental change in the country's political alignment cannot be attributed to any one event. Business interests, propaganda, political influence and intrigue, and most importantly the unbridled pursuit of submarine warfare by Germany, all played a role in bringing the United States into the war.

Although it officially maintained a strictly neutral stance from 1914 through to 1917, the United States played an increasingly critical role in supplying both Britain and France with munitions and in extending them credit to bankroll their war efforts. By

◀ *The* Los Angeles Examiner *highlights the turnabout in U.S. foreign policy in early 1917.*

▶ *Wilson had to move warily in going to war. He did not want to alienate the country's German-Americans, nor did he wish to be linked with the motives of Britain, France, and Russia.*

1916 Britain was obtaining some 40 percent of its military supplies from the United States, chiefly through the offices of the J. P. Morgan Bank. American businessmen grew rich on this trade, which was perfectly legal and was denied to Germany by a British naval blockade. However, the British policy of searching neutral ships and confiscating anything that was deemed to be contraband cargo destined for the use of Germany caused considerable resentment in some U.S. business circles, as it robbed them of valuable European customers. The U.S. government used angry protests but did little to oppose this policy or the many other ways in which Britain sought to control transatlantic trade. Germany found itself forced to exert its own influence on transatlantic trade through the pursuit of a submarine blockade of Britain.

Most of what Britain and France bought from the United States was bought on credit. By April 1917 the Allies' credit facilities with U.S. banks were almost exhausted, and their gold reserves were negligible. Some historians have argued that the United States entered the war at the behest of its leading industrialists to ensure that Britain and France would be in a position to

▼ *A U.S.-built tractor is put through its paces by the French military. U.S. trade increasingly favored the Allies rather than the Central Powers as the war progressed, partly because the British naval blockade prevented goods from reaching the latter.*

repay these debts, but many other factors acted to push the United States into World War I.

U.S. neutrality undoubtedly strongly favored the Allies, but both sides recognized the value of direct American support. With a total population of more than 100,000,000 people and as a pioneer of mass production, the United States had the potential to decide the outcome of the war. As such, both Britain and France—and Germany—struggled to win over the hearts and minds of the U.S. population in pursuit of their own self-interests.

Germany knew that the powerful and influential pro-Allied lobby in the United States would prevent any direct help for its cause and instead sought to dissuade the country from intervening militarily on the Allied side. Britain, France, and Russia, in contrast, needed vast quantities of U.S. arms, foodstuffs,

and raw materials and also clamored for American troops to join the fight against the Central Powers.

The U.S. press was generally pro-British, and its coverage of the war was colored by the fact that most of its reporters were based in either Britain or France. The British did much to encourage stories in the U.S. press of alleged atrocities committed by the German forces in Belgium. Much of the published material had a pro-British slant, which grew out of the long-standing links between the two and U.S. concern over affairs in western Europe. While some propaganda sympathetic to Germany did exist, it did not carry much weight with the wider American public. Germany was seen as a monarchy with militarist leanings, and, after the interception of the Zimmermann telegram in 1917 (see pages 270–271), an agenda to undermine U.S. power.

The U.S. political climate

Struggling against this growing tide of anti-German propaganda, President Woodrow Wilson was conscious of the need to maintain harmony among the diverse ethnic populations of the country, including the large number of German and Austrian immigrants, and also stood firmly by his non-interventionist policy against increasingly loud calls by interventionists for action to protect U.S. interests overseas. During 1916 the president pursued a peaceful resolution to the conflict through his closest political confidant, Colonel Edward House, who traveled to Europe in search of accord. U.S. isolationist foreign policy was also encouraged by Congress's apprehensions about allowing other countries a political door into U.S. policies. The leading voice among the various organizations that actively supported the full preservation of the

isolationist policy was a pacifist pressure group, the American Union Against Militarism (AUAM), but its leadership lacked the funds or cohesion to make a sustained public impact.

By April 1917 the AUAM had expanded to around 1,500 members but never had the influence of its political opposition, chiefly the Preparedness Movement and the National Security League, which were among those who argued that the country should expand the size of its armed forces in case of war. Formed in December 1914 by General Leonard Wood, the U.S. Army's former chief of staff, the National Security League called for universal military training and the introduction of conscription as a means of increasing the size of the U.S. Army. Wood was a close friend of ex-president Theodore Roosevelt, the influential Republican whose vigorous

▲ *A demonstration against deeper U.S. involvement in the war. The placards argue that the decision to go to war had as much to do with the profits that would accrue to big business as to any moral obligation to bring a swift and fair end to the conflict.*

▲ *A cartoon published in the British satirical magazine* Punch *in October 1916 rails against the president's neutral stance. It argues that he was failing to act against the growing German submarine menace in his desire to keep the United States out of the war.*

that his threat to impose full accountability in the event of a resumption by Germany of unrestricted submarine warfare amounted to an ultimatum. He strove again to pursue a resolution, but the failure of Wilson's "peace note" in December 1916 (see pages 246–247) demonstrated the gulf between the belligerents and helped convince the German leadership of the need to resume the submarine offensive.

More than any other factor the activities of Germany's submarines convinced the American people that war with Germany was necessary. Prior to 1915 German submarines had a policy of warning, allowing the passengers and crews of vessels under attack time to evacuate their ships before sinking them. However, in 1915 the *Lusitania* was sunk without warning, killing more than 120 Americans. One year later, the *Sussex* was sunk in the English Channel, again by a German submarine and with more loss of life. The American press of

support for the recently formed Preparedness Movement brought him into conflict with Wilson. As early as September 1915 Roosevelt had been moved to say: "The United States has played the most ignoble part for the last 13 months. Our government has declined to keep its plighted faith, has declined to take action for justice and right, as it was pledged to take action under the Hague Conventions. At the same time, it has refused to protect its own citizens; and it has refused even to prepare for its own defense."

Two years later America remained divided over the issue. In November 1916 the electorate voted Wilson back into the White House after a campaign that championed him as "the man who kept us out of the war." It was a stance that Wilson was loath to use, as he knew

all political persuasions expressed outrage at these flagrant violations of the rights of U.S. neutrals at sea.

Wilson thereafter took a stronger stance on foreign affairs by increasing the size of the military and issued a stern diplomatic warning to the Germans. He stated, "Unless the imperial government should now immediately declare and effect an abandonment of its present methods of submarine warfare against passenger and freight-carrying vessels, the government of the United States can have no choice but to sever diplomatic relations with the German Empire."

In response, Germany temporarily called off the unrestricted submarine campaign, but by the fall of 1916, the British naval blockade was seriously affecting Germany's ability to wage war. Germany's military leadership believed that it must risk attacking the neutral merchant shipping that sustained Britain's war effort while its own was being starved. Germany had, by its own reckoning, been left with little option but to resume the trade war against Britain. Inevitably, such an act was likely to lead to further U.S. shipping losses.

At the end of December 1916, Wilson again sought to achieve a negotiated peace by issuing his so-called peace note, which called on the various combatant nations to state the basis on which they might agree to peace. Ultimately this tactic failed. Although publicly Wilson continued to talk only of peace, in private he knew that in all probability he might have to lead the United States into the war once German unrestricted submarine warfare had recommenced. Wilson was also far too politically astute to argue for peace at any price.

Despite his growing reservations, the president continued to call for a fair and peaceful solution, notably in a speech to the Senate on January 22, 1917. Wilson emphasized that his goal

▼ Democratic Party supporters in New York attempt to rally support for Wilson during the 1916 presidential campaign. The election centered on the country's degree of involvement and role in World War I.

was "peace without victory," wherein the warring nations would settle on equal terms with neither side forced to accept the humiliation of defeat. The appeal was made to "forward-looking men and women everywhere." In effect, Wilson was appealing directly to the ordinary people of the countries at war, not their political masters. However, the president's speech fell on deaf ears. The

---

POLITICAL WORLD

"PEACE WITHOUT VICTORY"

On January 22, 1917, Wilson addressed the Senate. His speech was directed at those nations fighting World War I. Wilson's intention was to broker peace and establish basic international political principles that would prevent such a war from breaking out again:

"Victory would mean peace forced upon the loser, a victor's terms imposed upon the vanquished. It would be accepted in humiliation, under duress, at an intolerable sacrifice, and would leave a sting, a resentment, a bitter memory upon which terms of peace would rest, not permanently, but only as upon quicksand. Only a peace between equals can last, only a peace the very principle of which is equality and a common participation in a common benefit. The right state of mind, the right feeling between nations, is as necessary for a lasting peace as is the just settlement of vexed questions of territory or of racial and national allegiance.

"The equality of nations upon which peace must be founded if it is to last must be an equality of rights; the guarantees exchanged must neither recognize nor imply a difference between big nations and small, between those that are powerful and those that are weak. Right must be based upon the common strength, not upon the individual strength, of the nations upon whose concert peace will depend. Equality of territory or of resources there of course cannot be; nor any other sort of equality not gained in the ordinary peaceful and legitimate development of the peoples themselves. But no one asks or expects anything more than an equality of rights. Mankind is looking now for freedom of life, not for equipoises of power."

◄ *Count Johann von Bernstorff, the German ambassador to Washington, delivered a note on January 31, 1917, that announced the recommencement of his country's campaign of unrestricted submarine warfare.*

KEY FIGURES

SECRETARY OF STATE ROBERT LANSING

Robert Lansing (1864–1928), the U.S. secretary of state from 1915 until 1920, was a forceful advocate of American entry into World War I.

It was to Lansing on January 31, 1917, that the German ambassador to the United States, Count Johann von Bernstorff, announced the recommencement of unrestricted submarine warfare. Lansing later pressed Wilson to immediately sever relations with Germany over the issue, but Wilson was initially more circumspect.

Although Lansing was a forceful believer in U.S. involvement in the war, his role at the center of policymaking was over-shadowed by Wilson's own interests in such affairs and by the activities of Colonel Edward House, Wilson's special envoy to the warring nations in Europe.

Nevertheless, Lansing continued to serve within the administration throughout the war. He also accompanied the president to the Paris Peace Conference (1919–1920) to draw up the treaties to end the war. However, Lansing strongly disagreed with Wilson over the form and role of the proposed League of Nations, and relations between the two men soured. Lansing was forced to resign in 1920.

Allied leadership made no official response to Wilson's speech. Germany's reaction was much more warlike.

On January 31 the German ambassador to the United States, Count Johann von Bernstorff, delivered a note to Secretary of State Robert Lansing declaring that, as of February 1, unrestricted submarine warfare would be resumed, although there would be a period of grace lasting until March 2. The brief note made clear that all vessels, both passenger and merchant, whether neutral or belligerent, that were sailing in the various war zones around the British Isles, France, and Italy would be subject to sinking without warning. U.S. passenger ships, one sailing in each direction across the Atlantic

each week, would be allowed—but only if they were plainly marked and carried no war goods. Bernstorff justified such measures by stating that the United States had failed to exert pressure on the British to lift their blockade of Germany, which had been part of the agreement reached when Germany had halted its U-boat campaign in May 1916.

The decision to resume the submarine campaign had been made on January 9. Many senior figures in Germany believed that the war could be won in a matter of months—well before the United States could have any significant impact on its outcome—if the submarines were unleashed without restriction. The German naval minister of the time, Admiral Eduard von

Capelle, captured the mood in a speech to the Reichstag (German parliament) on the day Bernstorff delivered his blunt message in Washington: "I have always laid great stress on the importance of America's entrance into the war. But from a military point of view its entrance means nothing."

The U.S. reaction to this announcement, among the wider public, the media, and the Wilson administration, was measured. Many people seemed to support media calls for immediate action against Germany. However, some groups were more circumspect. The German-American media expressed the hope that the president would acquiesce in the German decision, while several pacifist groups demanded that Wilson do nothing to endanger the country's peace. However, the tide in mainstream political circles was turning against such sentiments. After two days of deliberation, culminating in a cabinet meeting and an informal gathering of several Democratic senators in the Capitol building during the afternoon of February 2, Wilson found that he could count on political support for direct action. That night he composed an address to be read before Congress on the following day.

On the afternoon of the 3rd Wilson spoke to Congress. He stated that the recent German announcement had left him no alternative but to sever diplomatic ties with Germany. Lansing was instructed to inform Bernstorff of his decision, which in political terms was one step away from a war declaration. However, Wilson also stated that he found it difficult to believe that Germany would sink U.S. ships and kill its citizens in what he considered to be an illegal campaign. If such events did occur, he warned, then he would ask Congress for the right to protect U.S. trade. Wilson's stance infuriated the British. Their war leader, David Lloyd George, remarked on the day after the speech to Congress: "And so he [Wilson] is not going to fight after all! He is awaiting another insult before he actually draws the sword."

Although Wilson's speech was received mostly favorably, both inside and outside Congress, it forced the wider U.S. public to confront the real possibility of war with Germany. Worse, U.S. involvement in the conflict now depended on German actions over which they and the administration had little control. Wilson opted to offer no provocation. The Departments of the

▼ President Wilson addresses Congress on February 3, announcing that the United States would sever diplomatic relations with Germany forthwith in response to the latter's decision to give its submarines free rein.

► *Clear evidence of the worsening state of relations between Germany and the United States—Germany's ambassador, Count Johann von Bernstorff (center) arrives at Hoboken, New Jersey, to begin the journey to his homeland after being expelled, February 14, 1917.*

Army and Navy were allowed to draw up plans for full mobilization, but a White House-inspired report published in the *New York Times* stated that German attacks on belligerent ships would be ignored even if U.S. lives were lost. Action would only be taken if U.S. ships were attacked without warning.

Wilson also refused requests from various U.S. shipping lines for the government to provide guns and men to protect their vessels, although he did permit them to arm their own ships out of their own pockets if they wished. However, demand for the arming of U.S. merchant ships steadily grew—captains were keeping their vessels in safe harbors, and trade goods were piling up in dockside warehouses and on wharves. On February 20 Wilson asked Lansing to draw up a memorandum regarding the arming of neutral vessels. The president planned to read his proposal to Congress six days later. However, war-related matters were now moving at an alarming speed.

On February 25 the British passenger liner *Laconia* was hit. During the war the *Laconia*, like several other fast civilian vessels, had served on occasion as an armed merchant cruiser as part of the campaign against Germany's commerce

raiders, and it had also recently served as a headquarters ship during the British-led campaign in German East Africa. The *Laconia* had reverted to its peacetime role just six months before, and on February 17 it had steamed out of New York, bound for the port of Liverpool. The voyage had been well-publicized and probably noted by the Germans. Whatever the case, the liner was torpedoed and sunk. Many of the stricken liner's passengers took to the lifeboats. After six hours adrift they were rescued by a British ship and taken to Ireland, where it was soon discovered that two U.S. citizens, a mother and daughter from Chicago, had been drowned. The story was relayed to the United States, from where it was syndicated around the world. Regardless of the fact that *Laconia* was but one of 230 ships, 70 of them neutral, that were sunk in February, its loss made a considerable impact on the U.S. public.

On February 26, when the news of the *Laconia* sinking broke in the United States, Wilson was preparing to address Congress on the issue of arming U.S. merchant ships. He was already outraged by recently revealed secret negotiations, yet to be announced to the wider U.S. public, between Germany

▲ *Two Austrian vessels are interned at New Orleans in February 1917, evidence of the growing rift between the United States and the Central Powers.*

and Mexico—the highly provocative Zimmermann telegram. This incident, together with the German unrestricted submarine campaign, would lead to a U.S. declaration of war.

Events relating to the secret correspondence dated back to the beginning of the year. On January 19 Alfred Zimmermann, the German foreign minister, had cabled Bernstorff in Washington instructing him to ask the German ambassador in Mexico, Heinrich von Eckhardt, to make overtures to that country's authorities inviting them to join an alliance with

Germany in any war with the United States. The telegram offered Mexico the U.S. states of Texas, New Mexico, and Arizona, once controlled by Mexico, in exchange for the right of German submarines to make full use of Mexican ports. The telegram also proposed that the Mexican government make secret approaches to Japan, with the same political objective in mind.

Unbeknown to Germany, its diplomatic communications were being routinely intercepted by the British. Zimmermann's telegram, after being encoded in Berlin, was sent in several

ARTHUR ZIMMERMANN

The telegram sent on January 19, 1917, by Germany's foreign minister, Arthur Zimmermann (1860–1940) to his ambassador to the United States, convinced Wilson that Germany was insincere in desiring peace. It suggested that Germany was willing to provoke war with the United States by creating an alliance against it.

"On the first of February we intend to begin submarine warfare unrestricted. In spite of this, it is our intention to endeavor to keep neutral the United States of America.

"If this attempt is not successful, we propose an alliance on the following basis with Mexico: that we shall make war together and together make peace. We shall give general financial support, and it is understood that Mexico is to reconquer the lost territory in New Mexico, Texas, and Arizona. The details are left to you for settlement.

"You are instructed to inform the president of Mexico [Venustiano Carranza] of the above in the greatest confidence as soon as it is certain that there will be an outbreak of war with the United States and suggest that the president of Mexico, on his own initiative, should communicate with Japan suggesting adherence at once to this plan; at the same time, offer to mediate between Germany and Japan.

"Please call to the attention of the president of Mexico that the employment of ruthless submarine warfare now promises to compel England to make peace in a few months."

ways to the German embassy in Washington, one of them through the U.S. State Department's cable office in Berlin via London, prior to transmission to Mexico. The British, who did not want the German and U.S. authorities to know that they had tapped their communications, waited until they had gained a copy from Mexico City before breaking the news.

The German telegram was deciphered by the Royal Navy's secret intelligence department, known as Room 40, with little difficulty and passed on to the U.S. ambassador in London, Walter

Hines Page, by Britain's foreign secretary, Arthur Balfour. Page sent the text to the United States, where it duly arrived in the State Department on the evening of February 24. It was read by an outraged Wilson during the early evening of the next day. The authenticity of the document was checked over the following days, and a transcript was passed to the U.S. press on February 29 for publication on March 1.

The decision for war

Thus when Wilson rose to address Congress on February 26 he was aware of the details of the Zimmermann telegram, if not its authenticity, but he did not announce its contents. However, the news of the *Laconia* reinforced his belief that U.S. commerce had to be protected by a policy of armed neutrality. Wilson stated that there was a need "to supply our merchant ships with defensive arms, should that become necessary, and with the means of using them, and to employ any other instrumentalities or methods that might be necessary or adequate to protect our ships and our people in their legitimate and peaceful pursuits on the seas." There was much support for the policy, with many believing it might reduce the need for war.

On March 1 Americans awoke to read startling banner headlines, among them: "Germany seeks an alliance against us; asks Japan and Mexico to join her; full text of proposals made public." Most were outraged, doubly so because the document had been transmitted by way of the U.S. State Department cable office in Berlin, access to which had been granted as a gesture of goodwill when, in 1914, the British cut the transatlantic cable linking Germany with the United States. Many who opposed the war were now convinced that Germany had gone too far, particularly after March 3, when Zimmermann himself publicly admitted sending the telegram.

▶ *The British foreign secretary, Arthur Balfour (second from left) is greeted by U.S. Secretary of State Robert Lansing (second from right) on his official arrival in Washington on April 23, 1917. Balfour had passed on the transcript of the Zimmermann telegram to Walter Hines Page, the U.S. ambassador to Britain in February, a decision that helped move the country to declare war.*

After his inauguration on March 4 Wilson became increasingly preoccupied with the policy of armed neutrality. On March 6 it was confirmed that he could, under his presidential powers, order the arming of merchant vessels; Wilson made such an announcement three days later. However, the viability of armed neutrality was being called into question by Germany's submarines. The *Algonquin*, an American vessel, was sunk by submarine gunfire while in British waters on the 12th, although with no loss of life. It was the first U.S. vessel to be lost since the full introduction of unrestricted submarine warfare on March 2. Between March 16 and 18 three U.S. vessels—*City of Memphis*, *Illinois*, and *Vigilancia*—were sunk, the last with considerable loss of life.

These events finally pushed Wilson and the U.S. public over the edge. There were nationwide public demonstrations and marches in favor of declaring war on Germany. Wilson gathered the members of his cabinet on March 20. As one they voted for war, leaving him in no doubt of their feelings. This is Lansing's memory of the meeting: "The president, during the discussion or at the close, gave no sign what course he would adopt. However, as we were leaving the room he called back [Postmaster General Albert] Burleson and me and asked our views as to the time of calling a session if he so decided. After some discussion we agreed that to prepare the necessary legislation for submission to Congress would take over a week and that, therefore, Monday, April 2, would be the earliest day Congress could conveniently be summoned. I asked the president if he would issue a proclamation that afternoon so it would appear in the morning papers on Wednesday. He replied smilingly: 'Oh, I think I will sleep on it.'"

Wilson probably made up his mind to go to war that afternoon. Historians suggest there were five reasons that moved him in the direction of U.S. involvement. First, as recent events had shown, armed neutrality was not preventing the sinking of U.S. ships and the deaths of the country's citizens.

▼ *The inauguration of President Wilson on March 4, 1917. Within days the sinking of several U.S. vessels by German submarines would leave him with no alternative to declaring war.*

Second, Wilson also believed, correctly, that Germany was ruled by ardent militarists, who were unwilling to negotiate terms that would lead to the protection of U.S. merchant ships. Consequently, as long as the war progressed, the United States would continue to suffer casualties at sea. Third, Wilson believed that the war was entering its final stages and that U.S. entry would hasten its conclusion and bring a speedier end to the bloodletting. Fourth, the Russian Revolution in March had removed a stumbling block to U.S. participation. Prior to the revolution, many saw Russia as a despotic, undemocratic state in which millions were kept in virtual slavery. Before the overthrow of the regime, many believed that the democratic United States could not side with the Allies when one of them was so patently undemocratic. The revolution seemed to offer hope for the creation of a more democratic Russia, and thus a major barrier blocking U.S. direct involvement on the side of the Allies appeared to have been removed.

Finally, Wilson also believed that the United States would have a greater opportunity to shape the peace that followed the end of hostilities if it took a direct part in the war. Wilson was probably little influenced by volatile public opinion in the United States, and he had few illusions that Britain and France, who were wholly of the view that Germany initiated the war, would demand that harsh peace terms be imposed on the defeated Central Powers, particularly Germany.

On April 2 Wilson delivered a strongly worded war message to a special session of Congress. Wilson's speech, delivered in his usual careful manner to a hushed assembly, chronicled the various acts of aggression by Germany against the government and people of the United States. Such violent acts, he declared,

▲ *The* Illinois *was one of three U.S. merchant vessels sunk by German submarines in quick succession during mid-March 1917. These losses and several others convinced many in the United States that Germany would not show any caution in its recently renewed unrestricted submarine campaign.*

Wilson Goes to War

By late March 1917 President Woodrow Wilson felt he had little choice other than to ask Congress to back a declaration of war against Germany. His various attempts for peace had failed, U.S. citizens were being killed, and the country's trade was suffering.

On March 21 Wilson requested the 56th Congress to meet in special session. The date was set for April 2. Wilson felt driven into such a position by recent events. Between March 16 and 18, three U.S. merchant ships had been sunk by German submarines, and it had recently been revealed that Germany's foreign minister, Arthur Zimmermann, was attempting an alliance with Mexico and Japan against the United States. It was impossible to remain uncommitted. Wilson's speech, a call for Congress to back war, reflected his view that the United States could not remain neutral.

"The present German submarine warfare against commerce is a warfare against mankind. It is a war against all nations. American ships have been sunk, American lives taken, in ways which it has stirred us very deeply to learn of, but the ships and people of other neutral and friendly nations have been sunk and overwhelmed in the waters in the same way. There has been no discrimination. The challenge is to all mankind. Each nation must decide. There is one choice we cannot make, we are incapable of making: we will not choose the path of submission and suffer the most sacred rights of our nation and our people to be ignored or violated. The wrongs against which we now array ourselves are no common wrongs; they cut to the very roots of human life.

"With a profound sense of the solemn and even tragical character of the step I am taking and of the grave responsibilities which it involves, but in unhesitating obedience to what I deem my constitutional duty, I advise that the Congress declare the recent course of the Imperial German government to be in fact nothing less than war against the government and people of the United States; that it formally accept the status of

belligerent which has thus been thrust upon it, and that it take immediate steps not only to put the country in a more thorough state of defense but also to exert all its power and employ all its resources to bring the government of the German Empire to terms and end the war.

"There are, it may be, many months of fiery trial and sacrifice ahead of us. It is a fearful thing to lead this great peaceful people into war, into the most terrible and disastrous of all wars, civilization itself seeming to be in the balance. But the right is more precious than peace, and we shall fight for the things which we have always carried nearest our hearts—for democracy, for the right of those who submit to authority to have a voice in their own governments, for the rights and liberties of small nations, for a universal dominion of right by such a concert of free peoples as shall bring peace and safety to all nations and make the world itself at last free."

"*We are coming, brothers, coming, A hundred thousand strong!*"

◀ *President Wilson speaks to Congress on April 2, 1917, outlining his reasons for taking the United States into World War I. Though some of those present had reservations, the speech was generally received favorably, and war was declared four days later.*

▲ *The impact of the declaration of war on the U.S. people was rapidly felt. This postcard was also aimed at Britain and France, both of whom were nearly at the end of their rope in 1917.*

Nr. 41   LXXI. Jahrgang

Kladderadatsch

Der Bluthund Morgans

Morgan: „Einen schärferen Bluthund hätte ich wohl nirgends finden können, um meine Dollars aus Europa zurückzuholen."

▲ *It was thought by some that Wilson's call for war was at the behest of big business. This German magazine depicts Wilson as a dog, controlled by business in the shape of John Pierpont Morgan.*

amounted to war. During the speech he uttered a phrase with which he and U.S. involvement in the war have since been associated. "The world," he said, "must be made safe for democracy." As Wilson finally sat down, Congress erupted in spontaneous applause. There were voices of opposition, but they were drowned out in the clamor for Wilson and support for the war. Theodore Roosevelt, once an opponent of Wilson, was moved to praise the president.

Nevertheless, Wilson had to obtain a declaration of war from Congress. Thomas Martin of Virginia introduced a war resolution to the Senate on April 3, the day on which an armed U.S. merchant ship, *Aztec*, was sunk by a German submarine. The congressional session continued well into the night. The mood among those assembled was generally for a declaration of war, with many speaking at length of their patriotism and unqualified support for the president's call to arms. However, there were some dissenting voices to be heard from the floor.

Few senators present at the meeting chose to question the wisdom of direct U.S. involvement in the war, except for three Progressive Republicans, Robert La Follette of Wisconsin, George Norris of Nebraska, and Asle Jorgenson Gronna of North Dakota, and also, from the Democrats, James Vardaman of Mississippi and William Stone from Missouri. The most eloquent among them were La Follette and Norris. La Follette, a very gifted orator and former presidential candidate whose state had a significant population of German Americans, was jeered at from all sides as for three hours he implored the chamber to consider its decision wisely.

Norris, after declaring that he was wholly "opposed to taking any step that will force our country into the useless and senseless war now being waged in Europe," reiterated that "if this resolution passes I shall not permit my feeling of opposition…to interfere in any way with my duty, and all of my energy and all of my power will be behind our flag in carrying it on to victory."

He went on to lay the blame for the outbreak of war in 1914 firmly with the British political leadership. This was based on the argument that "both Great Britain and Germany have, on numerous occasions since the beginning of the war, flagrantly violated in the most serious manner the rights of neutral vessels and neutral nations under existing international law as recognized up to the beginning of this war by the civilized world. However, the first war zone was declared by Great Britain and both of these orders declaring military zones were illegal and contrary to international law. It is sufficient to say that our government has officially declared both of them to be illegal and has officially protested against both of them."

Norris found little support for his proposal that the country was being forced into the war to protect the interests of the businessmen on whom the Allies relied for munitions and to whom they owed money. He and La Follette were loudly heckled, and had to field wholly false accusations that they were in the pay of Germany. The Senate voted overwhelmingly in favor of war by a margin of 82 to 6.

Next, the House of Representatives discussed the war issue. The session took place on April 6, and speakers were restricted to just 20 minutes of oratory. When the vote came, some 373 of those present backed war and only 50 voted against the resolution. Wilson now had the political support to take the United States into World War I.

On April 6 the United States formally declared war on Germany. The declaration was carefully worded, stating that the United States was opposing the German government and not its people. It also made no mention of any close alliance with the Allies, thereby reflecting Wilson's belief that he was taking his country to war not for selfish national objectives but to bring a swift end to the conflict and the creation of a more equitable world order. He avoided forming a fully binding alliance with Britain and France, and the United States fought in the conflict as what was termed an "associate power."

On the same day, diplomatic links with Austria-Hungary were severed, although war was not declared until December 7. Diplomatic relations were formally broken with Turkey on the 20th, although war was never actually declared against either Turkey or the fourth Central Power, Bulgaria, and no U.S. troops fought against them. Only a token force of regimental strength ever fought against the Austro-Hungarians.

The focus of the U.S. war effort would be directed against Germany. After 34 months of trying to maintain a neutral position, Wilson had been forced into committing U.S. economic might and its people to fight a war that was no longer distant. However, Britain and France wondered how long it would be before U.S. manpower could have an impact on the western front.

▼ Senator Robert La Follette of Wisconsin argued eloquently against U.S. entry into World War I, stating that public opinion was against such a move and the desire for war was generated by big businesses, which feared they might lose their overseas investments.

The U.S. Military Commitment

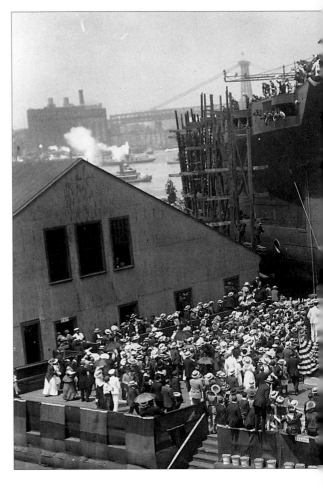

In April 1917 the United States was faced with creating a vast military machine virtually from scratch if it was to influence the fighting in Europe. The U.S. Army was small and the air service virtually non-existent; only the U.S. Navy was ready for a major war.

In 1914 the U.S. Army comprised some 98,000 men, of whom some 45,000 were defending the country's overseas interests in the Caribbean, Central America, and the Philippines. Some 29,000 others were committed to home defense, leaving 24,000 troops for deployment to potential trouble-spots. The U.S. Army was backed up by the 27,000 members of the National Guard, but this force, chiefly created for domestic defense, was considered generally inadequate by those who sought a more active worldwide role for the military. In December 1914 the most prominent spokesman for this point of view, General Leonard Wood, formed the pro-military National Security League and began arguing for conscription as a means of rapidly increasing the size of the U.S. Army.

President Woodrow Wilson responded in June 1916 with the National Defense Act. This envisaged the enlargement of the U.S. Army, in stages, to 235,000 men by 1921, although the president was allowed to implement the act more quickly if necessary. Enlistment was to be for three years, with a further four in the reserves. The National Guard was also to be strengthened to around 457,000 men split among 16 divisions. Costs relating to the National Guard were henceforth to be carried by the federal government rather than the states.

In contrast the U.S. Navy had grown into a rather more formidable force in the previous 30 years. A major construction program had been begun in the 1890s, which aimed at creating a modern battlefleet along the lines of those of navies from western Europe. Further expansion of the U.S. Navy was encouraged by the Spanish-American War of 1898 and by the need to protect and extend flourishing trade routes across the Pacific and Atlantic oceans. In 1914 the U.S. Navy was the third largest in the world, with some 300 warships in its service, including 10 powerful modern

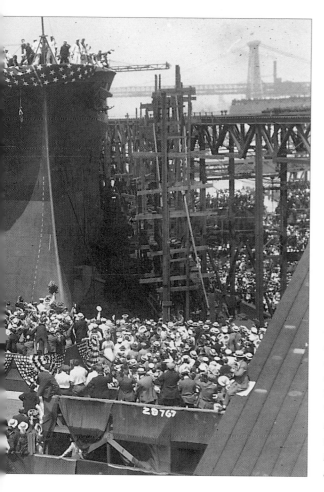

◀ *A large crowd surrounds the officials' stand at the prow of the U.S.S.* Arizona *during the dreadnought battleship's naming ceremony and launch in June 1915. The U.S. Navy was then already one of the largest navies in the world.*

▼ *In contrast with the U.S. Navy, the U.S. Army was small and far from battle ready. The most effective element of the country's armed forces was the U.S. Marine Corps (part of the Navy), seen here during the actions in Mexico.*

the limited provision of medical care facilities and a crippling lack of basic sanitation measures to prevent disease.

Mexico proved to be another major diversion for the U.S. Army, although the expedition made the reputation of its future wartime leader, General John Pershing. In 1916 the U.S. government sent Pershing and a force of 10,000 troops across the border into Mexico to hunt down the bandit leader Francisco "Pancho" Villa, whose men had inflicted casualties on U.S. citizens during a cross-border raid on Columbus, New Mexico. Having failed to capture Villa, Pershing's force found itself in direct conflict with the regular Mexican Army after President Carranza's support for U.S. intervention was withdrawn. By the end of August 1916 relations between the two countries had turned into outright hostility, and a full-scale war seemed a possibility. A total of 150,000 troops from the newly expanded National Guard were mobilized along the border with Mexico. In the event, Carranza was persuaded to adopt a more liberal constitution. Pershing withdrew in February 1917.

battleships (dreadnoughts). Another construction program was launched in August 1915, heralding the start of a massive wartime shipbuilding boom.

Creating a modern U.S. Army
One of the chief problems that faced the U.S. Army in 1917 was its very real lack of experience in large-scale military operations. Its last major conflict had been during the American Civil War over half a century before, and aside from more recent small and unusually brief wars and expeditions, it had no real experience of modern warfare. The basic inadequacies of the U.S. Army were first exposed in the fighting during the Spanish-American War, which although undoubtedly a victory for the United States, had cost it dearly in military casualties because of

Although its performance had been only marginally effective in Mexico, the U.S. Army had some inherent strengths. The first of these was a modern and progressive system of education for its officers and future leaders based on the Army War College, which was already producing high-caliber graduates tutored in the most modern principles of warfare. Its leaders also had the benefit during the first years of World War I of being able to watch and study the strategies and tactics employed by those countries at war in Europe, and they deduced that what was needed was a large force capable of fighting a protracted battle, something that no European military leader had grasped in 1914. Another advantage was that the U.S. public, from whose ranks any potential army would be forged, was not yet fully aware of the horrors and casualties that modern war could generate and did not as yet have to bear the anxiety of sending its young men to war. Any large U.S. Army entering the field would be fresh and ready to do battle—in marked contrast to the forces of those countries that had been fighting since 1914 or 1915.

▶ *President Woodrow Wilson (in white trousers) carries the U. S. flag over his shoulder while leading a draft parade through Washington, D.C., on September 4, 1917. The draft enabled the United States to field more than four million men during the war.*

In the aftermath of the Mexican expedition, the U.S. Army also benefited from a far greater degree of autonomy than it had enjoyed in the past. President Woodrow Wilson, who had very little experience in military matters, was widely criticized in the press for his overly restrictive orders, close supervision, and control of Pershing during the expedition, and had suffered politically as a result. Thereafter, he was particularly careful not to risk interfering too greatly in the country's military affairs again.

Such underlying strengths could not detract from the fact that at the time of the U.S. declaration of war on April 6, 1917, its army was poorly equipped to fight a war and faced considerable obstacles before it could offer large and tangible support to the Allied cause. Its total uniformed force, after two years of cautious expansion, amounted to about 307,000 troops if one includes reservists and the National Guard, and these were of a very widely varying quality. The best American soldiers were the 15,000 men of the U.S. Marine Corps, but they were widely scattered among the country's overseas possessions. Equipment was also in very short supply: there were no serviceable aircraft and insufficient machine guns, despite the pioneering lead taken by the United States in developing both weapons. Another problem, one that had already been suffered by both the British and French armies, was a shortage of artillery ammunition. Similarly, although the British Mark I tank was based on the drive system of

▲ *Men stand in line for draft registration in New York. Many were undoubtedly immigrants from a continent they were set to go back to, this time as soldiers for their newly adopted country. Those called to serve were selected by lottery.*

the U.S.-built Holt tractor, the U. S. Army did not have a single armored vehicle. Equally worrying was the fact that the United States lacked a dedicated armaments industry and was unable to manufacture the matériel needed by the country's armed forces.

Forging the Expeditionary Force

When President Wilson declared war, he was unaware that a mutiny in the ranks of the French Army was threatening to bring about an Allied collapse on the western front. Equally, by 1917 the British and French—both soldiers and

civilians—had become weary of the war. The prompt arrival of U.S. forces might serve to boost Anglo-French morale and help stabilize the worrying military situation. Although the president was not fully aware of the seriousness of the situation threatening to cripple the French Army, General Joseph Joffre, a former commander in chief and now head of a military mission to the United States, held a conference with the U.S. general staff on April 27 in which he appealed for the immediate dispatch of a U.S. division to the western front. At the White House five days later Joffre repeated his plea to Wilson, who agreed to petition the U.S. Congress for conscription to speed matters up. The Selective Service Act, which was drafted by Brigadier General Hugh Johnson, was passed by the U.S. Congress on May 19. This act instituted conscription to create a new national army, one separate from the regular force and the National Guard, which was to be deployed alongside the professional U.S. Army and the militia in a new American Expeditionary Force (AEF) to be sent to Europe.

The Selective Service Act required all males between the ages of 21 and 30 to register their eligibility for military service with a local registration board. Nearly 10 million did so on June 5. By September 12, 1918, 23,908,566 men, out of a total male population of 54 million, had signed up with the boards.

The process of selecting the first 687,000 men to fight began on July 20 through a national lottery drawn by the secretary of war, Newton D. Baker. Further registrations were held in June and August 1918; by the war's end the U.S. Army had swelled to four million men (more than three-quarters of them draftees), although only about half were in France and many others arrived too late to see action. These infantrymen were nicknamed "doughboys," a term coined by U.S. cavalrymen observing the appearance of soldiers after hours of marching along dusty roads.

Having committed itself to war in Europe, the United States was faced with the task of creating and equipping its force, transporting it across thousands of miles of ocean, and sustaining it at the front. Strong leadership was clearly needed, and Baker looked no further than General Pershing, recently returned from Mexico, who was appointed the AEF's commander on May 12. On the 28th Pershing left the United States for Europe on the SS *Baltic* with the 191 men of his staff, and after a brief stopover at Liverpool in

KEY FIGURES

SECRETARY OF WAR NEWTON D. BAKER

Newton D. Baker (1871–1937) was born in West Virginia. After graduating from John Hopkins University, he became a lawyer in Cleveland, Ohio. Baker was the Democratic mayor of Cleveland from 1912 to 1916, and despite his own pacifist beliefs he accepted the post of secretary of war under President Woodrow Wilson in 1916.

Baker was responsible for authorizing the expedition to Mexico in 1916. After the United States entered World War I in April 1917, Baker drew up plans for universal military conscription, resulting in the mobilization of more than four million men. However, Baker had his critics, particularly over his decision to appoint General Pershing commander of the American Expeditionary Force (AEF) to fight in France. Republicans attacked him for failing to appoint General Leonard Wood, a key figure in the country's Preparedness Movement, as head of the AEF. Despite these attacks, Baker stayed in office throughout the war.

In 1920 he returned to his legal practice in Cleveland, and in 1928 he joined the Permanent Court of Arbitration at the Hague. The following year President Herbert Hoover appointed him to the Law Enforcement Commission.

A blindfolded Newton Baker selecting those citizens who are to be the country's first draftees.

northwest England to meet senior British officials, he set foot on French soil on June 13.

An independent fighting force

Soon after arriving Pershing found himself at odds with his Allied counterparts, Britain's Field Marshal Douglas Haig and France's General Henri Philippe Pétain, both of whom entertained the notion—as did their political masters— that U.S. troops should be used as reinforcements for the depleted British and French divisions. This plan was justified, the Allies maintained, by the need to eliminate the time-consuming process of creating an independent U.S. force

▼ "I Want You for U.S. Army"—this now famous poster featuring Uncle Sam (the personification of the U.S. people) was created by the artist James Montgomery Flagg.

I WANT YOU
FOR U.S. ARMY
NEAREST RECRUITING STATION

with its own staff, chain of command, and logistical support. Pershing, acting under President Wilson's orders, refused and insisted that only an independent force would serve in France.

Resisting proposals for amalgamation, much to the annoyance of the British and French, Pershing set to work organizing the structure of the force that would be sent across the Atlantic. Because of the very real lack of senior staff (the regular U.S. Army had just 5,000 officers in April 1917 and few of them had any combat experience),

Pershing concluded that his divisions would have to be based on a strength of 28,000 men, twice that of the Allied divisions, split into two infantry brigades, an artillery brigade, an engineer regiment, three machine-gun battalions, plus a number of support units. Fewer, larger divisions would require fewer officers to lead them.

Pershing's staff was joined at the end of June by advance elements of the U.S. Army, some 14,000 men of the U.S. 1st Division, which paraded proudly through the streets of Paris on July 4,

1917. It was the vanguard of a force that would eventually swell to 42 divisions, but in July 1917 it did not seem much with which to confront the battle-hardened Germans, now being released in slowly increasing numbers from the eastern front as Russia faltered. The Americans were all drawn from regular units, but few of them had ever seen combat. Furthermore, the speed with which the U.S. 1st Division was raised and sent to France left its officers with virtually no experience of working with one another, or their men.

▲ *General John J. Pershing and his staff stand to salute while their vessel docks in June 1917. Pershing arrived in Liverpool, then traveled to France via London. The first large group of U.S. troops were in Europe by late June.*

Although the Allied commanders were fully expecting that the first divisions would be composed of professionals drawn from the regular U.S. Army and U.S. Marine Corps, these organizations had been badly understrength before the war and simply could not answer the sudden demands for both instructors and combat troops. U.S. Army and U.S. Marine Corps regiments comprised only 700 men, and to fill the ranks of the four 2,500-strong infantry regiments that were required for each of the large American divisions, as many as 2,000 new recruits were drafted.

Until the following spring the AEF would not reach sufficient strength to have a major impact on the western front, and its presence would be largely symbolic—laying down a mark for the scores of thousands of U.S. troops that would arrive in the future. It was an inescapable fact that most Americans were raw recruits, required combat training, and were led by inexperienced officers, but for Haig and Pétain there was also much reason for encouragement. The first incoming U.S. contingent promised up to a million men for France. They would provide much-needed backing for the Allies, and they offered in the long term a means to break the impasse on the western front.

Preparing for combat

By mid-July the professionals of the U.S. 1st Division were undergoing advanced training alongside French forces at Gondrecourt, close to St. Mihiel in eastern France, one of 20 such camps set up by the U.S. Army in the country. French officers could scarcely believe that the

▼ U.S. troops move into position on the western front. Once such fresh units had arrived in France, both they and their officers had to gain the necessary training in World War I tactics before being fully ready for combat operations at the front.

PEOPLE AND WAR

NATIVE AMERICAN INVOLVEMENT

Although large numbers of Native Americans were not yet U.S. citizens, many, often volunteers, served in the armed forces during World War I. Others also made significant contributions as civilians, serving in war industries, supporting the efforts of the Red Cross, and buying Liberty bonds to help finance the war.

Details of Native American participation in the armed forces are fragmentary and conflicting. Figures for those volunteering for service in the armed forces vary between 5,000 and 10,000, but it is known that some 6,509 were drafted into the U.S. Army once conscription was introduced in 1917. It also appears that substantial numbers elected to serve with the Canadian Army. However, it is not known how many in total actually served in France, although a figure of between 2,000 and 4,000 has been suggested. Something like 5 percent died in action, while many others died of disease. It is known that just 228 Native Americans who were called up for service and just 1 percent of all who registered filed a claim for exemption.

The evidence suggests that Native Americans served in all branches of the U.S. Army. One of the most famous incidents involving them relates to the 142nd Infantry Regiment. The unit had a company of Native Americans and these men relayed messages and orders in their own languages when it became clear that the Germans had tapped the radio lines the regiment was using.

◀ *Training their new body of men to high enough standards to prepare them for battle was the immense task facing the U.S. authorities. Veteran Allied soldiers assisted the process; here, at Camp Dick in Texas, a British sergeant major (left) provides instruction in bayonet fighting.*

division, whose soldiers apparently could not drill, salute, or march and lacked any military demeanor, constituted the cream of the U.S. Army.

In fact, as previously noted, the majority of the professional soldiers were kept at home to organize the 32 training camps built after conscription became law. The U.S. basic training camps, which received their first batch of recruits in September, were run under a tough regime, characterized by long periods of repetitive training with little recreation time. Many of the recruits, a lot of them recent immigrants to the United States, had to be given lessons in basic English. Training was conducted by regular officers and other instructors who had only recently qualified themselves. Ill treatment at their hands was a common complaint among the ordinary rank-and-file soldiers.

Once in France, another bout of training awaited, nominally 12 weeks but in reality usually no more than nine and in late 1918 often as few as six. Instruction, usually by French and British regulars, was usually very basic, centering on the use of such unfamiliar equipment as the gas mask and hand grenade. As he watched his men undergoing training at St. Mihiel, one of the U.S. 1st Division's officers (and later its

African American Recruitment

African Americans faced great discrimination in the U.S. armed forces and reluctance to recruit them. Nevertheless, many thousands did serve overseas.

One of the glaring mistakes made by the U.S. Army high command was the failure to exploit the willingness of ethnic minority groups to fight for their country. The most prominent of these groups was the African American community, of whom some 2,291,000 volunteered for service and another 367,000 were drafted. Completely segregated in U.S. service, some units fought with the French Army during the war, notably the four regiments, some 15,000 men, of the proposed 92nd Division. About 200,000 African Americans served in the U.S. Army in Europe, but only 42,000 were classified as combat troops. The U.S. Marines and the United States Army Air

▲ *A Bible class held among a group of servicemen. Many servicemen of all backgrounds were found to be illiterate.*

▼ *African Americans returning home in 1918 wearing the* **Croix de Guerre** *medals awarded to them by France.*

German lines and reach the Rhine. During 191 days of fighting, the regiment did not have a single man captured, nor did it lose an inch of ground by retreating. The military leaders in France were so impressed with the way the troops fought at the Battle of Maison-en-Champagne that they gave the regiment the *Croix de Guerre* medal, the country's highest award for valor. The regimental band led by James Reese Europe is credited with introducing jazz music to Europe, and among those who served in the unit's ranks was the noted painter Horace Pippin.

▼ *Lincoln's presence, in this print celebrating the fighting qualities of the African Americans on the western front, implies a parallel with the civil war.*

The Germans were well aware of how badly African Americans were treated in the United States and attempted to coerce them through propaganda. Leaflets were dropped on African American soldiers, which attempted to capitalize on the many lynching incidents carried out against the African American population of the United States. The tactic proved unsuccessful as not one African-American soldier deserted.

Training camps in the U.S. Army, like much of American society at that time, were segregated. Fort Dodge was the only training school for African American officers in the U.S. Army. Although many African Americans were commissioned, U.S. Army regulations did not permit the officers to be put in command of white troops.

Service refused to take black volunteers, and they were only offered menial tasks in the U.S. Navy, although warships were not segregated.

Three-quarters of those who served in the U.S. Army overseas worked as cooks, orderlies, and truck drivers. The Transportation Corps, which unloaded ships in French ports, was made up mostly of African Americans—18,451 of them by the end of the war. Their working day was arduous. At St. Nazaire, for example, the men were detailed in two shifts, one that ran from 7:00 A.M. to 6:00 P.M., and the other that ran from 6:00 P.M. to 4:00 A.M, each with a one-hour break and one day a week off work.

The first black soldiers to arrive in Europe were those of the 369th Regiment from New York (January 1, 1918). The regiment quickly built up an excellent reputation and was given the nickname Harlem Hellfighters. This unit was the first to break through the

"Liberty And Freedom Shall Not Perish"
A. Lincoln

RED MEN
irst Americans
Planted
Flag

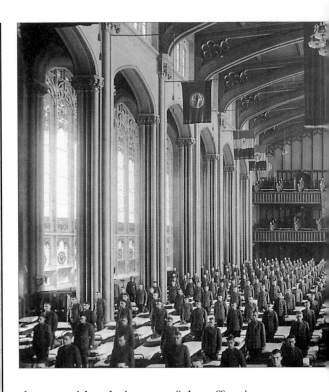

EYEWITNESS

SHERWOOD EDDY

Sherwood Eddy was a reporter and writer who was on assignment on the western front for the Associated Press. Covering the gradual buildup of the American Expeditionary Force in France during 1917, he recorded life behind the lines:

"In almost every valley sleeps a little French hamlet, with its red tiled roofs and its neat stone cottages, clustered about the village church tower. It is a picture of calm and peace and plenty under the summer sun. But the sound of distant guns on the neighboring drill grounds, a bugle call down the village street, the sight of the broad cowboy hats and the khaki uniforms of the American soldiers, arouse us to the realization of a world at war and the fact that our boys are here, fighting for the soil of France and the world's freedom.

"We are in a typical French farming village of a thousand people, and here a thousand American soldiers are quartered. A sergeant and a score of men are in each shed or stable or barn loft. The Americans are stationed in a long string of villages down this railway line. Indeed it is hard to tell for the moment whether we are in France or in the States. Here are Uncle Sam's uniforms, brown tents, and new wooden barracks. The roads are filled with American trucks, wagons, motors, and motorcycles, American mules, ammunition wagons, machine guns, provisions, and supplies, and American sentinels down every street.

"These are the men of the 1st Division, scattered along behind the French lines, being drilled as rapidly as possible to take their place in the trenches for the relief of the hard-pressed French. The nucleus is made up of the men of the old army, who have seen service in Cuba, Puerto Rico, the Philippines, Texas, or along the Mexican border. And with them are young boys of 19, 20, or 21, with clear faces, fresh from their homes, chiefly from the Middle West—from Illinois to Texas."

Extract taken from Eddy's With Our Soldiers in France, *first published 1917.*

commander), Brigadier General Robert Bullard, remarked that the "French count on nothing else than purely trench warfare. Plainly they show that they consider their part of the offensive of the war as done." Most of the French instructors had gained their experience in the trenches, but they appeared to the doughboys to be timid, scrambling from one shellhole to the next and exposing themselves as little as possible.

Pershing had made a careful study of the fighting in France and had concluded that "Victory could not be won by the costly process of attrition, but that it must be won by driving the enemy out into the open and engaging him in a war of movement. My view was that the rifle and bayonet still remained the essential weapons of the infantry." Accordingly, he ensured that his troops were tutored mainly in open combat, believing that the trench warfare tactics to which the British and French clung presented no opportunity for early success. He placed a particular emphasis on high standards of marksmanship.

One thing that was constantly noted by those observing the U.S. troops was their infectious enthusiasm for the fight and their general physical well-being. In France Pershing was eager to preserve

◀ *Temporarily accommodated in an educational institution in New York, recruits stand to attention prior to an inspection.*

Movement, which offered military training for those civilians who aspired to become officers.

The MTCA built its first training camp at Plattsburg in 1915 and in 1916 was awarded $2 million for expansion. After the declaration of war the MTCA camps provided the basis for a nationwide network of officer training camps, staffed by regular officers of varying ranks who conducted the 90-day assessment and training program that the U.S. Army judged was necessary. On May 16, 1917, the first of an eventual 43,000 officer candidates reported for training. The 90-day program often proved insufficient to turn raw recruits into top-notch leaders of men, but it was at least capable of processing a large number of officer candidates and weeding out the unfit.

Overcoming logistical difficulties

By early fall the British and French generals were becoming increasingly frustrated by the failure of the United States to provide troops quickly for France, and relations between them and Pershing's staff were cooling rapidly. However, the Allies failed to acknowledge that aside from the protracted training process, the AEF was hampered by enormous logistical problems. Central among them and the cause of considerable friction with Britain for the duration of the war was the problem of transatlantic transportation.

In 1917 the United States had a relatively small merchant fleet, inadequate to the task of transporting a potentially huge U.S. Army to France as well as supplying many necessities to the Allies. Ultimately, the movement of troops would be the responsibility of Britain, which controlled most of the world's merchant shipping. During the summer of 1917 Britain failed to provide enough transportation for U.S. troops, and there was no coordinated shipping plan for this complex logistical operation until November. At the heart of the

the fitness of his troops, and he pursued a zealous program aimed at keeping them free from venereal disease. Fraternization with prostitutes was banned, and any soldier who was found to have contracted a sexually transmitted disease faced court-martial and three months of hard labor.

The need for officers

General Pershing still had the problem of finding sufficient officers to enforce these strictures on the men in the ranks and lead them into combat. One of the greatest weaknesses of the fledgling American Expeditionary Force, which was never properly resolved during the fighting, was the lack of really capable, experienced, and competent middle-ranking officers. Fortunately, there was already the skeleton of a training organization for lower-ranking officers in the United States. Prior to the United States joining the conflict the Military Training Camps Association (MTCA) had been established on the initiative of General Leonard Wood, one of the leading members of the Preparedness

WAR AND RESPONSE, 1914–1916

▶ *The buildup of U.S. troops in Europe during the second half of 1917. The uptrend is unmistakable, from 14,000 troops in June, the first month for arrivals, to 49,000 men sent in December.*

▼ *The U.S. war-ships* George Washington *and* America. *By August 1918 U.S. forces had managed to transport more than a million men to France.*

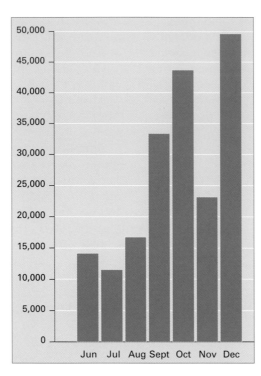

dispute lay Pershing's refusal to fight under British or French command. David Lloyd George, Britain's war leader, argued that if the United States was determined to have its independent AEF, then U.S. ships would have to carry it to Europe. When asked to justify their position, the British pointed to the fact that German submarines were steadily reducing the available shipping and that the remaining vessels were already fully stretched in meeting the demands of Britain's war effort. Nine months after declaring war, only 183,896 U.S. troops had been able to reach France. However, when the Germans launched their spring offensive in 1918, the British were suddenly able to free up ships to transport AEF troops to France.

Shortage of merchant shipping was not the least of the logistical problems facing the AEF. Inefficiency and poor

planning at the U.S. War Department were rife, and while the doughboys went short of essential supplies, ships were being sent across the Atlantic in August packed with floor wax, refrigerators, and other such items. Distributing the supplies, a process also hampered by widespread inefficiency, was left to the Services of Supply, a vast organization that by the end of the war accounted for nearly a third of the two million or so U.S. troops in France. Pershing's demand for an autonomous U.S. force led to the creation of an extensive transportation and supply network linking the sector of the front awarded to Pershing to the deep water ports of St. Nazaire, Bassens, and La Pallice. As part of this effort the Services of Supply imported some 1,500 locomotives and 18,000 freight cars to France, and the Corps of Engineers built more

▲ *U.S. troops line up at the dockside after their 1917 arrival in Europe. It took nearly a year to get one million men in place.*

than 1,500 miles (2,400 km) of track to get the supplies to the front. The results were remarkable: in the first seven months of the AEF's service in France only 484,550 tons were carried across the Atlantic; by the end of the war this figure was achieved every month.

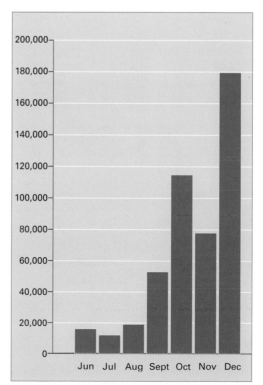

◄ *Aside from troops, the United States shipped thousands of tons of cargo to Europe in the second half of 1917. By the end of the war some 7.45 million tons had been shipped across the Atlantic to fuel the country's war effort. Some 48 percent of the total, largely food and clothing, was destined for distribution to the AEF by the U.S. Army's Quartermaster Corps.*

Added to the needs of equipping the growing AEF, U.S. industry faced increasing demands from both Britain and France. At the end of May 1917 French Prime Minister Alexandre Ribot demanded 2,000 aircraft and 4,000 engines per month from the U.S. War Department, and this from an aircraft industry that had yet to switch from peacetime to military production. The American armaments industry was still very small—only two factories produced the standard U.S. infantry weapon, the Springfield bolt-action rifle, and the U.S. Army had only 600,000 of them in April 1917. Artillery was in even shorter supply. Pershing estimated that to support a 500,000-strong AEF he needed 2,500 artillery pieces, but even at the end of the war when his force numbered four times this figure he had only 2,100, and most of those were bought from France. The U.S. Army also lacked many of the other weapons that had proved or were proving vital to the conduct of war on the western front—machine guns, tanks, trucks, mortars, and gas. Because of the serious equipment shortages U.S. soldiers arriving in Europe in 1917 were armed only with rifles, and initially they relied heavily on machine guns and artillery supplied by the French. Lack of weaponry and transport were a constant handicap.

In April 1917 the United States Army Air Service (USAAS) was tiny—just 65 officers and 1,120 men. The service had been steadily expanded and improved since its poor performance during the punitive actions undertaken in Mexico in 1916, when all 20 of its aircraft had been lost, but it was still far from combat ready. A $13 million grant from the U.S. Congress in the aftermath of the Mexican campaign funded the purchase of some 260 aircraft, but these were unsuitable for the aerial combats being fought in early 1917.

During the summer, representatives of Britain's Royal Flying Corps and France's Aéronautique Militaire traveled to the United States with recommendations for ways to improve the USAAS. As a result, the U.S. Congress voted another $640 million to build 22,000 aircraft to French design and voted to form 263 squadrons for operations. This response heralded a massive expansion in U.S. military aircraft production, and although the predicted targets proved to be optimistic, U.S. air power grew at a phenomenal rate. Much of this was due to the USAAS commander, General William Mitchell, who trained and organized the first pilots in June. On September 3 the 1st Squadron, USAAS, arrived in France. The USAAS was regarded as a sideline

▼ A Curtiss trainer aircraft, the Jenny, in 1915. Pilots from the United States were early volunteers for Europe's air war and performed with great daring. The gun here is an early example of one synchronized to fire through the propeller arc.

in the early fall of 1917. Equipment shortages were common, and despite the glaring shortfall in instructors, no one had the foresight to draft experienced U.S. pilots for foreign service. The first combat missions were not flown until March 1918.

The U.S. Navy goes to war

The mobilization of the U.S. Navy had a more immediate impact on the war. By April 1917 it was second only to Britain in terms of modern battleships, altering the balance of naval power in the Atlantic and North Sea irrevocably in favor of the Allies. Germany would have little chance of defeating them in a surface battle, a fact brought home in December 1917 when the U.S. Navy's 4th Squadron (the modern dreadnought battleships *Arizona, Arkansas, Florida, Nevada, New York, Oklahoma, Texas, Utah,* and *Wyoming*) under Rear Admiral Hugh Rodman joined the British fleet. Unlike the AEF, the U.S. Navy's forces in Europe were fully integrated with the Allies; elements of the 4th Squadron, for example, served under the British and were known as the 6th Battle Squadron.

In June 1917, despite the belated introduction of the convoy system, U-boats were still wreaking havoc in Atlantic and Mediterranean waters, causing losses that the Allies could not sustain. Between mid-1917 and the Armistice in November 1918, the United States' major contribution to the war at sea was the provision of warships for antisubmarine operations and, most crucially, merchant ships to replace those lost to submarines. The chief of naval operations, Admiral William Benson, implemented a major expansion program in 1915 that focused U.S. naval strategy on the Atlantic, but although six dreadnought battleships were launched by mid-1918 to join the 27 already available in 1914, wartime production concentrated on light forces. A year after the United

States had joined the war, its shipyards were launching 100 merchant vessels and warships every month.

Benson's essentially defensive attitude to the naval war against Germany ensured that for the remainder of the war, the bulk of U.S. naval forces was concentrated in home waters, tasked with patrolling for U-boats. Many civilian craft were temporarily commissioned for this work, and because of the manpower demands of the regular navy (conscription was not applied to the U.S. Navy), they were often crewed by the volunteer reserve. Benson's stance brought him into conflict with Admiral William Sims, liaison officer with the Allied navies from April 1917 and commander of U.S. naval forces in Europe from June, who demanded the release of antisubmarine forces from U.S. duties. Sims also encouraged operational integration with the British and requested greater U.S. commitment in the Atlantic and Mediterranean.

He was given the backing of Admiral Henry Mayo, who was the commander in charge of the U.S. Navy's Atlantic

▲ *Planned to be built in 17 days, this Liberty destroyer is at an advanced stage of construction after 14 days of flat-out work. Such was the phenomenal output of U.S. yards that three new vessels appeared daily.*

Fleet. In August 1917 Mayo returned from an Allied naval conference held in London with a number of recommendations, most importantly for the full implementation of the convoy system and concentration on the production of small warships. Calls for antisubmarine forces were later answered, but only after Benson had visited London in late 1917 on a fact-finding mission with the War Commission and been persuaded to adopt a much more aggressive stance. Subsequently, a variety of craft were mobilized to oppose the U-boats, some of which were operating off the eastern United States. Their value, when combined with other tactics such as convoying, may be gauged by the fact that not one U.S. soldier on his way to France was lost to submarine action. Escorted by U.S. destroyers, the Cruiser Transportation Force and the Naval Overseas Transportation Service participated in carrying over two million soldiers and nearly six million metric tons of cargo to Europe. In total 79 destroyers took part in the escort of convoys, and a further 135 operated in European waters on antisubmarine patrols. The contribution of these forces to the buildup of the AEF in Europe can be judged from the fact that they escorted 62 percent of all U.S. troops to Europe.

Into battle on the western front

By fall 1917 four American divisions were in France, but in truth none of them was really ready for full-scale combat, although small groups of troops were sent into the frontline on a regular basis to gain some experience of trench warfare. During August the British had suffered enormous losses at the beginning of the Third Battle of Ypres, and in October the Italians suffered a massive defeat at Caporetto, forcing the British and French to send reinforcements to shore up that sector of the front. To compound the crisis in manpower, a second revolution in Russia had swept the Bolsheviks to power, a party that would sue for peace and release more German divisions for the western front.

The first major U.S. unit to enter the line, the U.S. 1st Division, did so in September. One of its members, Alex Arch of the division's 6th Field Artillery, is credited with unleashing the first shot fired in anger by Americans against German troops on the western front on October 23. November brought the first U.S. Army fatalities in direct action—three men from the 16th Infantry Regiment, James Gresham, Merle Hay, and Thomas Enright, were killed during a raid by German troops against their trenches on the night of the 2nd.

▼ *American representatives of the War Commission, with Admiral Benson at the center, on a fact-finding mission in the European war zone. Also present is Colonel Edward House, the president's special adviser on European matters (fourth from left).*

GENERAL OF THE ARMIES JOHN PERSHING

John Joseph Pershing (1860–1948) was born in Linn County, Missouri. After a period as a schoolteacher he went to West Point where he eventually became one of its military instructors, and also gained a reputation for toughness and the nickname Black Jack, because he had once commanded the African American 10th Cavalry Regiment.

Pershing served on frontier duty against the Sioux and Apache Indians (from 1886 to 1898) and in the Spanish-American War of 1898. In 1903 he gained further military experience in the Philippines and as an observer with the Japanese Army during the Russo-Japanese War of 1904–1905. This service was followed by the military campaign in Mexico during 1916 and 1917. On May 26, 1917, Pershing was appointed commander of the American Expeditionary Force in Europe and oversaw its buildup over the following months. Pershing insisted that the AEF should remain an independent force—an argument he won.

Nevertheless, Pershing was flexible enough to "lend" units to the French in the spring of 1918, when a series of major German offensives threatened to cut through the western front. By mid-summer that year the AEF's buildup had been completed, and Pershing had a large force under his command, one that could play a major role in the defeat of Germany. Pershing believed that his fit, fresh troops could break the deadlock in the second half of 1918.

He won praise for his great victory at St. Mihiel in mid-September and followed it with the Meuse-Argonne Offensive, which was the largest and final U.S. operation of the war. Pershing was later granted the unique rank of general of the armies.

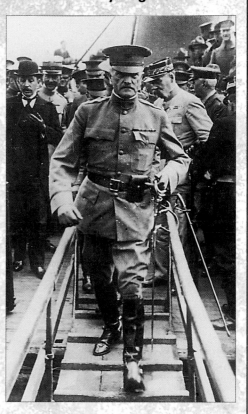

All three had been present at the July 4 Independence Day parade in Paris.

The AEF was still only a token force, but it was a growing presence in the Allied line at the end of 1917. During the winter the pressure mounted on General Pershing and President Wilson's administration to increase their country's commitment. The U.S. war effort was escalated further, and by July 1918 there were more than a million American soldiers stationed in France. More than two million U.S. troops eventually reached Europe. The AEF suffered 264,000 casualties during the war, of whom 112,432 men died. However, in 1917 the gulf between the expectations in Europe about the U.S. capacity to provide huge quantities of men, machines, and supplies and its actual capacity to do so was vast. Nevertheless, the potential was there for all to see, particularly among Germany's leadership. If the war was to be won, they recognized that victory had to be achieved before the full might of U.S. military power was available to the Allies on the western front.

The Search for Peace

◀ *Crowds gather in central Vienna, the capital of Austria-Hungary, at the outbreak of war, August 1914. Held aloft are portraits of their own emperor, Franz Joseph (right), and his German counterpart, Wilhelm II. Such scenes of support for the decision to enter into the conflict were common in many European capitals, but some groups were strongly opposed to the war.*

Although enthusiasm for war was widespread in 1914, there were voices of opposition that, as the conflict continued, gathered strength. However, popular peace movements and diplomacy all failed to bring the fighting to an early conclusion.

In the summer of 1914 earnest but ultimately futile attempts were made to avoid war through the normal process of diplomatic discourse. The conflict might have been prevented at any point during the five weeks of crisis that preceded the outbreak of war in August had the will existed or if moderation had found a voice. However, the rival nations had never created any systems for negotiation nor agreed on a code to regulate international affairs and policies.

One of the clearest failures was the lack of communication between the rival factions in the weeks running up to the war. In 1899 Czar Nicholas II of Russia had convened an international conference at the Hague in the Netherlands to discuss the limitation of arms and the settlement of international disputes through diplomacy. The conference and the international court that it established failed time and again in its ambitious aims, for international policy in the early twentieth century was chiefly guided, not by the search for peaceful resolution to areas of conflict, but by the quest for military superiority. Ultimately this quest led to war.

The search for peace motivated many disparate groups, from the grass roots to the highest offices of government. One of the first organized opposition movements was the Women's Peace Party. In February 1915 an international forum of women met in the Netherlands. Several of the British delegates, as well as others, had been active in the suffragette movement and the struggle for female emancipation before the war, including Chrystal Macmillan and Catherine Marshall. Millicent Fawcett and Emmeline Pankhurst, also prominent figures in the votes-for-women movement, both accused the pro-peace women of treason and urged their supporters not to attend. More than 180 women from Britain were refused permission by their own government to travel to the meeting. Nevertheless, 1,500 delegates representing Austria-Hungary, Belgium, Britain, Canada, Denmark, Germany, Italy, the Netherlands, Norway, Sweden, and the United States managed to overcome official attempts to stop them from reaching the peace meeting.

At the meeting the women discussed ways of ending the war. The delegates also spoke about the need to introduce measures that would prevent wars in the future, such as international arbitration and the state nationalization of munitions production to prevent an arms race. As a result of the conference the Women's Peace Party was formed. Other women who joined this party included Charlotte Despard, Sylvia Pankhurst, Olive Schreiner, and Helena Swanwick. In the fall of 1915 a number of the British women who attended the meeting formed the Women's International League of Great Britain.

However, at this stage of the war neither the wider public nor the political leaders of the combatant nations were willing to consider peace. Military victory was seen as the only way to satisfy national honor, and the peace movement was unable to achieve its aims.

The Catholic Church and war
One of the major sources of peace proposals was the Catholic Church. After

▶ *A papal emissary, Eugenio Pacelli (fourth from left), delivers a peace note to the German emperor in mid-1917. Pacelli was later to be elected pontiff and took the title Pope Pius XII.*

the death of Pope Pius X, Giacoma della Chiesa was elected as Benedict XV on September 3, 1914. The new pope was an able diplomat. At Christmas he tried to promote a truce, but without success. Throughout 1915, Benedict XV gradually lost his influence with the Allies, due in part to the role he played in separate negotiations between the Italian government and the Central Powers. In April, during the negotiations in London that committed Italy to declare war on the side of the Allies, a secret clause that prohibited the Allies from responding to any papal peace proposals was supported by the Italian government. When this clause was revealed to the western press by the Bolshevik revolutionary government in Russia, it caused the Italian government considerable embarrassment.

The only other major initiative that emanated from the Vatican was a peace note, which was issued to all the belligerents on August 1, 1917. Addressed to "The Heads of the Belligerent Peoples," it began with: "From the beginning of our pontificate, amid the horrors of the terrible war unleashed upon Europe, we have kept before our

attention three things above all: to preserve complete impartiality in relation to all the belligerents, as is appropriate to him who is the common father and who loves all his children with equal affection; to endeavor constantly to do all the most possible good, without personal exceptions and without national or religious distinctions, a duty which the universal law of charity, as well as the supreme spiritual charge entrusted to us by Christ, dictates to us; finally, as our peacemaking mission equally demands, to leave nothing undone within our power, which could assist in hastening the end of this calamity, by trying to lead the peoples and their heads to more moderate frames of mind and to the calm deliberations of peace, of a just and lasting peace." The note was considered but, although the Vatican tried to claim a major role in any postwar peace discussions, Benedict XV was not invited to the Paris Peace Conference of 1919.

At the highest level of government few attempts were made to find a peaceful resolution to the escalating crisis in the first years of the war. By 1916 the most promising hopes for peace

seemed to rest in the hands of two statesmen—the German chancellor, Theobald von Bethmann Hollweg, and the U.S. president, Woodrow Wilson. Bethmann Hollweg was appointed to the German chancellery in 1909, a position he held until 1917, and in the summer of 1914 had supported the idea of a short, limited war as a means to quell a growing economic crisis in Germany and thereby minimize any undermining of the country's international position. The threat of a protracted war on a large scale prompted Bethmann Hollweg to withdraw his support, but he lacked the personal or political authority to reverse the march to war in the summer of 1914.

Wilson, having proclaimed the neutrality of the United States in August 1914, strove for the next two years to maintain it, while engineering a peaceful resolution to the conflict. In 1915 and 1916 he sent his closest political adviser, Colonel Edward House, on several diplomatic missions to sound out feelings in Europe about the possibility of U.S. mediation between the various belligerents. As Wilson's emissary, House visited and met officials in the

▼ *Colonel Edward House (left) and his wife return to the United States from one of their fact-finding missions to Europe. As President Woodrow Wilson's most trusted envoy, House undertook a number of trips overseas in an ultimately futile attempt to find common ground between the warring nations on which peace could be built.*

▶ Edward Grey, the British foreign secretary between 1905 and 1916, depicted as a warmonger in *Simplicissimus,* a German satirical magazine. Grey had initially attempted to pre-vent the slide to war in July 1914, but in early August he argued success-fully that Britain should go to war if Germany violated Belgian neutrality. He later attempted to solicit U.S. sup-port for the Allied cause in negotia-tions with Colonel Edward House, President Wood-row Wilson's special adviser on Europe.

major European capitals. In early 1916 he was in London, where he conversed with the British foreign secretary of the time, Edward Grey. The result of their talks was the House-Grey memordan-dum of February 22, outlining the pos-sibility of U.S. entry into the war if Germany rejected an invitation to a peace conference. However, the sugges-tion was rejected by the British govern-ment and never communicated to the Germans. By mid-1916 the approach of the presidential election caused Wilson to suspend moves for peace.

In Germany, meanwhile, Bethmann Hollweg had argued, successfully but with difficulty, for the postponement of unrestricted submarine warfare. Wilson was reelected president on November 7, but another month passed without any new peace initiative. During this period German-led forces successfully invaded Romania, winning a victory that strengthened the already powerful position of the country's military leaders, Field Marshal Paul von Hindenburg and General Erich Ludendorff, and increased their influence over the easily swayed Emperor Wilhelm II.

Bethmann Hollweg hoped that the United States would initiate peace proposals before the military's control of the emperor became unchallengeable, but he was informed by the German ambassador in Washington, Count Johann von Bernstorff, that no action could be expected until after the U.S. approaching presidential elections. Bethmann Hollweg became increasingly impatient and sought approval to make a proposal of his own. After their victory over Romania, the leaders of the military high command also believed that Germany, from a position of strength, might now propose a settlement acceptable to themselves.

Germany's offer, issued by Bethmann Hollweg in the Reichstag (German parliament) on December 12, 1916, was undermined by the conditions imposed on its contents by the military. The militarists insisted that, if his proposals were rejected by the Allies, unrestricted submarine warfare must be resumed. The pronouncement underlined that Germany had been forced into the war to exercise freedom of national development and stressed that Germany should retain those areas of territory in Western Europe that it now occupied. The stumbling block was Germany's absolute insistence on being allowed to annex all of Belgium and the occupied portion of northeast France.

None of the Allied nations could accept peace on these terms. Furthermore, the tone of the offer stressed an end to the war on the grounds that continued fighting was futile, and no mention was made of peace terms or of the reparations demanded by the Allies for the illegal occupation of Belgium and France. The terms were so pro-German as to preclude the Allies' acceptance of them. Wilson was infuriated by German statements that suggested that in some way the offer was linked to his own recent peace initiatives.

▼ *The German emperor, Wilhelm II (center), pictured with Charles I, the ruler of Austria-Hungary (fourth from left) in mid-1917. Both of their countries had attempted to bring about an end to the war. Germany's somewhat insincere efforts had been rebuffed as too extreme by the Allies as they included clauses that would have allowed the Germans to take over certain already occupied territories. The Austro-Hungarian attempts failed because they did not include its stronger partner.*

EYEWITNESS

JAMES GERARD

Gerard was the U.S. ambassador to Germany for much of World War I and witnessed the ebb and flow of the country's political life and diplomacy. He later recorded conversations with Chancellor Theobold von Bethmann Hollweg concerning the basis for Germany's peace proposals in 1917:

"Finally in January, 1917, when he was again talking of peace, I said, 'What are these peace terms to which you refer continually? Will you allow me to ask a few questions as to the specific terms of peace? First, are the Germans willing to withdraw from Belgium?' The chancellor answered, 'Yes, but with guarantees.' I said, 'What are these guarantees?' He said, 'We must possibly have the forts of Liège and Namur; we must have other forts and garrisons throughout Belgium. We must have possession of the railroad lines. We must have possession of the ports and other means of communication. The Belgians will not be allowed to maintain an army, but we must be allowed to retain a large army in Belgium. We must have the commercial control of Belgium. We cannot allow Belgium to be an outpost of England. We are willing to leave northern France, but there must be a rectification of the frontier. We must have a very substantial rectification of our frontier. We shall leave Bulgaria to deal with Romania. A very small Serbia may be allowed to exist, but that is a question for Austria. Austria must be left to do what it wishes to Italy, and we must have indemnities from all countries, and all our ships and colonies back.'"

Extract taken for Gerard's memoirs *My Four Years in Berlin.*

Wilson's "peace note"

Only six days later, on December 18, Wilson issued his "peace note" inviting all belligerents to state their war aims, as a prelude to any cease-fire talks. The note made no reference to the German offer, thereby discrediting it. The Allies were also secretly encouraged by the U.S. secretary of state, Robert Lansing, to offer terms too sweeping for German acceptance, but delayed their reply. The Central Powers made their response on the 26th but, suspecting collusion between Wilson and the Allies, only agreed in principle to the opening of negotiations and left their statement of the 12th practically unchanged. Privately, they decided to insist that Wilson be excluded from any negotiation that he might bring about. The Allies declared their rejection of the German offer to Wilson but delayed in proclaiming their own war aims.

Having failed to elicit an acceptable response to their offer, on January 9, 1917, Germany's leadership adopted an unrestricted submarine campaign. The following day the Allies finally outlined their demands, which included the restitution of French and Belgian territory, and also made reference to the liberation of national groups from foreign domination. These demands were rejected, and by mid-January the peace overtures had ended.

Wilson's next appeal, which was made in a speech on January 22, elicited a confidential response from the British

▶ *Accompanied by his consort, Princess Zita, and child, Charles I is crowned emperor of Austria-Hungary on December 31, 1916. In 1917 he sought peace with the Allies to preserve his empire.*

who expressed their readiness to accept his mediation in peace talks. Austria-Hungary was likewise ready to listen to peace proposals. At the end of January, on the 31st, Bethmann Hollweg, who was an increasingly marginalized figure in German politics, restated Germany's peace terms and invited Wilson to persevere in his efforts, but his initiatives were nullified by the recommencement of unrestricted submarine warfare.

Austro-Hungarian peace moves

Franz Joseph, Austria-Hungary's long-serving emperor, died on November 21, 1916. At his death he firmly believed that a Central Powers' victory was impossible and that the survival of his polyglot empire was hanging by a thread. His successor, Charles I, was a humanitarian man with liberal tendencies, whose wife, Princess Zita, was the sister of Prince Sixtus of Bourbon-Parma, an Italian aristocrat with connections in the French government. Charles had deep reservations about his empire's increasing subservience to

Germany's military leadership, believing that to continue the war any longer would lead to the total collapse of the Austro-Hungarian Empire.

With his foreign minister, Count Ottokar Czernin, the new emperor sought a compromise peace with the Allies, but their initial list of peace proposals did, at least on the surface, attempt to preserve the prestige of the Central Powers. Through his wife's brothers, Princes Sixtus and Xavier of Bourbon-Parma, both of them officers in the Belgian Army, Charles began peace moves in spring 1917. The focus would be the French. Sixtus and Xavier first met Jules Cambon, the secretary-general of the Ministry of Foreign Affairs, on February 11.

The two princes conducted further secret meetings with Austro-Hungarian and French government representatives over the following weeks and met British Prime Minister David Lloyd George in April. However, the various efforts failed, chiefly because those privy to them disagreed upon the basis on which any move to peace could proceed. All had their own agendas.

Prior to the war, pacifism and conscientious objection were minority sentiments, identified with a number of religious or political groups, and could be taken to mean either a moral revulsion at war or else an opposition to conflict as the conventional tool of international diplomacy. Supporters of such ideals often faced ostracism in their communities. However, in the months following U.S. entry into the war in April 1917, calls for peace began to acquire a broader popular backing. The depredations forced on civilians by the war, most notably food shortages, coupled with mutinies in some armies and seemingly endless casualty lists led more and more people to question the wisdom of continuing the war.

The French Army mutinies in 1917, some unrest in the Austro-Hungarian, Russian, and Turkish armed forces, and disobedience in the armies of the British Empire and the German Navy were generally indicative of the erosion of the fighting enthusiasm displayed by the belligerent populations at the outbreak of war. Government propaganda had cultivated this enthusiasm, and media censorship was also used to varying extremes by all the belligerent powers. Pacifist propaganda invariably had less access to distribution networks or mass publication techniques, but some movements were able to make a considerable impact on European home fronts. With access to a printing press—and rarely with funding from enemy agencies—small groups of committed individuals could foment antiwar sentiments within the large, volatile populations of industrial cities and among frontline troops. Problems never really arose in Britain or in America, but in Austria-Hungary, France, Germany, Italy, and Russia seditious activity led to strikes that reflected war weariness.

Germany's peace resolution
In Germany, Matthias Erzberger, a leading figure on the left wing of the German Catholic Center Party and a deputy in the Reichstag since 1903, had, on July 7, 1917, tabled a joint declaration by the socialist and center parties that called for all territorial annexations to be renounced in order to facilitate peace. During the ensuing debates Bethmann Hollweg acted indecisively, and military and liberal factions conspired to force his resignation on the 13th. Emperor Wilhelm II appointed the next chancellor, Georg Michaelis, without consulting the Reichstag. Michaelis was the choice of the country's senior military leaders, Field Marshal Paul von Hindenburg and General Erich Ludendorff.

The Reichstag, which was offended by Michaelis's appointment, passed the *Friedensresolution* (peace resolution) on July 19 by a margin of 212 votes to 126. Erzberger issued this pro-peace statement: "Germany took up arms in defense of its freedom, its independence, and the integrity of its soil. The Reichstag strives for a peace of understanding and a lasting reconciliation of peoples. Any violations of territory, and political, economic, and financial persecutions are incompatible with such a peace. The Reichstag rejects any plan

▼ *The Reichstag (German parliament) in session during February 1918. The previous year its members had passed a peace resolution, but it failed to interest the Allies, chiefly because it did not clarify Germany's stance on occupied Belgium and the northeast of France.*

which proposes the imposition of economic barriers or the solidification of national hatreds after the war. The freedom of the seas must be maintained. Economic peace will lead to the friendly association of peoples. The Reichstag will promote actively the creation of international organizations of justice.

"However, as long as the enemy governments refuse to agree to such a peace, as long as they threaten Germany and its allies with conquest and domination, so long will the German people stand united and unshaken, and they will fight until their right and that of their allies are secured."

The resolution was little more than a loose collection of phrases expressing Germany's desire for peace but made no clear promise to relinquish occupied territory or pledges to pay reparations. As both of these were key Allied prerequisites, they took almost no notice of it. It had the added impact of placing the Reichstag in direct opposition to the military leadership and ended the *Burgfrieden* (political truce) that had existed between the country's various political parties up to this time.

Erzberger's proposal had been intended to pave the way for Pope Benedict XV's note to all of the belligerents. Dated August 1, 1917, the note advocated a German withdrawal from Belgium and France, an Allied withdrawal from the German colonies, and the restoration of independence in Montenegro, Romania, Serbia, and Poland. The governments of France and Great Britain declined to give any reply until Germany's position regarding occupied Belgium was clarified. However, the Germans avoided making any commitment toward Belgium or concrete proposals and the pope's personal initiative came to nothing.

The foundations of peace

Despite U.S. entry into the war in April 1917, Wilson remained committed to formulating a peace settlement. He

▲ *The new chancellor of Germany, Georg Michaelis (left), pictured on his way to present his credentials to Emperor Wilhelm II on July 14, 1917. Michaelis was effectively a puppet of the country's military leadership and had little backing in parliament. He resigned on October 17.*

made himself the chief developer of and spokesman for the war aims of the Allies and the United States, although he was often at odds with his Allies. Early 1918 saw Wilson's series of speeches on his war aims: the Fourteen Points on January 8 (see pages 310–311), the Four Principles (February 11), the Four Ends (July 4), and the Five Particulars (September 27).

Wilson's peace campaign, based on the Fourteen Points, was a factor in the collapse of German morale and the decision of the government, which also feared the growing U.S. military presence on the western front, to sue for peace in October 1918. Indeed, the Germans conducted their preliminary peace talks exclusively with Wilson, believing that his proposals would not lead to the humiliation of Germany. The armistice, when it came on November 11, was based on the Fourteen Points, although Wilson was later forced to concede some ground to his Allies, chiefly Britain and France, not least their demands that Germany accept responsibility for the war and be made to pay for the destruction it had wrought in Europe.

Wilson's Fourteen Points

By early 1918 a few farsighted politicians were looking to formulate the nature of the peace that would inevitably end World War I. Chief among them was U.S. President Woodrow Wilson.

On January 8, 1918, Wilson addressed the U.S. Congress, proposing the Fourteen Point Peace Program. The program had been devised to prevent the outbreak of any future world war. Although the points were wide ranging, at their core was a belief that peoples had the right to self-determination and that individual states had the obligation to engage in collective security through the offices of an international body, the League of Nations. The body was to contain diplomats from all of the world's nations and have the power to arbitrate disputes between any of its members. The individual clauses of the Fourteen Points were:

1) Open covenants of peace and the renunciation of secret diplomacy.
2) Freedom of navigation on the high seas in wartime as well as peace.
3) The maximum possible freedom of trade.
4) A guaranteed reduction of world armaments.
5) An impartial colonial settlement accommodating not only the colonialist powers but also the peoples of the colonies.
6) The evacuation of all Russian territory and respect for Russia's right of self-determination.
7) The complete restoration of Belgian sovereignty.
8) A complete German withdrawal from France and satisfaction for France about Alsace-Lorraine.

◄ *The full text of President Woodrow Wilson's Fourteen Point Peace Program as delivered to Congress on January 8, 1918.*

Program for the Peace of the World

By PRESIDENT WILSON January 8, 1918

I. Open covenants of peace, openly arrived at, after which there shall be no private international understandings of any kind, but diplomacy shall proceed always frankly and in the public view.

II. Absolute freedom of navigation upon the seas, outside territorial waters, alike in peace and in war, except as the seas may be closed in whole or in part by international action for the enforcement of international covenants.

III. The removal, so far as possible, of all economic barriers and the establishment of an equality of trade conditions among all the nations consenting to the peace and associating themselves for its maintenance.

IV. Adequate guarantees given and taken that national armaments will reduce to the lowest point consistent with domestic safety.

V. Free, open-minded, and absolutely impartial adjustment of all colonial claims, based upon a strict observance of the principle that in determining all such questions of sovereignty the interests of the population concerned must have equal weight with the equitable claims of the government whose title is to be determined.

VI. The evacuation of all Russian territory and such a settlement of all questions affecting Russia as will secure the best and freest coöperation of the other nations of the world in obtaining for her an unhampered and unembarrassed opportunity for the independent determination of her own political development and national policy, and assure her of a sincere welcome into the society of free nations under institutions of her own choosing; and, more than a welcome, assistance also of every kind that she may need and may herself desire. The treatment accorded Russia by her sister nations in the months to come will be the acid test of their goodwill, of their comprehension of her needs as distinguished from their own interests, and of their intelligent and unselfish sympathy.

VII. Belgium, the whole world will agree, must be evacuated and restored, without any attempt to limit the sovereignty which she enjoys in common with all other free nations. No other single act will serve as this will serve to restore confidence among the nations in the law which they have themselves set and determined for the government of their relations with one another. Without this healing act the whole structure and validity of international law is forever impaired.

VIII. All French territory should be freed and the invaded portions restored, and the wrong done to France by Prussia in 1871 in the matter of Alsace-Lorraine, which has unsettled the peace of the world for nearly fifty years, should be righted, in order that peace may once more be made secure in the interest of all.

IX. A readjustment of the frontiers of Italy should be effected along clearly recognizable lines of nationality.

X. The people of Austria-Hungary, whose place among the nations we wish to see safeguarded and assured, should be accorded the freest opportunity of autonomous development.

XI. Rumania, Serbia and Montenegro should be evacuated; occupied territories restored; Serbia accorded free and secure access to the sea; and the relations of the several Balkan States to one another determined by friendly counsel along historically established lines of allegiance and nationality; and international guarantees of the political and economic independence and territorial integrity of the several Balkan States should be entered into.

XII. The Turkish portions of the present Ottoman Empire should be assured a secure sovereignty, but the other nationalities which are now under Turkish rule should be assured an undoubted security of life and an absolutely unmolested opportunity of autonomous development, and the Dardanelles should be permanently opened as a free passage to the ships and commerce of all nations under international guarantees.

XIII. An independent Polish State should be erected which should include the territories inhabited by indisputably Polish populations, which should be assured a free and secure access to the sea, and whose political and economic independence and territorial integrity should be guaranteed by international covenant.

XIV. A general association of nations must be formed under specific covenants for the purpose of affording mutual guarantees of political independence and territorial integrity to great and small States alike.

▲ *A caricature of Wilson that depicts him as a peacemaker, but one out of step with his Allies, Britain and France, whose capitals, Paris and London, are depicted in silhouette in the background.*

9) A readjustment of Italy's frontiers on an ethnic basis.
10) An open prospect of autonomy for the peoples of Austria-Hungary.
11) The restoration of Romania, Serbia, and Montenegro, with free access to the sea for Serbia and international guarantees of the Balkan states' independence and integrity.
12) Autonomy for non-Turkish peoples of the Ottoman Empire and the unrestricted opening of the Dardanelles, but secure sovereignty for the Turks in their own areas.
13) An independent Poland with access to the sea and under international guarantee.
14) A general association of nations to guarantee the independence and integrity of all states, great and small.

The program was not well received by Britain and France. They had not been consulted and had several reservations about its contents. Nevertheless, the Fourteen Points were mostly accepted by them, but with two caveats. First, there was no mention of war reparations. France believed that Germany started the war in 1914 and should pay for the damage. Second, Britain was lukewarm to freedom of the seas. However, the program found favor with the Central Powers. Indeed, Germany sought peace in 1918 on the basis of President Wilson's earlier proposals.

▼ *Not all German commentators believed that Wilson wanted peace. This cover from a magazine from September 1918 shows the president as a vulture swooping down to destroy the dove of peace.*

BIBLIOGRAPHY

Albertini, L. *The Origins of the War of 1914*. New York: Oxford University Press, 1952.

Beaverbrook, Lord. *Politicians and the War 1914–1918*. London: T. Butterworth Ltd., 1928.

Bennett, G. *Naval Battles of the First World War*. Newton Abbot: David and Charles, 1972.

Bruce, Anthony. *An Illustrated Companion to the First World War*. New York: Penguin USA, 1989.

Farrar-Hockley, A.H. *The Somme*. Philadelphia: Dufour Editions, 1964.

Gilbert, Martin. *First World War*. New York: Henry Holt & Co., 1996.

Gilbert, Martin. *Atlas of the First World War*. New York: Oxford University Press, 1994.

Graves, R. *Good-Bye to All That*. London: Jonathan Cape, 1929.

Gray, Randal, and Christopher Argyle, eds. *Chronicle of the First World War*. New York: Facts on File, 1991.

Griffiths, W.R. *The Great War* (West Point Military History series). Wayne, New Jersey: Avery Publishing Group, 1986.

Haythornthwaite, P.J. *Gallipoli 1915: Frontal Assault on Turkey*. London: Osprey, 1991.

Herwig, H.H., and N.M. Heyman. *Biographical Dictionary of World War I*. Westport, Connecticut: Greenwood Press, 1982.

Hoehling, A.A., and M. Hoehling. *The Last Voyage of the Lusitania*. New York: Henry Holt & Co., 1956.

Joll, James. *The Origins of the First World War*. New York: Longman, 1984.

Joll, James. *Europe since 1870: An International History*. New York: Harper and Row, 1973.

Kennedy, P.M. *The War Plans of the Great Powers*. Boston: Allen and Unwin, 1979.

MacDonald, Lyn. *1914–1918: Voices and Images of the Great War*. New York: Penguin USA, 1991.

Pope, Stephen, and Wheal, Elizabeth-Anne. *Dictionary of the First World War*. New York: St. Martin's Press, 1995.

Preston, A. *Battleships of World War I: An Illustrated Encyclopedia*. Harrisburg, Pennsylvania: Stackpole Books, 1972.

Siney, M.C. *The Allied Blockade of Germany, 1914–1916*. Ann Arbor, Michigan: University of Michigan Press, 1957.

Stone, N. *The Eastern Front, 1914–1917*. New York: Penguin Books, 1998.

Thayer, J.A. *Italy and the Great War*. Madison, Wisconsin: University of Wisconsin Press, 1964.

Thomas, Gill. *Life on All Fronts: Women in the First World War*. New York: Cambridge University Press, 1989.

Tuchmann, Barbara W. *The Guns of August*. New York: Ballantine, 1994.

Winter, Denis. *Death's Men: Soldiers of the Great War*. New York: Penguin USA, 1996.

INDEX

Page numbers in *italics* refer to picture captions.